GODMEN OF INDIA

GODMEN OF INDIA

PETER BRENT

Quadrangle Books
Chicago · New York

GODMEN OF INDIA. Copyright © 1972 by Peter Brent
All rights reserved, including the right to
reproduce this book or portions thereof in any form
For information, address:
Quadrangle Books, Inc., 330 Madison Avenue,
New York 10017

PRINTED IN ENGLAND
First American Edition
Published in England by Allen Lane The Penguin Press

Library of Congress Catalog Card Number
73–190123
International Standard Book Number
0–8129–0258–0

FOR JEAN

*I would like to thank the many people in India
whose friendship, hospitality and advice
helped in the preparation of this book,
particularly Swami Ananda,
of the Bharat Sadhu Samaj in Delhi,
and Kulamarva Balakrishna,
writer and journalist,
of Bombay.*

Contents

I

The Background

'IN the midst of the highest heaven there is a shining light; he who has no *Guru* cannot reach the palace; he only will reach it who is under the guidance of a true Guru.' Thus Kabir, the fifteenth-century North Indian mystic, plainly sets out the Guru's status.

When we discuss world religions, we put Hinduism among them. The fact is, however, that although there are certain tenets held in common by almost all Hindus, they do not add up to a body of definitive doctrine, nor are they upheld by an authoritative hierarchy. The skeleton of Hinduism is the Guru. The continuity of divine awareness which runs through the succession of Guru by Guru is the chain which binds the religion together. Revelation is not, as among Christians and Muslims, something which occurred at a particular moment in history, a unique and seminal event from which the essential vigour of the religion flows. The continuous presence of self-realized persons gives Hindus access to a constant inspirational source. In a confusion of ideas, philosophies and sectarian beliefs, in a morass of idolatry and superstition, faith in the Guru as intermediary resolves all problems of doctrine.

There are, however, some essential beliefs which underlie the multiplicity of what Sri Aurobindo called in *The Foundations of Indian Culture*, 'that vast, rich, thousand-sided, infinitely pliable, yet very firmly structured system we call Hinduism'. The first of these is the certainty that there is an Absolute permeating or underlying the phenomenal universe. This Absolute is called *Brahman* and it is essentially neuter and abstract: Indian thought finds room for it as well as the more

I

concrete versions of the gods, sometimes including that of a Creator, Ishwara. In other words, Creation depends upon the fact of Being, not the reverse. The second is that souls transmigrate into new bodies after death, with the corollary that this birth–death–birth cycle can be broken if a certain level of spiritual development is reached. Such development – or lack of it – is the consequence of all one's actions in this and in previous incarnations: one's *karma*. One's liberation from the cycle is called *moksha*.

The third is a belief in the absolute authority of the *Vedas* and of the *Upanishads*, modified by the commentators who have founded their varying philosophies upon these sometimes ambiguous texts. The *Vedas* as normally understood are a collection of prayers and descriptions of rituals, the objects of which are a cluster of deities which include Agni, the fire god; Dyaus, the sky god; Prthivi, the earth god and so on. So important and basic were they, that Jaimini's *Mimamsa Sutra* which, somewhere between the fourth and the second century B.C., founded a whole school of thought, taught that karma lay in the rituals and ceremonies themselves without the practice of which knowledge was no use and human objectives unobtainable. The commands of the Vedas could not be questioned; they were a basic fact of the universe, a sort of natural law in themselves.

Also part of *shruti*, 'that which has been directly heard', are the *Brahmanas*, which lay down in detail, for the benefit of the priestly Brahmins, rules for conducting extremely complicated ceremonies. They are attached to the *Vedas* and from our point of view do not extend their significance.

The third part of 'that which has been heard' is the *Upanishads* which, though based on the *Vedas*, are much later and have been a seam of ore richly mined by philosophers and sages for at least twenty-five centuries. The ideas of the *Upanishads* about the Self and the universe are very different from those implicit in the early *Vedas*. It is in them that we first come across the doctrine of the transmigration of souls. Earlier, the emphasis had been on the blessings of this life, on earthly reward for proper observance of the Vedic rituals. 'Upon the earth men give to the gods the sacrifice, the prepared oblation; upon the earth mortal men live pleasantly by food. May this earth give us breath and life, may she cause me to reach old age', says the *Atharvaveda's Hymn to Earth*, and in its *Prayer for the Exemption from the Dangers of Death* it says, 'Rise up hence, O man! Cast off the foot-shackles of death, do not sink down! Be not cut off from this world, from the sight of Agni and the sun . . . Thy mind shall not go thither, shall not disappear!'

But in the *Chandogya Upanishad* we find, 'Those whose conduct here has been good will quickly attain a good birth, the birth of a *Brahmin*, the birth of a *Kshattriya*, the birth of a *Vaisya* (the three higher of the four basic castes). But those whose conduct here has been evil will quickly attain an evil birth, the birth of a hog or the birth of a *Candala*.'*

The *Brhad-Aranyaka Upanishad* tells us, 'When this (body) gets to thinness, whether he gets to thinness through old age or disease, just as a mango or a fig or a fruit of the peepul tree releases from its bond, even so this person frees himself from these limbs and returns again as he came, to the place from which he started back to life.'

Thus was established the ground of all Hinduism – that action in this life will be rewarded in one's next embodiment, but that the final reward is not returning, is taking up existence at the soul's real level.

That level is finally the level of Brahman, for, says the *Chandogya Upanishad*, 'Verily, this whole world is Brahman, from which he comes forth, without which he will be dissolved and in which he breathes. Tranquil, one should meditate on it.

* A Candala, having a *Shudra* father and a Brahmin mother, was considered among the most degraded of creatures. He was usually a hunter and lived in caves.

Now verily, a person consists of purpose. According to the purpose a person has in this world, so does he become on departing hence. So let him frame himself for a purpose.' And that purpose is, in the end, liberation from the birth-death-birth cycle and unity with Brahman: 'He, verily, who knows the Supreme Brahman becomes Brahman himself,' the *Mundaka Upanishad* tells us.

Upon these and many similar verses of the *Upanishads*, all Indian thought developed. 'They have,' Radhakrishnan said, 'dominated Indian philosophy, religion and life for three thousand years.' There is dispute about how old they actually are, since manuscript sources are comparatively recent in India, but the oldest certainly seem pre-Buddhist and are generally assumed to date from the eighth century B.C. onwards. Radhakrishnan says there are over two hundred *Upanishads*; Monier Williams thought there were about one hundred and fifty; Indian tradition says there are one hundred and eight, but the most important are no more than ten or a dozen; Radhakrishnan in his *The Principal Upanishads* (from which all quotations in this book are taken) has set out eighteen in full. With such antiquity and such number, originally forming part of an oral tradition, it is no surprise that ambiguities and contradictions have been found in them, fruitful grist for the commentators' mills.

BASIC PHILOSOPHY

The most influential of these commentators was Shankaracharya, who lived around the beginning of the eighth century and was the intellectual spearhead of the triumphant Hindu revival against the then prevalent Buddhism. The success of Shankara's philosophy may have been partly due to the amounts of Buddhist doctrine it managed to adapt to Hindu use: Madhva, place in this one, would become invalid; you could hardly be put into a low place by the unwinding of the universal causality unless there was an irrevocably low place to put you in.

It is, of course, not the case that this view of reality is the only one Indian philosophy has proposed – it stretches from this kind of monistic idealism to some quite tough materialistic philosophies, complete with their own evolutionary theory – but it is Advaita Vedanta which, both inside India and outside, is considered the major stream of Hinduism. Nevertheless, throughout the centuries, Shankara had his critics: before the tenth century Bhaskara was pointing out that the unreality of the world must include Shankara and his philosophy too; for him Brahman was the cause of the world and of all human souls. The most important of the critics, however, was Ramanuja, who died in the twelfth century.

Ramanuja founded the school of *Visisht Advaita*, or qualified non-dualism. This stated that the world has a pre-existing creator. The soul is not identical with Brahman; it is finite. It is however a fragment of Brahman and totally dependent on this Absolute. Thus there are three real things: Brahman, matter and the soul, the first singular and infinite, sustaining the other two, which must be an integral part of it, since besides Brahman there is nothing. Brahman is within the world, as gold is within golden objects. Matter has neither consciousness nor vitality, souls feel ignorance and sorrow – only Brahman is perfect. The world has been created out of this perfect Brahman as a web is spun out of the body of a spider. It is different from, yet part of, Brahman; there is dualism in unity.

What is very important to the development of one of the main elements in Hinduism is that Ramanuja taught that liberation came not through jnana, through knowledge, but through *bhakti*, devotion: the soul suffered ignorance and sorrow, and the sorrow was caused partly by the ignorance but mainly by lack of belief. Pure love of the divine, the most intense devotion, would therefore purify the mind of unbelief and so relieve the soul of sorrow. It could thus reunite with Brahman – this leaves intact the doctrine of liberation – but within that great totality it would retain its own individuality and consciousness.

The bhakti strain in Hinduism has contributed a great deal to placing the Guru at the centre of Hindu tradition, since he often becomes, as we shall see, the focus for that intense and saving devotion which Ramanuja prescribed. Bhakti does not of course start with Ramanuja; according to some authorities it has its origins in the non-Vedic cults of the Dravidian south. Ramanuja, however – who himself came from the South – gave dualism a philosophical status while subtly keeping it within a wider monism; and devotion is a subject-object relationship which is essentially dualistic. He thus provided a base of speculation upon which later philosophers like Madhva, Vallabha, Chaitanya, Kabir and Nanak, the founder of Sikhism, would be able to take a stand.

ROUTES TO LIBERATION

One attains moksha, that desired liberation from death and earthly life which comes from merging with the Absolute, by fitting oneself for it through bhakti or jnana (devotion or knowledge). Since one tries to raise oneself lifetime after lifetime, using the undeviating logic of karma as a handrail, the method of attaining moksha becomes part of the practical essence of Hinduism.

'Meditate thou on the Supreme,' wrote Kabir. 'Go to his house, that you come not again.' And Shankara, in his commentary on the *Bhagavad Gita*, told us, seven centuries earlier, what meditation was: 'Meditation is approaching the object of worship by visualizing it and dwelling for a long time steadily and continuously on the idea of the object alone in an unbroken current, like a flow of oil.' 'Meditation' is of course only an approximate word for what is meant. In English it suggests an object – 'meditation upon' – but what it represents in the Indian tradition is an attempt to reach a state of such singleness, such stillness, that there remains only the experience itself, a unity in which what is Self and what is not Self are both contained. The oneness of the universe is thus felt directly, within and without merge together, the pervasiveness of the Absolute seems to be confirmed by one's experience. Such a state is called *samadhi*.

As Radhakrishnan describes it, 'In worship there is a distinction between the worshipping self and the worshipped object, but in contemplation this distinction is held in suspense ... Meditation is not argument. It is just holding oneself steadily in front of the truth.' Swami Atmananda writes in his *The Four Yogas*, 'Meditation ending in the attainment of samadhi is the necessary and essential finale of all the three Yogas (that is, ways or paths) alike ... The highest step begins with concentration which has to become more and more uninterrupted and of longer and longer duration and finally ends in samadhi' – and 'samadhi' he translates as 'absorption'.

So important is the experience of samadhi in the Hindu tradition and for so long has it been so that, far from considering it one condition, always the same, Indians distinguish between the varieties of it. The two major categories of samadhi are *nirvikalpa*, in which the soul is believed to merge totally with the Absolute, and *savikalpa* or *samprajnata* samadhi in which the distinction between devotee and deity is maintained. Different kinds of trance state are associated with the path the devotee has chosen to make his own – bhakti yoga, for instance, may lead to *bhava* samadhi, a trance state in which the worshipper dances and gestures as *bhaktas* do to praise the Lord; and it is jnana yoga, the way of knowledge, in which the devotee will dwell on some ultimate abstraction or on pure awareness itself, emptying his mind of all ideas, which will culminate in nirvikalpa samadhi. If this becomes established by practice and long experience, it develops into *sahaja* samadhi, which is considered by some the highest state – the liberated soul is permanently in this final plane of awareness. In *samprajnata* samadhi one concentrates on an object with such intensity that all body-consciousness is lost; this in turn leads to *asamprajnata* samadhi, in which even that final idea, that concept so totally concentrated on, is purged from the mind. Thus the mind has, as it were, died, and the devotee will not return to be reborn – according to Patanjali, from whose philosophy the ideas of Yoga derive, it is this and not sahaja samadhi which is the highest state.

To define a spiritual condition, however, and proclaim it as desirable, without offering any clues as to how one may achieve it, is to offer heaven with no path to its gates. Hinduism does not do us such cruelty; indeed, the paths to samadhi and thus to liberation are many. The discipline which an adept accepts is called his *sadhana*, which has been translated as 'gaining'; he then becomes a *sadhaka*, until he achieves his aim, when he becomes a *sadhu*.

He may begin by attacking what is called *adhyasa*, the errors which flow from identifying oneself with one's body. 'I am rich' or 'I am a commoner', used as definitions of oneself, spring from a wrong understanding of what one is, and this has its roots in a self-awareness born in the infant before conscious intelligence began. So the sadhaka will hear over and over again, 'Thou art not this body; thou art not this mind; thou art neither the sleeping, waking nor the slumbering self; thou art that which continues even during deep sleep and wakes up at dawn; thou art the innermost consciousness.' He learns to reflect profoundly upon these assertions, until he reaches the point where he can meditate intensely upon a single truth.

The attack upon the deluded Self is not confined to the intellect: it is clear that from the orthodox Hindu point of view, a man's attachment, his affection or love for other people, is the consequence of the overall illusion, maya. To refine his capacity for love and to raise it to the required intensity, he needs to practise bhakti yoga. The problem for the sadhaka is how to alter the object of love from the mundane to the godly – and this may be done by conceiving of the godly as the mundane. The relationship with the divine is thought of in terms that seem the most natural – as Swami Sivananda puts it, 'According to the person's object of love upon the human plane the Ishta (God) is to be regarded as a master (the bhakta being his servant or slave), as a friend, as a child, or again as the beloved.' This increases in intensity, until 'even the sense of separation between the bhakta and love's ideal becomes dissolved in ecstatic union'.

Both the way of knowledge and the way of devotion are demanding, one of the intellect and the other of the emotions. Consequently, a third way is offered – that called *karma yoga*, the path of works, of action, 'of selfless, humble, self-abnegating, motiveless service of all beings', as Swami Sivananda calls it.

Finally, even harder to attain than the others, is what is called *raja yoga*. In this, Swami Vivekananda wrote:

The powers of the mind should be concentrated and turned back upon itself, and as the darkest places reveal their secrets before the penetrating rays of the sun, so will this concentrated mind penetrate its own innermost secrets. Thus will we come to the basis of belief, the genuine religion . . . It will all be revealed to us. This is what raja yoga proposes to teach. The goal of its teachings is how to concentrate the mind, then, how to discover the innermost recesses of our own minds, then, how to generalize their contents and form our own conclusions from them.

Swami Sivananda describes it similarly: 'If the initial mind wave . . . is made the target of attack, then the battle is taken, as it were, into the very camp of the enemy and it becomes direct and summary. Upon this firm premise was built up the technique of raja yoga. It constitutes a process of nipping in the bud all ideation itself.'

It is raja yoga which is said to give the adept special powers over nature, called *siddhis*; hence miracle-working yogis, the delight of magazine readers for a century. For the orthodox, miraculous powers are a side issue, rather embarrassing because so often used for the wrong reasons.

The logical possibility of the practise of raja yoga leading to great powers is expounded by Vivekananda: 'The external world is but the gross form of the internal, or subtle. The finer is always the cause, the grosser the effect. So the external world is the effect, the internal the cause. In the same way external forces are simply the grosser parts, of which the internal are the finer. The man who has discovered and learned to manipulate the internal forces will get the whole of nature under his control. The yogi proposes to himself no less a task than to master the whole universe, to control the whole of nature.'

A necessary preparation for the concentrated meditation of both raja and jnana yoga is physical control and the various positions which have been codified under the name *hatha yoga*. Hatha yoga is about control, and in large measure control of breathing – *pranayama*. We translate *prana* as breath, but it is much more than that – it is the heart's vital wind, the life-force itself, and thus a synonym for soul. In raja yoga, such physical skills are only the beginning: there is control of the sense organs (*pratyahara*), and there is fixing the mind on a spot within the body – the heart or the head – which is called *dharana*. Once one has made that spot the base, Vivekananda says, 'a particular kind of mental wave rises ... while all the others recede and finally disappear. Next the multiplicity of these waves gives way to unity and one wave only is left in the mind. This is *dhyana*, meditation. When no basis is necessary, when the whole of the mind has become one wave, one-formedness, it is called samadhi.'

THE GURU

There before the aspirant, then, stretch the four great routes –
jnana yoga, bhakti yoga, karma yoga, raja yoga; knowledge, devotion, work or the mind. Not clear-cut, either; no
demarcated paths, sign posted, fenced, hedges clipped and
verges trimmed by priest and theologian, but weaving in and
out, crossing each other, running parallel for a mile or two,
then wheeling away in a great curve that will bring them by way
of other hillsides and valleys to the same desired goal. You, a
would-be devotee, stand facing their complexity, drawn by
their destination but uncertain about yourself and your right
choice of direction. You are ready to make contact with your
Guru.

For almost all who embark on the long and rigorous disciplines of sadhana, the Guru is mentor, judge, the fact or the
symbol of the Absolute they seek, the glass which pulls together
the disparate rays of their sun into a single burning shaft. Their
need for him is total, their devotion to him absolute: he is both
centre and limit of their religious life. He is known as human,
but understood as divine. They say of him, 'Guru is greater than
God because he leads me to God.' Unless one realizes the
completeness of the disciple's absorption in and reverence for
his Guru, little that is written in the rest of this book will have
any meaning.

What is a Guru? The first thing to be clear about is that there
are different kinds of Guru, and that at the edges, as it were,
of Gurudom the definition becomes a little ambiguous. In one
sense, any teacher is a Guru. The word, however, has spiritual
overtones and this is necessarily so; the earliest Gurus were the
Brahmins who taught the Vedas.

But between Vedic and Upanishadic times, Hinduism
changed; its emphasis turned from the seen to the unseen:

immortality and rebirth entered the picture, Brahman became supreme, the whole philosophy changed from a dualism in which the gods' function was to enhance the devotee's earthly life, to a monism in which it was the devotee's endeavour to realize the non-earthly *atman* within him and so leave the body behind for ever. As the philosophy changed, so did the Guru. The path of knowledge demands one who knows and one who wants to learn, yet it had now become difficult of definition; the *Upanishads* are full of conversations between wise fathers and eager sons, between great sages and respectful kings, but suitable aspirants would henceforth always be few.

I suspect, however, that more important in raising the Guru to the high place he now holds is the development of bhakti yoga. As devotion in its most intense form became one of the main paths to liberation, and one the pure emotionalism of which opened it to the millions, so the Guru as the focus of devotion took on a new importance. And out of that devotion one strand of the idea of surrender developed, so often mentioned in the *Gita*, an idea central, as we shall see, in the relationship between the disciple – the *shishya* or *chela* – and his Guru. He surrenders his will and his future actions to the Guru and all his efforts are turned inwards in the attempt to make that surrender; it is the means by which he conquers that devouring self which anchors him so tragically to the heaviness and misery of earthly life.

The other intertwined strand in the concept of surrender leads back once more to the Guru of ancient times. As sole repository of all the world's basic knowledge, the fount of all right action, the *Vedas*, he was accorded a complete respect. He carried the divine word and as such was an awesome figure. Fertilized by the later development of bhakti, this respect grew into what may sometimes seem grotesque adoration.

THE BACKGROUND

SAD-GURU

The Guru who answers the disciple's need for surrender, is called the *sad*-Guru, the teacher of reality, to distinguish him from other, perhaps lesser, types of Guru. He is not the only kind of Guru there is; there are the teachers of dancing and music, of wrestling and other skills; more clearly within religion there are hereditary Gurus, who pass their religious role and mission down through the generations. There are the sectarian Gurus, and the mahants, the heads of monasteries or maths, whose line of succession sometimes goes back fifty generations or more. Again, as everywhere in Hinduism, these distinctions are neither absolute nor clear, nor are these categories mutually exclusive.

The sad-Guru with his own establishment – called his *ashram*, the name given to the retreat where in ancient times the Brahmin Guru lived, received his pupils and taught them the *Vedas* – seems curiously apart from the stricter institutionalized tradition. This is because he harks back to the time when a Guru was a lonely ascetic in some magnificent wilderness, attracting a few disciples of the right potential only as the fame of his holiness spread. Nowadays, with marble temples and showers in the guest house, many ashrams are a far cry from that original tree-veiled Himalayan retreat.

Apart from spiritual experience and the ability to teach others how to achieve it, there seem to me to be two factors either of which can determine who is and who is not a Guru; they are *succession* and *initiation*. A Guru is one who succeeds another Guru; a Guru is one who gives initiation. But so complex is the situation, and so fluid is Hinduism, that even so broad a definition can be attacked – for instance, by those who say, as they have said to me, that anyone or anything through which one approaches illumination is a Guru. But in general it seems true

15

to say that a Guru carries on the work of his predecessor, either by becoming the head of a sect or monastery in succession to him, or by setting up in or near his Guru's ashram after the old preceptor has died.

The history of the sad-Guru tends to fall into a general pattern. As a boy, he may be discovered to be religious, different from other children, as in the West artistically gifted children are different. Threatened with marriage, he will often refuse and leave home, to wander from one holy place to the next. Finally he will meet his fate – the Guru at whose feet he is destined to sit. Such a meeting may be early, he may leave and then return years later; or it may be after twenty years of searching. He remains with his Guru, he does all that is asked, he subjugates himself, he serves. When the Guru judges him ready, he receives his *diksha*, his initiation. He achieves longer and longer periods of samadhi, his holiness becomes apparent, people begin to speak of him with reverence. He may leave at this point and, while always retaining his connection with the Guru, set up in an ashram of his own; or he may stay and, when the old Guru dies, become the head and centre of his ashram. People come to him, he becomes famous and the ashram rich. Sooner or later, a new disciple of great potentiality will attach himself to him – the next Guru will have been found.

INITIATION

By initiating a disciple, the Guru recognizes his spiritual worth, his fitness to continue on the path towards liberation. In all formal initiations, the aspirant is given a *mantra* – that is, a verse from one of the holy writings, or a syllable considered to be of concentrated power. This mantra is usually kept secret and is never written down. It becomes the centre of the new adept's devotions – he repeats it over and over again, he concentrates upon it during meditation. It is not magic – its special nature is that it is one's own and that it has been given to one by the Guru to whom one has surrendered. It is in its particularity that its virtue lies, its precise passing over from Guru to disciple or new aspirant.

It is not the case, however, that all initiation involves the giving of a mantra, although all formal initiation does. In one classification three kinds of diksha are mentioned: *anavi*, *sambhavi* and *shakti*. The first involves the Guru giving the novice a mantra, the second is by some contact between Guru and aspirant – a touch, a glance, a word – which suddenly provokes a sort of divine revolution in him, and the third is when the Guru's divine power, his shakti, enters into the disciple, sometimes unexpectedly, even at their first meeting, sometimes after a long time – and sometimes even when the disciple is physically distant from his Guru.

Such informality of initiation indicates what is essential – that something of the consciousness of the self-realized man should enter into the eager consciousness of his disciple. A transfer of this kind is called *shaktipat* and can be very sudden and dramatic.

In the West, a teacher dispenses knowledge as a chemist might powders – he may have an involvement with what he is doing, but he does not need to, and even a professor of philosophy will not be discredited if his way of life does not exemplify the maxims of his favourite sage. Our preachers need not have the gift of prophecy, nor struggle for forty days in any desert of their own; if they know the right words and live in a manner not too obtrusively self-indulgent, they fulfil our expectations. But a Guru is his teaching. What he does, what he is, is more important than what he tells us.

It is true, of course, that Hinduism is a religion of the temple and, even more so, of the home, and that it is only a minority who find their way to the ashrams of the holy. But it seems to me that the religion is given a continuing vitality by the experiences of this comparatively small number; what happens to them happens *now*. Not only is this important for those who take a direct part, it is important for the millions who only know that it occurs. Hinduism continues to live because everybody knows that at this moment, in the very country, even the very town, where they live, people are in a state of exaltation and illumination which they owe to a direct contact with the godhead all Hindus worship. The unity of man and Brahman is not doctrine, it is experience, and if it may not be every single individual's experience, it is the experience of someone he sees, perhaps knows, can certainly bow before; it is the experience of men who walk his pavements, men who speak to him, men he can approach, whose feet he can touch in reverence. In this way the actual continues to extend the assumed, the assumed continues to manifest itself in the actual. And the only instrument by which one can learn how to take part in this constant intercourse between the mundane and the spiritual is the Guru.

All that the disciple expects in and from the divine, all that he has of love, is concentrated on this single figure. The disciple can do this because he understands the scale of the Guru – however divine, the Master is still in human shape; however unimaginable the Absolute may be, the Master has visible limits. Trusting him, surrendering to him, he accepts the criticisms he is given, tries to adjust his behaviour to the ideal the Guru sets out for him. As Kabir says, 'Regard your Guru as a knife grinder, let him grind your heart; cleansing the heart from all impurity let him make it as bright as a mirror.'

THE DISCIPLE

The Guru is only one half of the relationship – the other half is the chela, the shishya – the disciple. Mani Sahukar writes, 'The Guru is necessarily the perfect spiritual preceptor; but the disciple too must fulfil his obligations by cultivating in himself a true spirit of dedication to the Guru. The entire matrix upon which this relationship is founded is the familiar ideal of reciprocity. The gracious act of giving would lose much of its significance if the acceptance of such gifts were not equally gracious and spontaneous. The disciple must be able to receive without reserve.'

The aspirant needs also a kind of discrimination, or at least an openness to personal influence. He needs to know when he has found the man he can trust to be his Guru – a wrong choice will undermine the whole process, for a man is not a Guru until someone has chosen to be his disciple.

The disciple must have the capacity – something which, at the beginning, perhaps only the Guru can see – to develop his inner senses; what we might call his extra-sensory perception. This is necessary, because so much of a true Guru's teaching may be wordless, quite silent, even immobile. Radhakrishnan, in *The Principal Upanishads*, quotes an illustrative story: 'Bahva, asked by Baskali to expound the nature of Brahman, kept silent. Baskali prayed, "Teach me, sir." The teacher was silent, and when addressed a second and a third time he said, "I am teaching but you do not follow. The self is silence."'

There are levels of disciple, differing not only in the capacities they bring to their tasks, but also in the tasks they take up and in the intensity with which they approach the Guru. Many live ordinary lives, devoting only occasional week-ends to the disciplines of the ashram. The rest of the time they may meditate upon the Guru, follow the sadhana he has prescribed, knowing that he is with them, a source of certainty and joy. It would be wrong to assume that most of these will ever progress in spiritual ability to the point where they can attain the higher levels of samadhi.

It is only a few who renounce the world and go to live in the ashram, to serve in whatever way the Guru prescribes, filled with happiness to be serving the person they equate with God. With them are those who, in the fourth stage of orthodox life, have given up what they once possessed. Most of these retire into monastic institutions, taking the ochre robe to symbolize the spiritual efforts they are now making to fit themselves for rebirth at the high level which will be their karmic reward.

Often the renunciation of this fourth stage is made at a time of the Guru's choosing. It is only when other responsibilities have been fulfilled that they are told that they may take the ochre robe. It is not rare, therefore, to find venerable monks looking, with their shaven heads and bare feet, like saints or anchorites of life-long standing, who a decade or so earlier were civil servants or teachers, clerks or wealthy merchants.

Those not living on the ashram travel when they can to see their Guru. They go for his *darshan* – that is, to see him, to benefit by his presence. They may bring him their problems, or they may simply sit and look at him, concentrate on him, suck out of the air his radiating power. If there is an ashram routine, they will adhere to it. If the Guru gives an address, they will attend and listen. Most of them will bring him gifts, either of money or produce – a tape-recorder, a garment, a hand of bananas, perhaps – and acolytes will offer these in turn at a shrine which is often that of the Guru's own predecessor, the previous Master. In return, the devotees will usually live on the ashram for nothing, being given both food and accommodation. They will eat communally, and they will sleep in rooms provided, perhaps even in a guest-house or bungalow. There is usually a limit to the time casual visitors can stay, but a serious seeker may be allowed to live on the ashram for months, in return, perhaps, for helping with the work. From that condition, of course, it is a small step to becoming a probationer disciple, determined to remain until the Guru, by initiating him, accepts him fully, and in that acceptance underwrites his fitness to step towards a glorious eternity.

Should he be successful in that, his reward is moksha liberation; it is an alteration in himself so profound that few have been able to describe it. This is not the temporary dislocation, the sometimes long but always in the end passing loss of self which samadhi brings, but something much more fundamental and lasting. This description comes from a pamphlet entitled *Self-knowledge and Self-realization* and is written by Sri Nisargadatta Maharaj, a Guru who sits unpretentiously in his small darshan hall at the top of a metal stair in a house in a Bombay back street:

The ever-awaited first moment was the moment when I was convinced that I was not an individual at all. The idea of my individuality and welfare had set me burning up to then. The scalding pain was beyond my capacity to endure. But there is not even a trace of it now. I am no more an individual. There is nothing to limit my being now. With the disappearance of the evil signs of individuality, and the accompanying defects, the ideas of acquisition and renunciation have automatically dropped away. The ever-present anxiety and the gloom of the smouldering heart have vanished, and I am all beatitude, pure knowledge, pure consciousness.

My present experience of the world as the divine expression is not for any profit nor for loss, but is the pure, simple, natural flow of beatific consciousness. It has neither sex distractions nor of God and his devotees nor of Brahman and maya. It is the unique, blissful experience of the primal unity ... Every object in the universe has lost its objectivity ... He that once meditated on bliss and peace is himself the ocean of bliss and peace.

That is the kind of report the Guru brings back from the unknown lands to which he says he can guide us. Others travel there, but not all come back; in his desire to help us along the same path the Guru is unique. For thirty Indian centuries men have accepted what he said and gone where he led, despite the enormous demands on them the journey sometimes made. Kabir again has the relevant word: 'The house of God is distant, as is a tall palm; he who climbs to the top, tastes of heaven; he who falls is ground to pieces.'

SUMMARY

In a country where there are perhaps ten million holy men, many with their own devotees, acolytes and disciples, some of them Gurus with hundreds of thousands of followers, all of them the inheritors of a tradition thousands of years old, nothing that one can say about them in general will not somewhere be contradicted in the particular. What I have described is the broad basis upon which the institution of the Guru-shishya relationship rests, and it might be as well to summarize it, in case detail (bewildering in its unfamiliarity) has begun to obscure what is essential.

1. Hinduism believes in a universal Absolute, and calls this Brahman.

2. Hinduism believes that souls are born again and again in different bodies and at levels determined by their karma, which is the accumulated spiritual value of everything they have done in the past.

3. What seems to be the real world must be transcended, either because it is a total illusion, maya, or because it is a real but irrelevant emanation of Brahman.

4. If the unreal 'real' world can be completely transcended, the individual soul which transcends the world achieves moksha, liberation from the birth-death-birth cycle, thus merging after death with Brahman; opinion is divided on whether the soul loses or retains its individuality in that merging.

5. One fits oneself for moksha by selecting the right, balanced route from among those which Hinduism makes available: the most important are jnana yoga, in which one's ignorance of reality is dispelled; bhakti yoga, in which one's devotion to

Brahman is lifted to the most intense level; and raja yoga, in which the mind is controlled and finally stilled to the point at which the activity we call Self comes to an end.

6. The selection and supervision of your actual spiritual discipline, which at its most dedicated is called a sadhana, is a responsibility you normally hand to the Guru of your choice, or of your sect.

7. A genuine Guru (taking for granted a wide scriptural knowledge) must answer to at least two points in the following description: he is someone who proves his spiritual supremacy by frequently attaining the high and intense experiences you seek, who can teach you how to attain them yourself, who has succeeded the Guru who was there before him and who as a result has the power to give you diksha, to initiate you as his disciple. Alternatively, a Guru is anyone (or even anything) you choose to induct yourself into spiritual life and mystic experience.

8. If you are accepted by the Guru of your choice, you become his disciple, his chela or shishya. A disciple may be partly committed, living an ordinary life but seeing his Guru at intervals, developing his mystic or devotional nature and thus increasing his spiritual estate; or he may be a total disciple, renouncing the world, becoming a celibate and eventually perhaps even becoming a Guru himself. This means that he will surrender absolutely to his Master, will utterly give himself up, serving him in even the most menial ways and revering him to the point where he will see no distinction between his Guru and God. If you have selected the right Guru and zealously obeyed his wishes, your success will be observable by your subjective experience of bliss, increased awareness, non-attachment to worldly things, and by the states of intense trance, called samadhi, into which you will with increasing frequency and facility fall. You will as a result feel a great and continuing joy in this life, as well as attaining moksha after it – that final death-defeating liberation which is the bait and lure of the whole

23

process. In this, you will be realizing a potential for spiritual development which you may need the Guru to discover and almost certainly to develop – 'The pearl is found in the oyster, the oyster is in the sea; the diver brings him up; with no one else is the power,' says Kabir.

2

The Vedic Godmen

THE *Brhad-Granyaka Upanishad*: it details the succession, the shishyas made Gurus, through which the Vedic truth was passed – 'Pautimasya (received the teaching) from Gaupavana, Gaupavana from (another) Pautismaya. (This) Pautismaya from (another) Gaupavana. (This) Gaupavana from Kausika, Kausika from Kaundinya, Kaundinya from Sandilya, Sandilya from . . .'

*

The *Vedas* are very old. Deriving from the root word *vid*, which means to know, they have been taken as a body of knowledge, absolute as natural law is thought to be absolute. It is in the need to transmit that knowledge that the institution of the Guru is rooted. The *Vedas* pre-date the *Upanishads* by a margin wide enough to permit those who created the latter to develop a whole new body of beliefs. Since the oldest *Upanishads* seem to have existed before Buddhism, usually thought to have been founded in the sixth century B.C., the *Vedas* can be taken as dating from several centuries earlier than that; Max Müller thought they were composed at the latest around 3000 B.C., other estimates bring the date down to 1000 B.C., but hardly any authority offers a later date than that for them. An exception may be the fourth *Veda*, the *Atharva Veda*, its verses full of curious lore reminiscent of the spells of witchcraft and as a consequence thought rather less of by the orthodox; certainly ancient texts talk of the *trayee*, the triad of *Vedas*. What seems clear is that these first three *Vedas* have come down to us from a time almost uniquely ancient; other literature has lost its purpose as the cultures that produced it collapsed, and only the Old Testament, perhaps, can pretend to sections rivalling the Vedas in antiquity and continuing relevance.

The Vedic tradition begins in a period for which myth must do duty as history. The *Vedas*, it says, were produced by men able to raise their consciousness to the level at which they could reach the eternal and universal truths; these men were the *rishis*. From them descended families; at least families existed who claimed descent from them. Each of these families had the duty of passing on one section of the *Vedas*. In this way the *Vedas* came to be called shruti, 'what is remembered'.

As society stratified into the four main castes, those who had this duty of handing on Vedic knowledge, knowledge of and about Brahma, came to be known as Brahmins; in the early days, they did not have the special place in the caste structure they were to take later; it was, if anything, the Kshattriyas, the warriors, who were the top-dogs. In time, probably because it was their astrological sums which decided seed time and harvest, and their rituals which plucked success from the gods, the Brahmins became more and more powerful. The Brahmin teacher embodied the *Vedas* and so was given the same respect as the *Vedas*, thus perhaps laying the foundations for the Guru's later veneration. The student went to him at a very early age, usually when he was about eight. The 'thread ceremony', now a sort of Brahminical initiation, was in those early days the sign that one was going to a teacher, a Guru.

The teachers were in the main householders with families, living on what their students gave them. Later, there were also universities, staffed by monks and, as the *Upanishads* demanded more philosophical contemplation and more subjective meditation, their doctrines tended to be taught by celibate ascetics living in forest retreats. A man became a teacher without much qualification except maturity, but if he taught the Vedas he would gain pupils mainly because of his renown as a scholar;

through debates (*shastrarta*) at which he defended his opinions about the meaning of some verse or portion of the scriptures.

The Guru, once established, was held in high honour, but he had his obligations – some writers say that no one qualified could be turned away, and certainly the poorer students had to be fed, clothed and housed. Secular teaching had to begin before the first year of a student's stay in the Guru's house was over; it was considered wrong to make any pupil wait longer than that, and the *Chandogya Upanishad* tells how Upakosala, denied his Guru's teaching after twelve years, was finally instructed by the sacred fires themselves. For doctrine that was more mystical, more philosophical, the Guru could wait longer, presumably to test the fitness of his student to learn such esoteric knowledge and technique.

The students would get up before the Guru, around half past four in the morning, and they would usually go to sleep later than he did. They would bath before their morning prayer, then tend the fire altar, then go out to beg for the Guru and his household, bringing back to him each noon what they had been able to collect. This was because no one could be paid for teaching nor pay for being taught – there is uncertainty, however, whether the students always actually did beg; it may be that only the disciples of the spiritual and ascetic *sannyasis* did so, or perhaps only the really poor students of any Guru – the rich may well have been exempt, the sophistry of this being that, in 'begging' from their parents who then paid for their education, they were doing what was asked of them. All students were expected to be chaste, clean and truthful, not to gamble, not slander or insult anyone, to avoid the fashionable, to wear their hair long and matted or to have it shaved off, to go barefoot, to eat simple foods. They had to salute their teachers by complicated prostrations, sit lower than they, remain subservient at all times. Their obedience did not have to be blind; Charaka, the first-century court physician whose writings help form the basis of ancient

Indian medicine, wrote that a student was free to ignore a Guru's orders if they jeopardized health or were against the law. One suspects, though, that it would have been difficult for a student so trained in obedience to decide when the time for rebellion had come.

The Vedic Guru, in return for being thus supported, reverenced and obeyed, took over a great range of paternal duties. Eight years was the minimum period for a young Brahmin's education, and during that time the Guru had to oversee his health, his sleep, his diet, the company he kept, the places he visited. It was normal for a boy to stay as long as twelve years under this autocracy; in earliest times this was how long they thought it took to learn one of the *Vedas* thoroughly.

It is clear that the position of the Brahmins depended to some extent on the absence of writing. Once there was writing and thus books, it became theoretically possible for anyone to learn the *Vedas*. In practice, though, there were some pretty tough defences against anyone who wanted to pull down this holy and profitable Guru-chela system. The intonation of the words had to be precisely right, and so could only be learned from someone who could show you how to do it; secondly, the *Vedas* by their nature were not for anybody – the lowest caste, the Shudras, should, it was commanded, have boiling oil poured in their ears if they heard a recitation of the *Vedas* even by accident. Only Brahmins were allowed to learn them – I heard of an American who was recently refused tuition in Vedic recitation by an old Brahmin in Benares; he found another teacher and, once proficient, returned to the teacher who had turned him down. The old Brahmin refused to accept that the American had learned the *Vedas*, even when he heard him recite the verses – 'When I recite the *Vedas*,' he said, 'they are the *Vedas*; when you recite them, they are not.' So strict was the attempt to hold onto this Brahminical preserve that the

Mahabharata, one of India's two great holy epics, condemns to hell anyone writing down the *Vedas.*

Nevertheless, once writing was established, despite the continuing Vedic tradition, some of the urgency must have gone out of the need for Brahmins to take up their sacred duty. At the same time, post-Upanishadic commentators were beginning to hammer out the terms of India's monism, the single mystic heart of its diversified, proliferating pantheism. For them, meditation became more important than knowledge alone, and certainly more than ritual. As the view form of Guru began to flourish, the other remained static, even declined. The great *bhaktas* of the fifteenth and sixteenth centuries, men like Chaitanya and Kabir, by stressing love and undermining the caste position, perhaps gave a final, decisive impetus to the development of the Guru as he is today.

In India, however, all is coexistence, and although the spiritual nature of the teaching and the teacher gained in emphasis, the line from Guru to Guru, through which the Vedic verses and their attendant rituals were passed, continued to flourish. Even today, many orthodox families will have a son at one of the Vedic schools, and there are still centres of traditional learning tight-packed with schools and ancient maths.

*

'. . . Ghrtakausika from Parasaryayana, Parasaryayana from Parasarya, Parasarya from Jatukarnya. Jatukarnya from Asurayana and Yaska. Asurayana from Traivani. Traivani from Aupajandhani. Aupajandhani from Asuri. Asuri from Bharadvaja. Bharadvaja from Atreya. Atreya from . . .'

*

The grammarian Panini was, legend insists, a dull student. One day, despairing of ever becoming a scholar, he was sitting alone in the forest when he heard the god Shiva, in the form of the dancer Natraja, rattling his hand-drum. Panini heard the sounds as language, leapt into scholarship and codified a grammar on the basis of those drumbeats. If he was the man responsible, he certainly constructed a difficult language for following generations to struggle over.

What Panini codified was the Vedic language which preceded and led into *Sanskrit*. Perhaps the main difference between the Vedic language and classical Sanskrit is the absence in the latter of accents. In the Vedic, there are three levels of intonation: *udatta*, which means 'brought up' and is the highest level, the middle level, *swarita*, and the lowest, *anundatta*. When written, the anundatta syllable usually comes first, then the udatta, with the swarita last. If you get these wrong, then the meaning of the word changes – a demon determined to kill the god Indra tried to gain power by chanting a mantra which meant, 'Make the enemy of Indra strong'. Unfortunately the demon was more wicked than educated, he gave the last syllable of Indra's name the udatta instead of the anundatta accent and so reversed the mantra's meaning. Paying for his incompetence he died in the subsequent battle between them – confident, one supposes, to the last.

In the Vedic schools, the boys learn these accents; they are taught the metre and how long each sound should be held while chanting. This is based on the *matra*, the time it is supposed to take to pronounce a short vowel. They learn twenty or more sentences every day, depending on their age and capacity. The technique is simple – it is endless repetition. Each sentence is chanted ten times over while the Guru listens or, breaking in, sharply corrects. When a boy has learned a chapter, a *shukta*, he repeats the whole thing ten times. The final stage of this level of education is called *ghana*, when a pupil may be asked at random to recite any chapter from any *Veda*. If the pupil is really proficient, he is called *ghana-pathi*; this only means, however, that he knows the texts by heart. He then moves on to learn their interpretation.

Because the *Vedas* are instructions for rituals as well as prayers, hymns and theological speculation, the Gurus who teach the *Vedas* are often asked to perform those rituals. Many of the latter are extremely complicated and nowadays rarely done. Not only is this perhaps a cultural loss, it also reduces the money the Vedic Gurus can earn and so pushes them a step nearer extinction. The Gurus often have a group of families, called their *shishya varga*, for whom they perform this priestly duty and which they inherit from their fathers, as the families inherit the Guru and his sons from their forefathers. Centuries ago, the priest and teacher functions among Brahmins were kept separate, but nowadays, as the number of people who know the rituals goes down and as the number of families who want to perform them does the same, the Guru has taken on the priestly function as well.

In the normal, everyday rituals, fire plays the significant part, the most important is, perhaps, the fire permanently kept burning by a householder (*garhapatya*). There are many fire ceremonies, called collectively *prajapatya*; some of these are for ancestor worship, others are directed to Brahman. Each has its own clutch of Vedic hymns, and the young Brahmin must learn which are the right hymns and how they are to be intoned during each of the different rituals.

There are, perhaps fortunately for the sanity of the pupils, days on which one may not study. The lunar month is divided into two fortnights, called the white and the dark fortnight, that is from the dark of the moon to the full, and from full to dark again. These free days are called *anadhyaya* and they fall on, for instance, the eighth and the fourteenth day of each fortnight, on the day of the full moon, on the first moonless day, and so on. And you are not allowed to study the *Vedas* on the fourth, seventh and thirteenth night of each fortnight.

Meeting the Gurus who teach in the Vedic schools, one has the sense of glimpsing one last, already tottering, dodo. That is

31

not to say that there are not young people who come, or are
sent to the schools, nor that the scholarship displayed is not
impressive and even vigorous. But today it relates to little
outside itself; one might see the same exactitude, the same
sense of precedence and repetitiveness, in some forgotten office,
part of the collapsing bureaucracy of a once-great empire. It has
that feeling of glory and importance now shrunken into mere
habits of behaviour, of men continuing to act in a particular way
because others a long time ago acted thus, of a way of life from
which the virtue has drained, leaving only tired, inbred custom
to sustain it.

*

'... Vatsya from Sandilya. Sandilya from Kaisorya Kapya.
Kaisorya Kapya from Kumaraharita. Kumaraharita from
Galava. Galava from Vidarbhikaundinya. Vidarbhikaundinya
from Vatsanapat Babhrava. Vatsanapat Babhrava from Patah
Saubharat. Patah Saubharat from Ayasya Angirasa, Ayasya
Angirasa from ...'

*

Gokarna is one of the holy cities of South India, a place of
temple, monastery and legend. It is a famous *linga* shrine, a
place where Ravana, the ten-headed king and hero, put down the
atman-linga granted him by Shiva and, having relieved himself,
turned back to see that it had not only changed into a stone cow,
but in that shape was sinking into the ground; he grabbed its
ears and held it, so only these now remain visible – enough to
make the place a centre of pilgrimage. It is this story which gave
the town its name, 'cow's ears'.

Gokarna stands beside the sea, its beach of deep yellow sand
long and empty, the breakers sometimes garlanded by the faithful but otherwise left to beat and flurry undisturbed. The streets
twist among a wilderness of temples and maths, each it seems

with its white-clad acolyte peering out lazily from the tiny terraces beside the doors. There is a wide main street, lined with low, two-storied houses. Each has a terrace in front of it, shaded by the long sweep of the tiled or palm thatched roof. The cement floors of these terraces glitter; they were ground smooth when the cement was first laid by daily working with the *pallekai* seed. Inside the houses, women polish the earthen floors, bending straight-legged as they work wristily away with a flat stone.

And as their wives work within, bare-chested Brahmins watch the passers-by outside – swaying, hard-breasted women, near-naked sadhus, some sullenly wrapped in the acridity of hemp smoke, small girls in gay, calf-length dresses, dignified elders with oiled top-knots smoothed over their napes, their shanks moving with harmonious deliberation within the white and glittering draperies of their *dhotis*. At their feet scuttle the grey-black crows and curious, nervous, yellow-brown dogs.

Between the houses, shops display religious curios, rosaries of *tulsi* beads, finger-cymbals, bells; and spices, or coconuts to drink, the soft meat in its shell then held out for some grateful, passing cow to lick clean; bare tables wait in the tea-shop, where the sweet-meats, blandishments for flies, lie in a dusty glass case and a watchful Brahmin sits near the cash-desk.

We had come to see Khare Shastri, the old Guru, more than seventy years old, who is the respected head of a school and of an old teaching family here. One of the touts who roam the Gokarna streets, looking for holy tourists, pilgrims in need of a minor priest to perform a ceremony, picked us up. With his help we discovered that the old man was not in Gokarna just then, that his son was not at home and that our best course would be to see Khare Shastri's senior chela.

We walked down a narrower lane, leaving the main street. The temples crowded closer; from doorways framed in ancient twisted wood came the sound of bells, and through the shadows a glimpse now and then of the colour and sharp glitter of an idol. We passed under an archway, to see before us Kotihirtha, the central sheet of holy water, the tank, its sides steeply stepped, a shrine islanded upon it, the resort of the devout, of those washing clothes or children or themselves. Its name means 'ten million varieties of blessed water' and the story is that the eagle of Vishnu, carrying this powerful liquid to heaven, let one drop fall here, a permanent, if accidental, benison. The water, though divine, was greenish, disturbed by ripples marking the upsurge of a spring; now and then dark fish showed on the surface, turning, then disappearing in darting, disciplined schools perhaps appropriate to such a place of learning. Children played on the steps, pilgrims poured the blessed water over their heads, women ducked into the dark ripples, their clothes floating in a breast-high frill about them.

The house we went to overlooked this water. It was grey, stone-built, and belonged to the chela, a householder in his forties called Kodelkere Ramachandra Shrouti. He was strongly built, solid, of middle height. When he smiled, he displayed large, blackening teeth which thrust outwards about his words as if to give them an emphasis of their own. On his forehead he had the white bars of the Shaivite, with a red dot below; more bars and symbols were painted on his arms. He was bare to the waist, except for the sacred five-fold Brahmin thread which he may never take off.

He had studied with the absent Khare Shastri for fifteen years before he reached the stage of being ghana-pathi. His actual surname was Bhatta, but he was given the name Shrouti as a sort of title, in the same way that a university graduate gets letters after his name. It testifies to his proficiency in the Vedas.

Brahminical families are said to belong to the *Veda* for which they have ancestral responsibility, and this makes them into a kind of sect. Ramachandra's was the *Ajur Veda*, his Guru's the

Rig Veda. Despite this – a difference which can prevent marriage even between equally high caste Brahmin families – and a difference of native language, which in Ramachandra Shrouti's case was Kanada, they did have links in common. The most important, he said, was their acceptance of the Advaita philosophy of Shankaracharya. They co-operated in the rituals; he lived on his earnings as a priest. He was married, with four children, so this was no small point, since this income is actually rather chancy; it is called *dakshina*, is voluntary and supposed to depend on the merits of the man in charge of the ritual. Since it is the client who decides this merit or lack of it, these payments have become hard to separate from charity.

He had three brothers, all of them out in the world in ordinary occupations; in this, he saw signs of the collapse of his tradition. Now it was usually only the eldest son who had any real Vedic training, and this often just to fit him for a career as a practising ritualist, someone who knew the right way to run a ceremony. The Guru-chela tradition had thus become an assembly-line for priests who would cater for the surviving orthodox; in some cases so emptily it had become more a matter of folklore than religion. Those who did not learn the *Vedas*, usually the younger brothers, were educated in the normal way – that is, on the Western pattern – and followed ordinary commercial careers; even those in the Vedic schools were learning English privately or through correspondence schools.

Ramachandra believed in pranayama, the control of breath, the vital wind, but not in the complex *asanas* of yoga: they were for ascetics, or for those following the Tantric ways. Shankara had said this, and his philosophy was the last word – Vedanta, the end of the *Vedas*. Nothing had been revealed or discovered since – the *Vedas*, the Brahmanas, the *Upanishads* and Shankara's philosophy were held to be the crux and basis of the whole religion.

'When I was a student', he said, 'I used to study and learn

35

(adhyayan) all the time. Now I am married, there are ceremonies and readings I keep up. I do the householder's fire
worship and *devarshipitru*, a propitiation of God, the rishis and
my ancestors. And I must recite various parts of the *Vedas*.
All this adds up to the normal Brahma *yagna*, the expected
devotions, and if I don't keep them up I am given a small
imposition – some small sacrifice to perform – by my Guru.

'The basic duties of a Brahmin are study, teaching, keeping
up one's own rituals and helping with other people's, giving to
those who need and accepting what is given to one. He has no
other prescribed duties. Of course, if he has no means of earning
a living, he must look for work. He should always be ready to
fulfil the demand of any Brahmin for a religious ritual and he
should not expect to earn a living from this. Still, if there is no
other way of earning money, even this is permissible, although
there is the duty of the holy man to beg – that has been laid
down in detail. In any case, a Brahmin can always do the work
of other castes – it is the other castes which can never do the
work of a Brahmin.

'The first duty, study, means collecting knowledge in order
to fulfil one's second duty, teaching. Giving is a part of one's
duties, but one expects dakshina to go with all rites, and that
means one has to be ready to receive as well. But one shouldn't
accept *dana*, the donation, with the intention of amassing money.
Teaching, on the other hand, must be free – it is laid down that
no one should take cash for teaching, no one should pay for
learning.

'A Guru can have more than one student – he can have a
hundred. There are methods by which a teacher can teach
many students at the same time – *dassavadhana* or *shatavadhana*,
which means the simultaneous or the consecutive teaching of
many students in different subjects by organizing one's mind.
In this way, by proper concentration, many subjects can be
taught at the same time. There are still people today who teach

by these methods, who have these powers of the mind. There is a
gentleman from Kurundawada, he has got such a powerful
memory that he can recite anything: the *Vedas*, the *Gita* . . . His
name is Edurkar; Sakharam Bhat Edurkar and he is over
seventy years old.

'When a Guru accepts a shishya, there is a fire ceremony laid
down, a *homa*, and another given for Saraswati, the goddess of
learning, to ask that his intellect develop properly. But I didn't
begin my studies in this way and they are largely extinct now.
When we learn the *Vedas* we divide the process into five sections
and if the student is not very bright he can give up and go home
after the first one, which takes about a year to complete. Not
many learn all five sections, or *kandas*, these days, although
traditionally if a young Brahmin didn't learn them, he wasn't
considered qualified for marriage. He was expected to know the
Vedas; if he was not quite intelligent enough for that, he ought
to have learned at least the rituals. The very intelligent were
expected to learn both. Now, whoever hasn't been able to
graduate in at least one of these three ways is given a token
graduation just before marriage, so as not to disbar him.'

Now Ramachandra brought out manuscripts on which he was
working, all carefully wrapped in cloths, and he and Bala
pored over them and discussed them. From outside came the
chatter of the bathers, worshippers, pilgrims, workers, washers,
idlers; and the steady slap of clothes on stone.

In the afternoon, Ramachandra suggested, with the character-
istic humility of the shishya, that we should meet someone more
qualified than he to answer our questions. Since his Guru was
away, he had recommended another, and would take us to him
himself. We met Ramachandra, therefore, outside his door and
he led us round the far corner of Kotihirtha to a house which
directly faced the arch through which we had first come to that
central, holy reservoir.

This house was set back from the road; concrete steps led

upwards into gloom; a gallery ran the length of the building and
Ramachandra took us to the room that lay behind it. The gallery
took the place of one wall of the room, its wooden ballustrades
and arches set between stone uprights. Narrow wooden pillars
supported the ceiling, which was crossed by low beams on which
hung the white garments of the students. Through a half-open
sliding door of creaking wood I could see piles of books and
manuscripts littering a long trestle table.

There were six men in the room, aged between twenty and
fifty; they were grouped round their Guru, Ganapathi
Subramanya Sharma, a man much older than the oldest of them.
We were greeted as members of a court might greet the pleni-
potentiaries of some doubtful friendly power. Bala and I sat
behind a table, the old Guru on my right, while the others
moved restlessly, stood, then sat, readjusted their positions,
shuffled closer to each other, until they finally settled hunched
like hens in a corner, the sunlight gleaming on the water of
Kotihirtha and on the pale-coloured stone houses on the far
side.

Subramanya Sharma had that appearance, which some learned
men get, of having reached an absolute in time, as if he had paid
every tribute age could demand and now lived on in a dry and
perhaps sensationless eternity. Only death, one felt, would
alter him – if he survived for twenty years, he would look
exactly as he did now. The cheeks would be no more shrunken
about the toothless mouth, the brown eyes would not fade more
than they had, the ceaseless, unconscious plucking of his left
hand would be no more fretful than it was today. His forehead
was white with Shaivite marks, he chewed his gums, looked
sharply at us with a scholar's cunning, his eyes behind the oval
lenses of his spectacles little more than a pale gleam. When asked
a question, he would lay his shaven head back, his glasses almost
at the tip of his long curved nose, his chin jutting like a trireme's
prow, and look at his interlocutor as though measuring him for a

thrust; but he answered peacefully enough, the network of veins in his neck standing out as though with the effort of such benevolence. Now and then he made what must surely have been donnish jokes. After each, his face gaping into an ancient's baby smile, he would look round in some pride at his audience and they, to be fair, laughed honestly and as if they meant it.

He told us he was sixty years old, although if he had put it at forty years more I should not have been surprised. Then he gave us some more preliminary information. 'I began studying the *Vedas* when I was ten; I studied them for fourteen years. Since then, I have kept up the holy Vedic fire. I follow the six duties of the Brahmin (which Ramachandra had already outlined for us), I follow the *Yajur Veda*; but I don't worship as a business. My own Guru was my father.'

The others interrupted to say that he was the Guru of all the followers of this Vedic sect. Subramanya Sharma smiled, pointed his chin at them, then at me.

'There were various ceremonies when I began my studies – one of gratitude for the rishis, one to declare my intention of working well, one for the goddess of words, of learning. Then came the study of the *Vedas*, first learning them by heart, then understanding their meaning. If a student could understand, if he had the capacity, words and meaning might be taught at the same time. But there aren't many who are sufficiently intelligent, so we teach the words first and the meaning later.

'I used to beg as the tradition demands when I was a student – I used to beg from my mother. Since my parents loved me, they never let me go out to beg; it was not my pride that prevented me. I had eight classmates, who were from this place and were my friends. It was believed by the *Mimamsakaras* that one could learn the *Upanishads* only until noon; hymns and prayers could be studied even in the evening. So we worked in that way; and we had the prescribed days and nights off, and any day which was thundery, or when there were visitors at the ashram. We used to wake up at five in the morning, and then do the dawn worship, the fire and the ancestor worship; then the teaching would begin.

'It used to be that the first three castes would have the same elementary education, then each would specialize in what most concerned them. Today, they say that only the first and the last castes remain. There is a story in the *Chandogya Upanishad*: Satyakama Jabala was a boy who went to Gautama's ashram and asked for education. Gautama asked him about his parentage, but the boy only told him that he was known as Satyakama Jabala. Gautama, however, considered that the boy had proved his Brahmin origins by coming to him for learning and so he took him as a student. But this was at Gautama's discretion – there is no Vedic mandate that the Guru should accept anyone who comes along and asks for learning. There is no such rule.

'It is laid down that self-denial, knowledge of the *Vedas* and birth into the Brahmin caste are the three conditions of being a Brahmin. A person who doesn't know the *Vedas* or practise self-denial is known as a Brahmin "by birth", that's all. "*Janmana jayate shudra samskarat dvija uchyate*" – "At birth one's condition is that of a shudra; by education and observance one becomes twice-born (i.e. a Brahmin)". Only a person born of a Brahmin father and mother should be given Vedic education. I have been entrusted with the duty of not teaching the *Vedas* to non-Brahmins. There are stories of Gurus who have been deceived about the caste origins of their students.'

The quiet, slightly querulous voice droned on. Outside, the sun yellowed, the shadows stretched as though desperate to detach themselves and seek a freedom of their own. In the back of the room, a young man in a dhoti sat on a bench, leaned on his right arm, picked his nose slowly with the middle finger of his right hand. A long-faced older man, his hair greying and no teeth in his upper gums, stood in the corner and made what seemed sardonic remarks about our inquisition. Sitting apart from the others, a man whose cheeks were creased with the harsh lines of fanaticism nodded slowly in the ceaseless, involuntary assent of burgeoning nervous disease. He compared a text with Ramachandra, checked a reference: Ramachandra bent anxiously over the manuscript, gold-rimmed glasses on his strong face. Finally satisfied, he leaned back as if delighted that it was not he who now had to answer our questions.

Subramanya Sharma said, 'I have six students. I wanted more students than that – the *Vedas* instruct us to pray that we may get many good students. There is also a ritual for getting better students. In the *samavartana* (the pupil's last ceremony; the literal meaning is "returning" – the boy goes back to his home) it says, "As rivers get tributaries, as the month is made up of days, as a mother desires a good son, so a Guru desires a good shishya." There is also a prayer asking that I get better shishyas than myself, and another asking for Guru-shishya unity. At the time that he is learning, the student should think of the Guru as God; and the Guru should think of the pupil as his son. What the student learns will be of no use to him if he abuses the Guru. It has been said that if the shishya will consider the Guru as God, then he will become famous. If they don't consider the Guru as God but abuse and insult him, then nothing they learn will be of any use later.

'This relationship between Guru and shishya goes on to the end. And even after the Guru's death, the shishya is expected to perform the ancestor worship of the Guru as though he were actually descended from him. Daily ancestor worship consists of a prayer for the Guru as well – though the parents are also considered as Gurus, of course. And if a Guru has no children, then he should certainly consider himself the father of his shishyas.

'There are men in and out of monastic orders who go about as Gurus. They do not have the approval of the *Vedas*. However, some say they are *turiyateetas*, that is, totally beyond the four orthodox stages of life, which are irrelevant to them. Since they went through the entire process in earlier births they may still be carrying the benefits of those past lives. Therefore, we shouldn't question their good faith; but neither should we follow them. We don't know about the present Gurus; we don't want to pass remarks about them. But there are those who simply go about in the garb of Gurus – the *Upanishads* have warned us not to fall into the trap of people who go about dressed as Gurus. And moksha, liberation, can come to the householder too.

'The true Guru is like God; he is not God himself. It is clear from the saying that we should consider the Guru *as* God that he is not God himself. The Guru-shishya relation should be informal, according to the scriptures. It should be natural. That's how it has been maintained. At the time when a Guru accepts a student he says, "With all my heart I will teach you; let your mind follow mine, with concentration follow and worship my words; I am the holy Guru, you are under my instruction." That is why Shankara said that the Guru's motto should be "Guide always". The Guru's mantra says, "I work for your progress, and you follow me in mind and follow my instructions without confusion. Let God give us the strength. May God give you all confidence in me."'

A breeze wandered through the room, bringing with it the slapping noise of clothes beaten against stone by a late laundress and, from somewhere below, a cricket commentary from Calcutta; India's Test Match against Australia incongruously relayed here through some errant pilgrim's transistor. A bespectacled young scholar leaned against the small, carved, wooden arches of the gallery. Through its bars I could see, lining the other side of Kotihirtha, the brown and pink and yellow houses, each with its shifting mackerel-speckling of reflections from the water below. The houses seemed small, crowded together, defensive despite the serene light. They had narrow windows, barred with heavy wooden stakes, and tiny doors let through their thick stone walls; above, the eaves jutted out as though forming a protective porch. A small, grey temple dome punctuated the line of their red-brown tile roofs; behind these, bright palm trees drooped, then gently shook in the small and sunny afternoon breeze. Beyond them again, the red and pale green of a worn escarpment, spur of the distant hills, and above that the slow traverse of the travelling clouds.

With a soft clatter, three cows slowly passed by on the road below. Subramanya Sharma was saying, 'It is not right that the rituals are performed by hired priests; it isn't approved by the *Vedas*. Of course, in the case of kings it's different. Kings must be guided by priests. There are procedures laid down by which a king should accept his Guru. But today there are no kings of the pure warrior caste. There are only Brahmins and Shudras. As for the Brahmins, they should try and keep up all the rituals themselves, if necessary seeking help from experts. But there is no Vedic sanction for teaching oneself. The *Veda* says, "Under a Guru learn the *Vedas*." Even a single word, spoken by an experienced Guru, will open the eyes of an ignorant youngster. It says in the *Katha Upanishad*, "*Navarenaavarena prokta bahudha chintyamanopi naesha bodhdhum shakya*" – "Unless it is told by someone greater, even if one thinks in various ways, one will not understand it."

'The world has not given up the Vedic way of life or the *Vedas*, though some people misunderstand and think it has. As for me, I adopted this life under the instructions of my Guru. There is a text: "When one's father and grandfather and many generations have walked a particular road, the son should take the same path. By travelling the established way one does not perish – that road is without thorns."

'My father lived as a *shroutriya* for seventeen years and taught over a thousand students. For seventeen years he kept the fires burning. Then his wife died. Finally he had to give up the domestic fire, as well as the funeral fire of his wife. That's why he asked me to carry on the fire. I was the eldest of four brothers, and so he asked me to take on the responsibility of preserving the Vedic fire. He said, "You should have no hesitation – that is the rishis' word." I accepted, and since then I have continued the fire worship.

'It isn't an easy job, as a matter of fact. There are three fires. You have to select cow dung, and then prepare the cow dung balls. Each of them should be about as big as a coconut. There should be no dust in the cow dung, and the balls should be dried in the sun. And every evening and morning the three fire pits should be fed with these balls, while the ashes inside are removed. Every morning and evening the fires must be worshipped ritually and then covered up. The fire then goes on smouldering; a cow-dung ball fire can be preserved for thirteen hours. If the fire goes out, there is an imposition which the *agnihotri* faces – extra ceremonies and so on. Every fortnight there is an *ishti*, a special ceremony.

'One should render service to the Guru – once, it is laid down, the shishyas had to dress him, anoint him, bath him, and eat his leftovers, but this isn't practised today. But the shishya should be a shadow to the Guru – if the Guru runs, the shishya should keep pace with him; if he walks the shishya should follow; if he stands the shishya should stop. The shishya should not eat before the Guru does. However, none of my shishyas go out to beg. One should not beg to fill one's belly. All the same, one ought to be without shame, even if one is rich, and beg when one is *brahmacharya*. And if there is no charity, one should beg from the wife or the mother of the Guru. That is the tradition.'

*

'. . . Abhuti Tvastra from Visvarupa Tvastra. Visvarupa Tvastra from the two Asvins. The two Asvins from Dadhyanc Atharvana. Dadhyanc Atharvana from Artharvan Daiva.

44

Artharvan Daiva from Mrtyu Pradhvamsana. Mrtyu Pradhvamsana from . . .'

*

At five the next morning, by the light of a weak electric bulb, the
son of the house sat, repeating some verse over and over again
in a toneless chant. Respecting his devotions, or religious
instruction, it was some time before I recognized what he was
saying as sentences from his English text-book.

We swam; by seven thirty we were walking down the main
street again, overlooked by the low, carved galleries which
made up the top storeys of some of the little houses. One or two
of the buildings looked rough, reached by steps which were
only rocks piled for easy access before the unpainted doors; but
most were painted, clean, with pillared terraces, the women
already at work sweeping and smoothing and polishing until
their steps and porches shone. On floors or benches or string
beds, the comfortable Brahmin husbands, bath and early duties
over, watched the quickening street, while next door their
neighbour cleaned his teeth with a busy, stretched finger and
spat with intensity into the gutter.

We passed by the cluster of temples at the end of the street,
turned left, stopped before the school we had passed the day
before; outside the school, his house, the Guru sat, his deerskin
spread over stones on the left of the entrance. He greeted us. He
was also toothless, sharp chinned, but peered through dark
spectacles with the dazedness of incipient senility, or perhaps
blindness, at the curious manifestations of a world he knew
could be comprised in a Vedic chapter.

Barefooted, we went in. To our left, five white-clad boys,
Shiva marked, sat on a low stone platform. Each chanted in
unison with the others, their thin bodies moving with the
effort and the rhythm. Their eyes watched us curiously while
their lips repeated again and again the prescribed, inflected

45

sentences. But tradition degenerates – each clutched a long oblong of paper on which the complex characters of Sanskrit toiled in heavy rows; there was no proscription of the written word here.

Behind them, a long, barred window looked out into the street from which we had come, face-to-face with the blank temple wall opposite. Octagonal pillars supported a dark, wooden ceiling low above the platform; everywhere else, beams cracked with age held up the frame of the roof, so that between them we could see the grey underside of the tiles. The old Guru came slowly in and joined the boys on their platform, hunkering down long shanked, then adjusting his dhoti; with its edging of green printed leaves, one end of it flung over his shoulder, it looked so much like a toga that he might have been an old, corrupt member of the Imperial Senate, busy about some esoteric affair ordered on the whim of a distant, impatient Tiberius.

Opposite him, a ladder reached up through the dark ceiling to the next floor, and above him hung a row of lanterns, some on long ropes, others on string, or on chains, large and small, square and oblong – eight or ten of them. From a wooden cross-piece supported by a pair of whitening antlers hung pictures of the gods; others gleamed above the heads of the still chanting boys. From the ceiling drooped an electric fan, not needed, in the freshness of the morning.

Facing us as we entered, about twenty feet from the front door, was one end of a terrace. Leading off it, to the left, were doors into the interior of the house; to the right was a high wall and at the end of the perspective thus formed stood an open shed full of wood. To the left, behind a window, an opening bordered by a purple pattern of conventionalized flowers and leaves and protected by thick, wooden bars between which floated the filmy threads of cobwebs, was the holy, permanent fire, its slow smoke curling from under the basket-like damper which covered it.

The Guru's cousin approached; a fat man in middle age, he was bare to the waist, and grey hair lay across the stretched mound of his belly. Round his neck hung two strings of wooden beads, presumably of *tulsi* seeds, and above them his head, though powerful, seemed too large for his body; with his jowls and shaven skull he looked to me like a gentler Mussolini. His small eyes lay within shallow caves of drooping flesh, their depth not lightened by any sparkle of intelligence. But he was open, devout, concerned about the tradition of which he was one of the hereditary keepers. He spoke placidly enough, his voice was even; but one knew that he could see the end of what he stood for, and that he thought its coming was inevitable. I got the feeling that he saw himself as one of a rearguard fighting doggedly but hopelessly throughout a forced and final retreat.

'The children come to learn the Vedas at about eight years old. There are eight students; they begin at seven, work till nine, then again from ten to twelve and in the afternoons from two thirty to five thirty. The house is the Guru's, Narayan Sitaram Yagneshwar; he is my cousin. The pupils don't live with him, they live with their parents; but they work for him in the traditional way, helping with the housework and so on.

'We came here from Ratnagiri (for me, a line of distant lights gleaming on a mysterious shore) near Goa, about 150 years ago. We brought the *agni*, the sacred fire, with us when we came; how long it had been burning then nobody knows. Now there are about fifty members of the family, of whom about thirty-five live here in this house. So, for the future, the fire is safe for another two or three generations. But it's difficult – for instance, cow's milk is necessary for the rituals and it's hard to get . . . Though if you really can't get it, it's permissible to use rice. And then you must have the ishti, the fortnightly ceremony at which four Brahmins must be present who, between them, really know the four Vedas – and they'll get more and more difficult to find.

'All the ceremonies are becoming a problem to keep up. The Guru here has performed *soma-yagna*; that's very rare, because it takes nearly a week and costs a lot of money – about five thousand rupees (roughly £250 – which is much more in Indian terms). You have to hold the mouth of a sheep, so that you stop its breath. The sheep's stomach distends and you hit it and it dies. Then you bore a hole into the body and take out its liver and a portion of that is put on the holy fire. The piece that's left is then eaten by those who have taken part in the ceremony. You have to kill a sheep a day for six days – you can see it costs a lot. My cousin performed it in 1963 – he's one of the few people alive who have done it.

'Ceremonies like that used to be paid for by the princely states, but of course they don't exist any more. Rich business-men now pay the expenses – men who want the tradition to continue. But our responsibility to the traditions is inherited – we work for the whole world when we perform the old ceremonies. The traditions must be continued. In the North there are very few people who keep up their fires; only in the South are the traditions preserved. But everywhere pressure of time and many different distractions keep people away from them – and how can you teach the rituals if you never perform them yourself? And how can you demand that other people should perform them?

'The young now come very reluctantly to learn the *Vedas* – the pressures on the culture are too strong. Of course, there's a demand from the lower castes to be taken on as pupils, but they don't have the cultural tradition, so they have diffi-culties with the Vedic sound system. In any case, we don't really want to teach them . . . and they aren't very good at it. But in the meantime the rituals have been eroded, there isn't the support; finally, we may have to accept anyone who wants to learn the *Vedas* – especially if we end up by taking a Government subsidy. Then we may have to take even

Untouchables. And that would really put us at the end of a tradition.

'Here, things may go on in the old way another fifty years – farther South, perhaps a hundred. Though there is a chance we will go on – they're really a very stubborn people. Look at Matunga – it's been swallowed up by Bombay, but the Brahmins there go on putting the *tripundra* (the Shaivite marks) on their foreheads and wearing the dhoti and going bare to the waist, despite all the pressures of the city . . . In the North, they don't even know how to tie a dhoti – we have to teach them when they come here. But we don't have to teach people from the South things like that – they haven't lost their culture yet.

'Of course, we welcome the new interest in Hinduism that comes from the West. And though our traditions may go, a skeleton may be left. Most of the old rituals, even the sacred thread ceremony, are going already, but an abstract interest in the Hindu religion remains; and people, of course, want to preserve that. But they don't want actively to take part in the religion, although they don't mind bowing before the god. Here too, you see, the trend is not to perform the *pujas* (religious ceremonies) fully. The interest in philosophy grows, but the rituals are being lost. And the first preference must be for the rituals; it tells us that in the *smritis*. If we can't preserve them fully, even a proportion will be worth preserving.'

He turned suddenly and pointed to a window about two feet square, barred by heavy staves of wood and covered by half-closed shutters, beyond which I could see a dark, bare room. 'Look how the idea of uncleanliness has gone. It's laid down that a menstruating woman should live apart for four days. That's what that room is for. But in the city, people don't have the space to spare for it, so they give up the tradition. In this way the area of observance is shrinking all the time, and eventually it will vanish.

'And the consequences are economic, too. These chelas

should beg for the Guru; they get their money from their families, so we say they are begging from their relations. But what happens when there are not enough chelas? When there are not enough rich people prepared to pay to have the ceremonies kept up? Then the Guru has to solicit for work; formerly, people came to them, now they must go out and pester people.

'For years now this economic pressure has been forcing the Guru-shishya relationship itself to decline – because of the rivalry it breeds between them. The area of activity is declining, so they have to share out whatever Vedic ceremonies are arranged. It's naturally going to cost less to get a chela who knows a ceremony to perform it, than to get his teacher. But in the old days, if you had approached a chela, he would have said, "I'll do it, if you ask my Guru's permission." Now, because the pressure is so acute, often the Guru won't allow his pupil to perform the ceremony – he will take it himself. So that starts mistrust between them – and after a while, if the chela is asked, he doesn't refer it to his Guru or ask his permission. And, after all, they know they can trust the chela, they've seen him perform as his Guru's assistant, the Guru will have introduced him to Vedic followers, perhaps all over the country, and he is obviously a Brahmin – why shouldn't they go to him? But in the old days it would have been impossible except through the Guru.

'And the orthodox families are breaking up. Some fifty years ago, my father's eldest brother was a magistrate; he'd studied, he spoke English. He was still a rarity – he had to travel fifty miles to High School. But a High School was opened in this area about forty years back, and now there are three or four children in every generation who leave orthodox families and go into the ordinary world – the Guru here has six sons, but three have left to work at other things. As I said, there are fifty in our family, but they don't all live together as they did in the old days – fifteen have gone. We have some land, of course, but nowadays, since Land Reform, it's hard to make that profitable. We used to lease it out on a yearly basis, but now the tenant is protected and his rent fixed, so we can't do that. And if he says one year that his crop has failed and he can't pay us, there is very little we can do. The laws are too cumbersome, it's become very hard to collect the rents, and so the family grows and its income doesn't ... It gets harder and harder every year to keep on ...'

*

'... Ekarso from Vipracitti. Vipracitti from Vyasti. Vyasti from Sanaru. Sanaru from Sanatana. Sanatana from Sanaga. Sanaga from Paramesthin. Paramesthin from Brahma. Brahma is self-born. Salutation to Brahma.'

3

The Godmen

Steam hurls past the windows, old-fashioned, exciting, the white banner all journeys used to carry. Trains fit into India, match its distances without dwarfing them; already they seem artifacts out of history, part of this landscape more than that of the West.

Outside, a man with a green cloth wound about his head lifts a forkful of straw to a low rick; it splays, lit about him like a halo as he swings it through the sunlight. Brown paddies wait between harvest and seeding. Trees stand close, scrubland passes, then scattered patches of rough grass curling into the hollows and valleys among low hills; in a dark-brown cluster, two or three thatched huts. Below us, the foam of bamboo catches the light as the land drops. On a path that winds away at right angles from the railway line, a boy in wine-red, holding a staff, stands still and stares at the train, at the me he cannot see but can, perhaps only just, imagine – a me who is an impossible himself, rich, travelling, with choices.

Two tall chimneys, a row of trucks in a siding; suddenly, beside the embankment, men in crisp white shorts stand poised for volley-ball, watching us as if anxious that we might in some way cut short their free time. Piles of sand, a grey-black crow at a puddle, a curly-bearded man in a loose pink *kurta*; then the long platform, crowded as if with nomads, unstirring men crouched, sunken cheeked, long shanked, among filthy bundles, ear-ringed women, red-turbaned porters. A visitation of beggar children in khaki rags – '*Paise, sahib! Sahib! Paise! Memsahib!*' None of us stirs until, the train already moving, I relent and hand out – what? A penny? – to the smallest and most persistent.

Then on again, past waterlogged paddies and bonfires and running children and the lines of slow oxen off for their evening bath, as the sunlight reddens and the sparse bushes roll long shadows across the plain.

After dark, trees whirl by like cloaked riders fat with messages of disaster, their humped silhouettes seen against the paler sky, then gone. Across the blackness, single distanced fires burn, the bivouacs of dark-faced men in headscarves, sacking thrown across their shoulders, and of the thin-thighed women who pass to and fro all day under their loaded baskets, green saris flapping as they walk into the breeze; or who pause, bent double, with sickles halted in mid-stroke, to watch us hurtle past.

VRINDABAN

Derived from the Sanskrit for 'herd forest', Vrindaban, on the banks of the sacred river Jamna, is the place where the god Krishna spent his boyhood. Brought up by the cowherd Nanda and his wife Yashoda, it was in this countryside that he played his pranks, enticed the *gopis*, the milkmaids, and especially his great love Rhada, enacted his miracles and so proved his godhead.

At Mathura, cross-roads of so many cultures and religions, home of art and of devotion, sixty miles and half a dozen centuries from Delhi, we get off. Outside the station, on a dusty concourse, the cycle rickshaws press around us. Swami Ananda picks one – all our luggage, his thin bones, my twelve stone, crush into the narrow seat. Standing on the pedals, hunched, the rickshaw man stamps us into motion. The street closes in – shops, cows, *tongas*, strollers, veiled women, goats, pigs, peddlars, priests. The rickshaw man gets off, begins to push. Guilt crushes me; with a few rupees, I buy my comfort, his pain. Swami Ananda talks of chastity, of celibacy. Below him, the man bends and sweats, tugging. I want to get down and walk until the going gets easier, but Swami Ananda does not let me. Nor, when asked, does the rickshaw man.

We pass brickworks, open scrubland, patches of sparse meadow: hereabouts Krishna's milkmaids grazed their cows, it is holy ground. Temples sprout, well rooted in such soil, and tiny ashrams. Sadhus march, ochre robed, festooned with tiny packages, the last possessions left them by non-attachment. The miles rub slowly past, paid for in sweat and aching muscles – not mine.

We turn a corner, roll down a dirt road, between low walls. A boy standing on the corner splashes me with dye – it is the *Holi* festival this week-end. The ashram opens before us: an archway, a wide courtyard, the place crowded for the festival. To our left, up steps, two temples stand, the nearer one of marble. Opposite these is the low house of the Guru. On the tiled verandah squat perhaps a hundred devotees. But the Guru himself, Swami Akhanananda, is resting or in meditation.

We are put in a cell, perhaps ten feet by fifteen, whitewashed, with two wooden beds in it. A red and blue bedspread brightens the bleakness. Ventilation is through holes left in the brickwork, patterned into a grille almost Moorish in design: a Moghul legacy. Just inside the brown, wooden doors there hangs a naked bulb. Outside, there is a narrow terrace with a pale blue wooden seat on it. Facing this cell and its row of identical neighbours is a high, whitewashed wall; peeping above it, a small dome marks a shrine. Lines are strung along the wall, and on them hang the drying, orange robes of sadhus.

I feel decision draining from me; I am culturally outnumbered by many thousands to one and I sense the odds like a constant pressure. A bowl of food is brought me and, having eaten, I stand on the terrace to wash my fingers with the remains of my drinking water. Swami Ananda comes back from greeting colleagues.

'So you are getting used to the ways of the Hindu!' He begins to peel an orange. 'Though they may be riddlesome.' He pauses, then repeats this. 'Riddlesome.'

'Yes', I say. 'Riddlesome.'

'Yes, yes.' He nods his head and, juice on his fingers, hands me half his fruit.

*

Swami Akhanananda's devotees have produced a booklet, *Glimpses of Life Divine*, which gives details of his origins and development. The followers of most Gurus bring out such pamphlets; sometimes even a biography, a full-fledged book. The story is always set out with great affection, eulogistically; no roughness is allowed to blur the hagiographic intention.

He was born on 25 July 1911, corresponding to Shravan Krishna 15, Vikram Samvat 1968, in a devout Brahman family in a village named Mahrai in the Varanasi District of the State of Uttar Pradesh in Northern India. His grandfather and father were well versed in scriptures and followed the vocation of priests and spiritual preceptors in the town and neighbourhood. His grandfather and parents performed some religious observances and as a result of the grace of Lord, our Shantanu Behari was born exactly nine months after the completion of the penance. Shantanu Behari, however, lost his father at an early age of seven and he was brought up by his grandfather who also died when he was about seventeen years old, leaving the responsibility on the mother, a devout Hindu lady who lived a long sacred life and later took up yellow robes and became a disciple of our Swamiji himself.

Sri Swamiji as a young boy did not receive much school education but he acquired a great proficiency in Sanskrit literature, Astrology, Puranas, Srimad Bhagwat, Maha Purana etc., at an early age and later followed it by a deep study of the *Vedas* and Vedangas from the erudite scholars of the day . . . His training and education in spiritual practices was done under the guidance of famous Sri Swamiji Yoganandaji Maharaj and realized souls like Sri Baba of Mokalpur, Sri Baba of Maghayee, Sri Swami Puranand (Sri Udiya Baba), Sri Swami Shankaranandaji Bhikshu and others.'

It goes on to describe his sadhana, and tell how at one period, 'he used to get up at about three in the morning and do meditation for some time; have a bath and perform sandhya and little Gayatri Japa and then sit down for Anushthan of his Mantra and continue till about eleven o'clock. After a glass of milk, he would soon do the Saptah Path of Srimad Bhagwat till late in the evening. Then he would have a small meal and a little walk and come back and perform sandhya and hold sankirtan. His intense sadhana soon yielded fruits. Lord Sri Krishna appeared and graced him. He put his hand on his forehead and gave him the *Maha Vakya* for self-realization and attainment of moksha.

The booklet tells of his devoted spiritual practice, of the addresses he has given and the people he has helped. It tells of the visions he has seen and the miracles he has performed. 'On one occasion a boy who had been dead for some time became an evil spirit and started haunting and troubling his mother. No amount of treatment could cure the mother and ultimately the spirit of the dead boy spoke and requested recitation of Srimad Bhagwat by a learned man. For this purpose a request was made to our Swamiji and he recited the Bhagwat Saptah and at the end the evil spirit declared that he had been freed from bondage and thereafter he never troubled or haunted anybody and his mother at once felt completely cured.'

Worldly people, too, we are told, have been much helped by him 'and many a desire has been fulfilled and many a trouble has been averted by his grace and it has been learnt that sick persons got well and barren ladies got children and unhappy social relations of father and son – brother and brother – husband and wife have considerably improved and become sweet and smooth by his advice. Some have indeed received gainful employment, profits in business, and monetary and other help by following the path and practices prescribed by him. Still his greatest desire and contribution to humanity is instructions towards upliftment of the soul, so that happiness and peace be real and eternal.'

*

In the morning I walk down a lane, past two cows and across a railway line, to a yellow temple standing at the end of a long garden. I wait in a sandy forecourt, surrounded by the worn sandals of the respectfully unshod within, until I am summoned. My sandals join the rest, then I pick my way around and through the crowded devotees who sit, two hundred strong, on the carpeted marble floor. Their curiosity fills the hall like fog. The walls are covered in marble to a height of about four feet, then for the twenty feet above that are painted a pale green. From the white ceiling, electric fans droop unmoving. At the far end, in a high, marble shrine hung with pale green, silver embroidered tapestry, stands an idol of the Lord Krishna.

The dais is covered with a cloth patterned with printed, yellow-brown leaves. Alone upon it sits the Guru, Swami Akhanananda Saraswati. I bow, palms together in respectful greeting, then sit at the foot of the dais. The Swami smiles in an easy, avuncular fashion at the gathering. The ochre jersey he wears bulges in a jolly roll over his stomach. In his broad face the long, mid-brown eyes, their shape emphasized by that of his glasses, gleam acutely, with humour and, once or twice, with a concentration which forces me as if in cowardice to turn away. Behind him, an old attendant, ochre robed too, his face fallen in about the absence of teeth, grey stubble gleaming, fans his Guru with a clutch of peacock feathers. Sunlight and bursts of shrill birdsong penetrate from outside. As the interview begins, a close-cropped young sadhu beside me slips straight-backed into meditation; after a moment, he begins to sway jerkily to and fro.

'If the disciple wants to attain something, is it true or is it not that somebody else has achieved it before him? If there is somebody who has already achieved it, then he must be the Guru. If the disciple wants moksha, then it is the Guru who has got those divine attributes. If the disciple wants to achieve something that nobody has ever achieved, then it is hopeless; but if he wants to achieve some of the divine virtues which have been attained by somebody, then they are certainly contained in the Guru himself. And the feeling that the disciple himself has about that will bring about the necessary result in him. The disciple realizes the divinity of the Guru when he himself achieves those divine attributes. Till then, it is not possible for the disciple really to know the divinity of the Guru. It exists there absolutely, but until he experiences it, there is no way of establishing it by any empirical method.

'So far as other religions are concerned, there are two aspects to be considered – they get the disciples, they initiate them into the religion for the purpose of putting them on the path of right conduct and away from evil deeds and evil thoughts, and finally to become a servant of God or in some such relation to God – to be one of his. There are some aspects of the Hindu religion which cover these elements also, but a special phenomenon of this religion is that the shishya is brought in, not only to put him on the path of right conduct, but to get rid of all conduct. To get rid of all bondages, good or bad. Whether the chain is of gold or the chain is of iron, he must be completely free of all of them, all bondages, particularly the bondages of birth and death. And this will enable him to live in bliss in this life. All that will be achieved by his realizing his identity with the Super-Being – with God. Not by becoming a son or a slave of God, but by becoming identical with God. So you have actually to attain Godhood itself.

'The relationship of Guru and shishya in India is unique and of a special significance. The significance is that it is not the intention that the disciple of the Guru should remain a disciple for ever. Neither is it the intention that the Guru should remain eternally the Guru, and the relationship so established should be everlasting. In the course of time, the disciple has to give up his discipleship and himself become a Guru; the Guru has finally to give up his Gurudom and the relationship developed on that basis. Both will in the end find themselves identical with God. The relationship is only a means to an end. Of course, as far as formality and courtesy are concerned, the Guru and the shishya will show a sufficient affection for each other, and that courtesy will continue. But as far as the truth is concerned, both will be identical and there will be no question of one being subordinate to the other.

'The objective of the Guru is to enable the disciple to experience that he is complete God, that he has absolute knowledge and absolute truth. The finite elements in the shishya which kept him from experiencing that are to be eliminated. For that purpose, the Guru will not keep the disciple for ever, but having taught him all this, both will enjoy this bliss and perfection. This awareness is not circumscribed by history, geography, time or place. This knowledge absolute, this truth absolute, will be the same in Europe or America, this will be the same ten thousand years before and ten thousand years after; it transcends the various Gurus also, it is not confined to any particular master of the religion or to any particular subject. It transcends all categories and removes finity – it is infinite knowledge. And it is this that has to be attained. It transcends caste, sect, religion – it is this that the real Guru must teach.'

In the evening, I go for a walk; beneath a tree in which six

59

vultures sit in a brooding row, the dusty road curves to the highway. Sadhus in white, in rags, in loincloths, in ochre pass, their hair wild or matted or shaved off; and around them the people trot, laughing now, their eyes bright, their clothes spectacular with the arbitrary hues of Holi. A small group comes by, singing a lugubrious 'Hari Krishna, Hari Ram' to the sound of a portable harmonium and a small drum. A swami in an ochre turban, flat faced, with a down-turned gangster's mouth and quick-silver eyes, embraces a plump devotee. On a canopied platform, dancers in red and gold perform; one sings and the microphone sends the high voice raucously across the dusk. A calf scratches against a tree trunk. On temple steps, three sadhus discuss, their forcefulness canonading to and fro, their laughter like broadsides.

Another morning, the sky crisp, the air still clean and sharp. Once more Swami Akhanananda sits on his dais, answering the questions of his devotees, once giving way to another speaker, then without effort taking his audience back. Why not? It is his audience, come to hear him; now and then they laugh, more often they cry out their admiration at this Guru's lucidity. They seem to enjoy his easy way with theology; when he has answered their questions, they look round, gleaming with satisfaction. I sit as before, and today there are nods here and there, greetings; I too, it suddenly occurs to me, am a celebrity, my foreigner's curiosity respected and, for them, perhaps adding its small weight to the Swami's sum of worth.

'Although the Guru is identified with absolute God, in order to teach the disciple he has to bring himself down to the level on which the disciple can follow. That is why disciples see Gurus of various levels. And that is the reason for so many religions and sects; they have to explain it to particular sets of people, and descend to their level on that account ... The Guru acts both as the father and the mother to the spiritual life of the disciple. He really creates this spiritual aura about the disciple and rears him as a mother does; he really creates that climate round his disciple, and in that sense he is both the father and the mother. If a teacher of a M.Sc. class in mathematics explains something, he may do so in a very complex way, but if he has to explain the thing to a lower class, he has naturally to go down to that level . . .

'It is impossible to advance spiritually without a Guru, but it is possible that the Guru may be one out of your past life who has instilled his energy in you; or the Guru may be some invisible being not yet known to you. But to have a Guru is essential on this path of achieving godhood and so on . . . There are instances of persons who have gone to some Guru not apparently of a very high level, but they also attained the necessary knowledge because it was the Guru of their past life or some other invisible, eternal Guru really granted it.

'Even an inanimate object can be a Guru; but consider the case of a person who wants to rely on an inanimate object: it shows he has no faith in any living, human being, and that will show that he is so egoistic himself that he will not bow to any living being. Now this lack of devotion will be an obstacle in achieving results even from the Guru as an inanimate object.

'You can leave the Guru if you are unable to achieve what you came for. So far as the priest who initiates you in the religion is concerned, who gave you the mantra and so on, he is of a different category – there is no reason to leave him or stick to him – but if you come to a Guru in order to ask for things of God, to achieve identity with God, if you fail to do it within a reasonable time in spite of your best efforts, then you have no option but to leave.'

These are some of the things Swami Akhanananda said to me. When the interview was over, I thanked him for taking so much time and trouble. He smiled, waved his right hand.

'Make whatever reply is suitable in European etiquette,' he said to the high court judge who had interpreted for us.

In the narrow streets of the town, *Holi* unfolds, rainbow coloured. It is a spring festival, a relic of aboriginal religions, now taken over by Hinduism. Because it commemorates the youthful games and pranks of Krishna, the people of Vrindaban particularly enjoy it. It is a time of noise, of shouting, of obscenities, of flung aside inhibition. It is a time of music, of dancing, of abandon. Above all, it is a time of colour – powdered dye or dyed water flies in every direction. Children and young men perch on walls, spraying passersby. Others stand at barricades, planting their red or yellow palms on anyone's cheeks and foreheads. Like chips in a kaleidoscope the colour-stained shirts of revellers pass to and fro in the crowd.

I am the one foreigner in town; squirt gun and flung powder focus – I have become a chance too good to miss. A powerful man leaps from a singing group and lifts me, swings me to and fro (movements perhaps left over from coital dances of ancient fertility rites). A masked dancer bends and jigs in the centre of a clapping crowd. Round a corner, gigantic in the narrow street, a decorated elephant ponderously walks. At last I turn tail, hurry back through the gauntlet at the edge of the town, to arrive at the ashram multicoloured, a Holi fool.

But in the great courtyard too they have brought out the coloured powders. They laugh at me. 'Today is a time for happiness,' they say. 'The colour is a sign of joy – you are covered: it means they love you!'

They give me a pinch of the powder. 'Put it on Swami,' they call, as if to a nervous child. 'Come on. He won't mind – today he doesn't mind at all. Look, he wants you to do it.' They are talking about Swami Sadananda Saraswati, a follower of the Guru, a realized man himself, a big-bellied man about six feet tall, with a narrow, clean-shaven skull and a big chin. He smiles, nods. I daub his forehead; a small cascade of coloured powder lands on his nose.

Now on the verandah of the Guru's house, these solemn men place points of colour on each other's foreheads, each other's hair. They move from one to another, senior executives in this business of religion, daubing each other's serious, smiling faces: a sort of shuffling, absurd but benevolent dance.

They take me in to the Guru. 'Go on – you have his permission. You may put colour on his forehead.'

His devotees crowd at his feet, while he sits, smiling faintly, on a bed. They daub his forehead gently, then do obeisance.

'Only a little – come on, it's all right, we've asked.'

I take powder on a fingertip, put colour on Swamiji's forehead. Someone calls out his approval. I salute him, palms together. He smiles, then hands me a fading, pale pink rose.

Later, I talk with Brahmacharya Premanand, broad shouldered, always to be seen marching, barefoot and busy, through the ashram: the arranger, the supervisor, the man who gets things done, who sees to it that there are beds enough, and food for those who are to occupy the beds, that visitors are spaced, that the Guru has peace, has comfort. He sits opposite me and smiles, displaying curiously divided teeth. When he stretches he shows smooth armpits; his chest, too, is smooth, and his skull clean-shaven, but there is down on his belly, not today covered by the vest he sometimes wears. He watches the door nervously, his concern not over me and my questions, but for the running of the ashram; he waits for a crisis, for a summons. He is, one imagines, a happy man; what he does fulfills him. Everyone calls him Dada. He is shy about his English, but knows more than he thinks; soon he is speaking quite freely:

'My family are orthodox Brahmins. So we are from ... our blessed predecessors are all Brahmins, so we are supposed to be most religious. Not every Brahmin is religious, but they are

63

supposed to be. My family is. I have left my family, but my elder brothers and sisters, my parents, are all religious persons. So that I came under religious influence from early childhood.

'Actually, I'm not a sannyasi, but I'm the disciple of my holy preceptor. I came in touch with him in the year 1940. Yes. When I was only eighteen or nineteen years old. I attended a lecture. Before that, I didn't like these sannyasis and saints. Like the modern youth; I didn't like these saffron coloured persons. (He laughs.) But my well-wishers, my elders, used to insist on me to attend his lectures. And they were divine lectures. Such saints are rare in India, or in the world, I think.

'I didn't think to leave the family or anything, but I intended to spend a few months or a little time with him, as a result of the lectures. His behaviour and love towards me and to us all affected me so much that I decided to live with him. In the year 1941 he was staying there, he was spending his . . . In the monsoon season, the sannyasis are supposed to stay in one place and not to wander here and everywhere, not to travel, so he was staying on the banks of the Ganges in a village. So – before that I didn't have . . . I didn't travel in train. For a mile, even a mile, I didn't touch the train. So that was my first trip – to Swamiji.

'Up to then, I had been serving in military: M.E.S. – Military Engineering Services. I'd signed a bond. By law I couldn't leave the service. So I fled away. Now they can't catch up with me because the Government has changed. (He laughs.)

'That was the period of the Movement. The "Quit India" Movement was being organized all over India. I was not in touch with the politics, but my elder brothers and other friends also were interested in it.

'I spent one year, one and a half years, with Swamiji. Then suddenly my mother's memory attracted me, so I couldn't live with him and I again went back to my home, and again lived with the family. For about six months I lived with my parents, and one day, my family, my elder brothers asked me to serve, to go into service, earn money and feed the people. They wanted me to go to work. They said, "If you don't like to work, you can't live here. You must leave the home and go away wherever you like. The doors are shut and we can't manage to feed you . . ." My elder brothers said this because my father died in the year 1941. The same year that I . . . he died in 1940 and I left in 1942 . . . I don't remember the date entirely; it might be 1945 or 1943, '44 or . . . But then, I decided that I can't fit in the family. This was not the proper place for me to stay. So I then decided to come back to Swamiji. I changed my garb (i.e. took to ochre robes), and since that time I am staying with him and I have now become one with him.

'I did not marry, but the world is the same! Because I am eating, drinking, sleeping, you know – and, so to say, all the facilities are here – accommodation, much accommodation, much facilities of clothing, food, etc. All are more, and rather more, than in a small house, small cottage. And there we were only thirteen or fourteen persons. We are about hundred here. There, one *dal*, *chapatis* and little rice, one vegetable – here, so many; you are seeing daily how many varieties are here. So this is not to say renunciation.

'But I am not attached to it. There's no attachment towards it. And if there's only one thing to eat, only one clothes to cover the body, there's no harm. If I have got much cloth, so I am covering others also.

'Through service I have become one with Swamiji. Through service only. And I say this is the grace of Preceptor, this is the grace of the Lord. Through him only I could realize this.

'I have taken diksha and so I have renounced the world in that sense, that I cannot go back home but I must spend my life till death; till my last breath exhales or I breathe my last, I am bound to be with the Preceptor and in this garb only. This is my determination.

'He doesn't insist on teaching. According to the liking of the man, of the disciple, he teaches. I am in the opinion of serving mankind. So I am doing all that . . .

'I used to do asanas; yes, I liked about forty asanas. I used to do it every day, morning and evening, but now as I am too busy all the day I cannot spare time to do those asanas because it takes one and a half hours, so I can't spare so much. But I do meditate.

'In the year 1946, I learnt all those asanas, and I used to do them till 1950, 1960, '65. Now I got old; I got forty-eight or forty-nine years old. And I do not wish to live long.

'What is the good of living on this earth so long, for a long time, being old, growing old with no teeth or eyesight or other things? Then I would require help from others, to serve me, give me assistance – so I would not like to live long. As long as my limbs are able to serve others I must live. But if they refuse to work, I must not live. My service is with the Swami, to my clients, to my colleague saints, to Swamiji's devotees.

'I see the God in them: that same God is in you also. I will not serve you as Mr Brent, but I serve you as you have come to Swamiji and the same supreme soul is in you. And I am serving that soul.

'This is the bliss. I have attained nothing, I do not know anything, because I can't express what I know.'

One of the women comes in, high voiced, her gestures agitated. His summons has come. He smiles, apologizes, goes to the door: tomorrow the Guru is leaving to tour other ashrams, address meetings of the devoted, and everything must be ready for his departure. Buoyed up by the possibility of further service, Dada hurries away.

*

Later, Swami Sadananda Saraswati sits with me, smiles his narrow eyed, small toothed smile – a big man, broad bellied, heavy chinned, who seems to sergeant-major through life, his

66

voice deep and penetrating and insistent. He appears to me a sort of religious alderman, a sort of self-justifying beadle – but then I remember the discipline, the hours spent in hardship, in self-examination, the rigours of learning and meditation . . .

'In my earlier life I was a guard on the railways. I hated all these monks and sadhus – I hated them very much. But afterwards when I came in touch with them . . . Because I did logic in my college life and without reasoning I was not ready to believe anything. But then by logic, by reasoning, by science, our Guru proved for us all these things – there was no question of not believing. When it is proved by reasoning, then there is no question. And for us, it is important that the Guru lives what he says. There are three things: what he says and what he thinks must be in what he does, in his actions.

'I began looking for a Guru when I began to question. I would question any sadhu I met, and when I found that because of my questions he became somewhat angry, or his mood became somewhat bad, or he was not replying to me, then I thought that I would tell him "No". But when I came across my Guru, he said to me, "Why do you worry about the world? Why do you worry about the world? Your mind has created this world. You get your mind quite all right, and you will find the world is all heaven for you, and all the world *mukta* for you – the centre is here, not there." That is one thing he told me. And the second thing – I put so many irritable questions to him to check how his mood was, how his eyes were; but he was always pleasant, and always very kind to me. I vexed him so much and he was always kind. He was always in bliss, loving, smiling, and I said, "Well, I will be living with you for six months."

'And he said, "Yes, yes – you'll see me."

'When I had been living with him for six months or one year, I saw how he speaks, how he sits, how he stands, how he . . . So I found that what he speaks, in his accent as well as in his thinking, his speaking as well as his actions, are all one. And he can answer me in the language in which I could understand. Then it was easy for me to understand. That was about thirty years ago.

'That was Swami Akhanananda – and his Guru before him. I have been with him ever since – since 1945, '46. I started looking for a Guru because, first, I come from a Brahmin caste. One day, a sadhu came from Karachi. I started questioning him very severely, but he was not worried. I said, "This God . . . this God . . . it's your business, I think. I think there is no God – can you show him to me?"

'He said, "Yes. Do you want to see him?"

'So I said, "Is he there, or is it only your business to make a fool of all these persons and so have money in your pocket? There is no God."

'"Yes, there is. Do you want to see that proved? Please bring me just a little milk."

'So I went on my motorcycle to the milkman and he gave me milk, pure milk, and I brought it to him.

'He said, "You have brought me milk without cream?"

'"No sir – there is cream. It is pure milk."

'"Well, where is it? There's no cream here . . . or here . . . Is it here, on this side?"

'I said, "Yes, it's there."

'"Is it on that side? And on the bottom?"

'I said, "Yes. It's all through it – in this milk, the cream is everywhere."

'So he looked at me. "Although I cannot see it, it is there?"

'"Yes."

'"Similarly with God – God is everywhere in the world, but you cannot see him. And how can you see the cream in this milk? And how can you see the butter that is in it? By this-and-this process. Similarly, by meditating and by sadhanas you will find everything to be God in yourself. Everything in this world is nothing except God. What is this world, then? It is nothing but your angle of vision. Because you have a certain angle of vision you see God as a world – it is not the world, it is God and yourself."

'And that convinced me. And I told him that I wanted to see God, I wanted to do that, but that I wouldn't be going to temple and I wouldn't be doing this and that, that these things embarrassed me . . . He said, "Good, then don't do that."

'But then, what to do?

'"Nothing except surrender. Just surrender yourself to God. Whatever you do, do for God. Everything that you do must be dedicated to God."

'There did not seem to be any great difficulty in that – dedicating each and every thing to God. But you see, psychologically, what ought not to be dedicated to God went away from life – it disappeared. I could not dedicate cigarettes to God, so they went out of my life – whatever it was; whatever could not be dedicated to God was away from life.'

In mid-afternoon, I am on my way back to Delhi; the bus has gone, I have to hire a cycle rickshaw. I choose someone strong, vigorous, a young man, but he turns out to be a tout. When we set off, me and my luggage perched on that narrow silent seat, the rickshaw man is old. He has an iron-grey moustache, a few projecting, yellow teeth, hair cut very short, like an ex-soldier's. After a while, he begins to cough, a dry, intermittent bark high in his chest; heart disease, I think, watching him strain, trapped in my guilt but having to reach the station.

On the road, lines of women pass, some carrying children; silver bracelets adorn their ankles. Families sweep multicoloured down the verge; sadhus walk, some muttering a mantra or the endless name of God; a man leads his brood, a transistor to his ear, the aerial high. A small girl pisses behind a tree, and everywhere innumerable men crouch to the ditch about the same errand. Girls pass in quiet groups, their clothes like particles from some exploded, unimaginable rainbow; small boys run, hang on the backs of rickshaws, throwing stones at last when they drop off. The *tongas*, two-wheeled passenger cars, pass slowly, the horses' hooves clapping on the metalled road. In one, three women sit in a row on the backward facing seat; when they see me, they smile with curiosity and derision. Moslem ruins, a distant Hindu shrine; then an enormity, a bright red-and-white temple at the roadside, built to put some millionaire right with heaven while not compromising his memory on earth; a dreadful pastime, this, of the rich and devout, whose memorial follies litter India with their hideous architecture. Soon there are garages, high walls, the sloping roofs of factories – the twentieth century sits on Mathura after all. I climb down at the station, overpay the rickshaw man, watched by smiling locals who calculate my innocence, admire his duplicity, but have no more idea than he that guilt is the meat of our transaction.

HARDWAR

Swami Ananda hurries me past the clustered rickshaw men outside the station, across the road: shops, kerb-side stalls, a sight of piled, green vegetables, the air cool and thin, something damp in the atmosphere; to the lungs, this might be England. We pass through an archway into the ashram – a central courtyard, cluttered with bricks, washing, trees, tenants and the children of tenants; one or two sadhus lie stretched on stone benches. Beyond them, an arcade with doorways curtained or closed by ancient wooden doors, leading into the dark rooms beyond. The last but one door to the right is where Swami Shyam Sunderdass, the head of the ashram, receives visitors.

The Swami is an ochre-cowled figure with a strong nose and

chin, grave almost sad eyes, the stubble on his face just beginning to go grey. There is not about him the obvious, twinkling
joy that there is in some sadhus; instead, great gravity, now and
then broken by a laugh which comes easily, then subsides. His
stillness seems no pose, but of himself. There is a hint of effort
in his face from time to time, an expression of strain, of conscious
control; but then, he has great responsibilities. He is, after all,
part businessman, landlord of all the shops that burrow into the
monastery's outside wall, of all the families who hang their
washing in his inner courtyard. He seems to have no vanity, nor
to care what I might think about him. At some later time,
possibly he might want to think about me. My gadgets – electric
razor, tape-recorder – please him. He looks at them with grave
delight – he does not want them, they delight him as themselves,
splendid but irrelevant toys.

His room is narrow, green walled, white ceilinged. There is a
telephone on a table, two chairs, a cupboard with blue double
doors. Beyond a barred window at the back of the room,
children laugh and quarrel, then recite in discordant unison: a
school. Under the window stands a bed, the place where the
Swami sits cross-legged and offers himself to the questions of the
devout. On the right a door leads to his bedroom, on the left to a
lavatory. In the walls, small niches hold a telephone directory,
an ochre scarf, files and ledgers, a cardboard box labelled
'Foamtreads', a bright yellow tin, a black nameplate on which
white letters spell out, 'Dr S. S. Dass, M.A., B.I.M.' He speaks
some English, but refuses to use it now; his gravity crumbles,
he becomes almost coy. Swami Ananda interprets, sitting keenly
by the other's side, considering my questions like an examiner.

'When a disciple comes to the Guru, then the Guru not only
teaches him, but in particular cases he may also have what you
might call a loving relationship, one of mercy and kindness and
deep love, and through that he passes his own knowledge to

him. From having been a nonentity, the man therefore develops until he has become somebody – his inner being is brought into existence and developed. And that is due to the Guru entering into the self of the disciple and so bringing the disciple into being, as it were.

'It is the Guru who releases a man from his bondage and gives him a way out of his attachments, through his teachings and through his mercy and compassion. In India, sometimes, people consider the Guru as greater than any Creator; greater than the Creator, figuratively speaking, since God has set us in bondage and the Guru has released us.

'In one of the sermons given by the founder of my own sect, Haridasji, he mentions a particular kind of bird; when it finds a dead bird, it carries it back to its own nest, which is covered with earth. And then, in the nest, it gives its own warmth to that other dead bird, and so gives it a new life; and in the course of time, the bird it has rescued and revived takes on the form of its rescuer's species. And he compares this to the Guru-disciple relationship – if anybody comes, if any man comes, the Guru creates a new life in him. Out of animality, he develops a human soul, the divine element, as the bird was revived by the living warmth of the other bird. That is the power of the Guru.

'Now, the Guru is God, the Guru is the director, the Guru is supreme because of concentration – he concentrates the whole of the universe into one point. And for the disciple, it is as if the Guru represented the whole world, the whole universe – something like that. Otherwise his mind is diverted here and there, he lacks concentration, and without concentration further development will not be possible.

'Anybody who comes to the Guru with respect and humility is accepted. And then the course of the teaching can begin. Each has to be taught according to his capacity and capability. And when anyone comes to him, the Guru can see whether he is capable, whether he is fit, whether he can take up the teaching with any speed. Anybody who comes to the Guru and wants to be taken up is assessed by the Guru, who has the power to do that; and the work allotted to him will be according to his capacity as the Guru decides it. Of course, some would-be disciples are rejected. After all, disciples come for different purposes.

'My own Guru was not a man of outstanding personality: he was restrained, a man of devotion, a good teacher, who used to give lessons in Vedanta; and it was in this way that I first made contact with him. I came into contact with him, that is, as a student in the ordinary way, not chosen particularly to be a disciple. But in the course of time, by associating with him day by day, we came more closely into contact. Then, in the last days of his life, he called for me. He was living here as mahant of this institution and I was living in Benares; and he called me and asked me to take charge of this institution. He thought I was the right person, the best fitted person, to be his successor. But I was afraid. I felt that I had not the capacity, the capability – I was too young. But he blessed me and told me that I was not to worry, I would be able to manage. In a way, this was an example of the transfer of power. I was just a student of Sanskrit and Vedanta. Of course, he had initiated me, but I was not one of the close disciples, one of whom might have been expected to be appointed here as mahant. He gave many people the mantra, many disciples, and there was nothing special about my position with him. But when he had given me his blessings and his assurances, I felt more confident that I could do what he asked. Now I have been doing that work for twenty-eight years – at that time, I was only eighteen years old!'

Hardwar got its name after it was rebuilt in 1399, on the ruins Timur had made of the previous town; it means 'the gate of Hari'. It is a place of pilgrimage itself, and the starting point of a pilgrim route to other holy places like Gangotri and Kedarnath.

73

It lies at the foot of the Siwalik hills, where the Ganges finally flings out of the valleys and winds across the plain.

Temples and maths overlook the river; I walk there with Swami Sunderdass. The sun goes down in a northern sky. A sadhu in a loincloth walks through the cool dusk. 'Look, naked man!' the Swami says. 'Look!' He repeats this, until I look. A small temple, like an ornate summer-house, stands at the top of a flight of steps – it is a temple of Hanuman; sure enough, a little way farther along, two monkeys sit on a balcony and peer gravely down at us.

Later, we drive in a taxi out of Hardwar, past the lines of cycle rickshaws, the waiting tongas, bullock carts piled high with branches, past sadhus, cows, maths, the endless cluttered shops, their keepers lying, toes high, on their rope strung *charpoys*; finally we arrive at the bright, templed Ganges. Between road-way and railway, a blackened hut stands on a slope; in front of it, white clad, a holy man sits motionless. Beside him, another bends, washing a dark, skinny leg. A little farther along, a thin man in a soaking, hang-buttock dhoti washes at a pump, while a sadhu, hair and beard wild as hurricanes, plods past with his cloth bag, stick and begging bowl. On the river, a raft slides across the diamond bright waves, poled through the current by a crouched man in vest and shorts. Beyond the railway lines, on a green bluff covered in straggling bushes, two grey and curly tailed monkeys watch, then, bobbing, scuttle off. So on, down the wide roadway, lined by the multifarious houses of religion and crossed by cows and cow dung, with ahead of us a dark ridge, first step into the towering, invisible Himalayas.

DEHRA DUN

Open country, heavy with cane and tended by flat faced moun-tain people. Sugar mills push bulbous, monstrous chimneys towards the grey sky. Hills, then mountains, come hog backing closer. Forests shut out the view, allowing us only occasional glimpses of a mist bowl valley, two dimensional ridges marking off the grey and dimming distance. Lightning cuts a complex mesh across the sky, the wind rises; leaves scuttle across the road like frightened women in russet saris. We drive on, through rain now, the first I have seen for months. At the roadside, a damp sign proclaims, 'Hotel Aroma – Western, Indian and Continental Cuisine'.

The cane fields end, rows of garages take their place: 'Tata Mercedes Service'. Then the piles of rusting spares are past, the ramshackle *chai* shops, the mounds of mouldering bricks. Scooter-taxis rattle by, canvas sided against rain, their competition tongas, whose soaking horses clip confidently through the traffic, the backboards of the little carts bright with painted patterns. Shops gleam, green with peas, spinach, cabbage, lettuce, bright with tomatoes. Everywhere, a delicate architecture of intricate tracery and precisely calculated gallery sinks out of sight under advertisements, shop signs, flat fronted modern buildings.

Guru Ram Rai is an enormous complex of temple, ashram, guesthouse, school: a palace. Ram Rai, a sadhu during the Moghul Empire, was given the whole of Dehra Dun by his patron Nawab. The present mahant sits in slightly shrunken state within these walls. But only slightly shrunken – the place is a maze of marvellous, pillared arcades, god-covered ochre walls, marble floors, a bustling of beggars in the courtyard. Above the gatehouse stands a mosque-like dome and beyond rise slender towers, truncated minarets.

The room we sit in is about fifty feet long. Three french windows lead out to a wide, flagged terrace, bouganvilia floating along its balustrade. Two inner doors lead to a large room full of enormous, scarlet Victorian furniture. Inside each door, the figure of a god stands in a glass case; above each, the life-size

75

model of a dog lies crouched on petrified guard. On the left, beyond the dog, I can see an enormous plywood cut-out of the Guru, tinsel garlanded and standing beside a black, upright piano. There are various carved heads and figures on this instrument, the high point a standing ibis. Peering over the top are the preserved heads of antelopes and deer. The wall is crowded with the relics and mementoes of a religious seigneur: whatnots, stands, shelves, tall tables; a gilt-framed mirror, a second ibis, wooden idols, a second cluster of furred heads, victims of some long gone sporting occasion. A smiling, ear-ringed man in a dressing-gown bustles in: Mahant Indresh Charan Dasji. He has short cut dark hair receding a little, smallish, lively eyes, a short dark beard sprinkled like his hair with grey. He waves me to a seat beside him – an honour, the gracious offer of an equality all of us know is only one of the fictions of etiquette. He seems cool, speaking reluctantly; then he begins to bend forward, the gold ear-rings glistening. His square, broad-browed face, firm and still youthful, serious at first, slowly begins to bend into a smile. Soon, he is pleased – with his answers, perhaps my questions. He begins to glow. His eyes glitter. He speaks quickly, with immense confidence: no one will contradict him here.

'The divinity of the Guru consists of faith – the faith of the disciple. And the self-confidence of the Guru. These two things constitute the relationship between Guru and disciple. The self-confidence of the Guru is based on his own personal attainments, which he has accumulated during a period of years, through study, through austerities, through experience gained from other people and through the knowledge he has acquired from his own Gurus.

'It is the choice of any sadhu whether he will accept anyone who comes to him as a disciple. Before he undertakes to train up a man as his disciple, he will see whether he is eligible, whether he is fit enough to be taken up as a disciple. Once the shishya says, "I am at your disposal, I am at your feet," then it is the responsibility of the Guru to lift him up to the highest status; and if anything is failing in the disciple, it is not the failure of the disciple, it is the failure of the Guru. I mean, if there's a pickpocket and he wants to train up a novice, he will take up the right kind of person. If he feels that this boy will betray the whole gang, then he will not accept him. If this is so with a pickpocket, how about people wanting higher attainments?

'And then who can work with whom, that's also the point. Anybody unsuitable would not be able to stand it; just as we have to send people to the moon and naturally they have to be tested – they found merely half a dozen men, or a dozen men, out of a very large number. The rest couldn't stand the test.

'The Guru will judge the chela from the face – that is the first thing. The first thing. Then he will ask questions. Then of course he goes through the family history, the background of the family. For instance, I know a boy who is probably from the gipsy clan – because he had a broad forehead, a smart looking boy; one of his friends put him in charge of a scholar, a *mahatma*, where he got his education. He got his M.A., but the deviation started, the turn in the life came, when he had done his M.A. and he thought of going to France, he thought of going to England, this thing and that thing . . . and ultimately, of course, he landed in disaster.

'So first comes family background, secondly comes the educational career. A boy has been in a school – why did he leave? Did he join the 1942 Congress Movement? Did he go to prison? Did he stay there as a good prisoner? If he did it, then of course he is good for any other job – if he is a patriot, he will do well anywhere. If he is a scoundrel, if he is a swindler, if he is a thief, he won't do any good anywhere. The world belongs to those who are fit to live in this world, but who also concede that

77

whoever is born in this world must be given his right to exist in this world.

'Of course, someone who has aspirations but comes from the wrong background can manage it. He can manage it, certainly. There's no right type of family background – but there's will. And if that will is there and if it has been developed, it comes to the highest mark and it defeats those who have the best family background.

'Often the relationship between Guru and shishya is largely unspoken – it is said of Ramakrishna, when Vivekananda came to him to be accepted as a disciple, he accepted him. A person like me would have to put questions – the best thing is to put questions and what you speak from the lips gives you away to a great extent. But once the relationship is developed, then you don't bother. Then you don't bother, whatever happens. Both are persuaded. It is just like Tensing and Hilary climbing up Mount Everest – there is a lot of nonsense going on about who stood on the top first. What does it matter?

'The Guru and the chela have to be very, very clear about one aspect: what is their pursuit? Does the Guru have plenty of money, and does the chela want to grab it? Does the Guru have plenty of respect, and does the chela want to have it? Is it just asking about easy affairs? Is it all this, or is it high attainment towards spirituality, towards God, salvation and all that? If that is so – spirituality, salvation and all that – there is no danger for the Guru or the disciple or for anybody else.

'If out of this whole world, ten men would achieve salvation through my efforts and I at the end achieved nothing, well, I would feel that I have done more than any professor ever did. But I won't find those ten men achieving salvation through my efforts – not ten. Not ten, I say! Did the prophets themselves achieve salvation? That's the point. I wonder if they did. I doubt very much if they did. They had their own claims, sponsored by their own disciples, but I do believe that there were many prophets, and that there will be many more in the future, who claim salvation and yet they have never reached anywhere near salvation.

'The Guru has to be particular about one thing; that the disciple does not draw out from the reservoir of goodwill of whatever establishment or organization he has set up. He does not draw out of it, he does not become a handicap to it. He does not become a parasite, more or less. Of that he has to be very careful. But as far as higher attainment is concerned, there is no enmity, there is no jealousy – nothing of that sort. We're all the same, we are all walkers on the same road to God, to divinity. We have nothing to worry about. If it is really meant, there is no competition about salvation or higher attainment, no going in front or going first. If Lord Krishna lived hundreds of thousands of years ago, he did what he did in his time; and if I live hundreds of thousands of years later, I don't bother about what he did then – I am going to do what I can do now. I am not envious of him. He never became envious of me, who would be born several thousands of years on. That's the point.

'Of course, the human devotion of the chela for the Guru can sometimes stand in the way of his spiritual development. After all, the Guru is the Guru – and if he does something wrong, say, well, he's a human being. And the chela may be blinded by his devotion to the Guru. By the barriers of the human frame which are placed before the chela, his vision is limited and he can't see through the limitations of flesh of the Guru. He can't go ahead – he has stopped there. That sometimes happens.

'There are certain lines of teaching that I consider more important than others – no doubt about it. The first thing is, we should study the *shastras*; it is the shastras which have opened the way for us. But then you have to have the practice. Studying alone won't do. For instance, detachment is there. What is there to be taught or learned about detachment if a man is shut in this room here? He might read a hundred books – and yet when he comes into contact, that detachment goes to the winds. He will be drawn by attachment.

'The birds sing on the trees – that gives us some joy, some pleasure. But the birds are not going to tell me which way I am to follow. The Guru, after he has given me the basic concept about my line of action, leaves me free. It is for me to consult him every now and then, whenever I so desire, whenever I need his advice. It is for the Guru to give me that advice whenever he thinks it is necessary for me to have it, otherwise I might make a mistake and then it might take a long time to repair the breach. But normally, let the Guru follow his own line and let the disciple follow his own line, with consultation only when it is necessary.

' Sometimes it may be necessary to be angry with the disciple – why not? Even hard words have to be used; but of course hardness, harshness . . . the degree of harshness will depend upon the person who is going to use it, and the person who is going to be used by those harsh words. Suppose I am using harsh words against a person, and that person is incapable of standing those harsh words, then I must change my mode. As to this person, another way is to be found. I am not making an experiment with my speech, with my temper, with my anger, my controlled temperament – I am making an experiment with the boy. He has to be improved. And I will use the method which will best improve him, if I am capable of adjusting myself.

'I have told you that the Guru-shishya relationship is a process and it really depends on the potentiality of the two. Anybody who claims to be a Guru, anybody who claims to be a disciple, will not make it so. As to whether there is a higher spiritual potential in Asia, for that also I will not make any tall claims. If you have time enough to spend in touring the length and breadth of the country, then that is your own affair. But I won't claim anything. And for one reason only – how am I going to believe that a person born somewhere in Jerusalem, Jesus Christ, attained a higher degree of religion and spirituality and things like that because he was born in Asia? Had he been born somewhere in South America, would that have made any difference?

'We talk of prophets, and so the prophets are born here. Those who don't talk of prophets, they don't have any prophets there. No prophets are born in Russia – they don't talk of prophets ... We have a proverb, "They haven't thrown grass to the animals," so the animals cannot feed off that grass.

'But if a scoundrel gets up tomorrow and claims to be a prophet, and he finds half a dozen more scoundrels to proclaim him as such, there are a dozen persons who are foolish enough to believe and ready enough to believe that he is really a prophet. The scoundrel does not believe that he is a prophet, the half a dozen scoundrels do not believe that he is a prophet, but the dozen unsuspecting persons are ready enough to accept him as a prophet. If that is the history of prophets and prophecy, then of course I don't have very much to say.'

We travel south from Dehra Dun by train. In these hill regions, military by tradition and not so very far from Kashmir or the northern frontiers, the Army is everywhere – big toothed smilers in burgeoning beards and green turbans, tough looking, in some way unIndian in their fitness. Saw-mills line the rails, log littered; at barely marked stations, small groups in multi-coloured clothes wait under trees to begin their journeys. Forests and hills crowd close, then slowly recede. The sky, grey-blue, familiar as the north, widens. Above my head, in the luggage rack, white bearded Swami Ananda sleeps like some nodding saint on the edge of a majestic Veronese ceiling.

DELHI

Through the Old Delhi evening: lights reflecting on sweets, fabrics, tins, jars, coils of electric wire, torch batteries, religious pictures, steel bowls; each coruscating pile of goods set in its high, square framed shop front as if on a stage. About us, cycle rickshaws, scooter rickshaws, motorcycle rickshaws, taxis; and about them, laughing walkers, hagglers, loungers, sellers, thieves, children shouting, then running, their noise just one more amidst cried wares, hooters, raucous transistors. All this is run together into one enveloping warmth, and in turn overlies an unconscious hopelessness, kept from the packed together people only by their ignorance – which I, corrupted, do not share – of what life might be like, given more choices, more chances, more money, more time. I sentimentalize? Watch and wait – these people too are learning how much they'll never own.

We stop outside the Gangeshwar Mission, an Udasi ashram. Udasis are an order with a Sikh connection, since they were begun by Sri Chaudra, one of the sons of Guru Nanak. They are ascetics – their name derives from a word meaning 'indifference' – and a reforming order unconcerned about the caste and background of aspirants. Their teachings have a revivalist streak in them, and in their philosophy they adhere to the doctrines of Vedantist monism. On initiation, it is said, the disciple sips a little water in which his Guru's feet have been washed – but to which a little sugar has been added.

We pass an assembly hall, open sided, pillared; on a dais a bearded man, ochre robed, speaks in soft bursts to an over-flowing audience. The building rises another three stories above the hall, taking in two sides of a square. It is heavy with sadhus and their flocks, settled in tiny rooms or in the open, the devoted gathered with rapt faces about those bare, holy feet.

The Guru of the sect, Swami Gangeshwaranand, has been

blind since he was five years old; despite this, he early became a prodigy of learning. Now, over eighty years later, he sits in this narrow tiled room, cross-legged on a bed covered with a white cloth, on which there is printed a design of pink flowers. He sits very straight, his head back; he is thin, his slight movements somehow cramped. Despite his empty eyes, folded in on themselves, he seems to peer about the room, his chin high, the movements of his head abrupt. He has a grainy, heavily hooked nose; his face is contorted into a smile of effort or anguish, almost as though he has spent his lifetime trying to outstare the dark. His fingers lie clawed, right hand on left arm. For a while we sit with him; the discussion is slow, academic; then, suddenly, the Swami must leave, there is a train to catch, time is pressing. Helped by a dozen hands, he moves out of the room. Devotees flood to him: women, middle-aged men, young girls. More are clustered on the long landing outside, an ambush of the faithful. Swami Gangeshwaranand, his arms feebly extended, his blind eyes high, swims through all this devotion.

We follow, under protection of the Guru's assertive right-hand man, Swami Arvindanand, called Military Sant because he was once in the Army. He takes us to his room, where he sits straight backed and dignified; the flowers on his bedspread are green. The walls are covered with photographs in which he hobnobs with India's great; Nehru and Lal Bahadur Shastri and Indira Gandhi smile at followers, or look serious during some religious moment. Beyond closed, wine red curtains is the small office of the Mission. On the wall hangs a calendar presented by the Military Radio Corporation.

Swami Arvindanand is a large chested, self-assured man, full cheeked and full lipped, so that he looks, with his grey beard, as though he might at any moment begin 'Ho-ho-ing' like a Santa Claus. He has a good brow, a steady eye. While he talks, he sometimes glances down and away, so that his profile shows his strong and fleshy nose – he looks through and through a sensualist, and somehow square and competent, not in the slightest spiritual. He begins, however, with great swathes of generalized metaphysics, a kind of self-indulgence, a showing off. I am happier when he gets to the details of his own life.

'If Guru so chooses, through his eyes' radiation he can pass knowledge to an individual. If I want my thoughts to be conveyed or communed to you – well, that can be passed on to you. And, similarly, if Guru wants you to be radiated, then of course you will feel and find that experience where you feel absoluteness and compactness with the entire universe. That is the experience which Guru can give . . . Even if *you* want this experience, even you can have it. No, it depends on your own background, whether you are prepared for that. It's only on that basis. It's not only my belief, because I have done it; to hundreds and thousands of people, I've done it! It's all his grace, his Holiness's grace. This is there. This is a part of, say, yoga, that you can through your vibration, through your radiation, and through unspoken language perceive God – unspoken language, the thought which can be passed on to another man. And you can be related to that evaluation.

'As for me, my very life from the childhood started with sadhus all round me. All round in my environment; where my house was located, just abutted to that there was a great sadhu. He was known to be Sadhu Ramjani. That sadhu was a great magnet of his time. And even now, up to this time, I couldn't find a match for him. He used to speak only one word – that was "*Govind, Govind*". And for forty-six years he didn't speak out any other word besides "*Govind*". So whatever he would like to say, it would be "*Govind, Govind, Govind, Govind, Govind, Govind*" – through that manner he would pass the message.

'Or he would write; if, sometimes, you didn't understand, he would write it. And his life initially influenced me. While I was, say, a child of a year and a half, my mother and grandmother would give me food only if I would sit in meditation and utter "Ram Ram" for half an hour or one hour. So then this thing started – of course I didn't have the consciousness of this life. So somehow this thing got into my blood.

'Naturally, there did exist a discipline that in our particular *mahala* no one took meat and wine, people were pure vegetarian. And no one could be given any house, even to rent, who would eat or drink any of these things. So this thing dominated my character from the very beginning. Then I joined High School, and what I then had from my environment was given more force and I developed a liking for all that atmosphere. My life has been one of a great struggle, quite a great struggle; I have been a very hard worker, worked in various lines. Almost all my lines were technical and then, at the same time, manual, intellectual, and even . . . yes, I must say – wrestling; at the same time I have been a good athlete, good sportsman. And then I have naturally had contact with different people. I have worked just as an ordinary labourer, a coolie, for four annas, five annas a day. And then I have worked as a conductor, bus conductor. I worked as a bus proprietor, then I worked as a schoolmaster. I worked as a sanitary fitter, then I worked as a technician; till the time came when I joined the Army.

'And there I found that I had had the impression that only our Indian people tell lies. But when I joined the British regime, I found that they too can tell lies. It's not only with the Indians. And that thing hurt me. I thought they were people who, because they were white, were great because of their whiteness.

'I joined as a commissioned officer – was a commissioned officer. I was in various sectors, and not me alone but even my generals and the people wherever I have stayed, they have been proud of my loyalty, sincerity, character, honesty. But nothing paid me. It all went . . . everything went against me. So naturally that thing gave rise to a different thinking.

'Until the time came that a man of my name, after drawing

85

his gratuity, he died. After drawing gratuity from the government, he died, and the government pinned me down, because my name was similar and I had a very similar number. So they said, "Well, recover that amount from him – debit his account!" It took me about two years to prove that I am alive and he is dead. And what one can psychologically think in those days you can very well imagine. Except for the fact that traditionally, from my lineage, from my very environment, I have been saying "Ram Ram" or some mantra . . .

'Then I was asked by the government to give my proof that I am alive; I was sent to my centre at Bangalore, and that was a boon to me. There I learned that there was a sadhu known as the Baswi Baba and his age was 194 years at that time – 194 years old. Then I was told that there was such-and-such a man in Mysore and someone informed me that I should see him. And when he told me that, I recollected that I had been with that man. So naturally, without asking for any leave from the army headquarters, I left the place, disappeared and I reached that man within about seven hours.

'And the moment I entered that environment, I reflected that I had been living over there. I recollected all that environment. Then of course I went to meet the sadhu. He embraced me. He naturally recognized me. I recognized him and then we met like anything! He said I should sit in his room, and he would be coming in a few minutes. I sat in his room; there was his footwear, wooden footwear, and I took one of those sandals and put it on my head. As soon as I did that, automatically I got into a sort of trance – and that state continued at least for . . . I understand for ten, twelve minutes or even more than that. Then I seemed to have an absolute peace of mind and a strange atmosphere and a strange recollection. I took off that *khram* and naturally then we had a very hard talk. I said I wouldn't go back from that place, and I would stay for the rest of my life. Then he ordered me that since he's . . . he reminded me of so

86

many things, he said since I am his disciple, I should go back –
and, say, take so many years more, spend so many years in my
service, and then of course retire. And I did that.

'The time and date he gave me, naturally I got retirement and
thereafter I took to this order – after retirement. Then I was a
free sadhu, a naked sadhu when I started. His Holiness had had
a real link with that man and I of course took it in that sense –
that I must come and join him. He had already hundred
thousand of his sadhus, chelas. But within a year I toppled
almost everybody. And I made myself stand over here just like a
rock – in spite of the entire opposition – not only opposition
from my camp, but even from throughout the country, from all
and every . . . from all sadhus. Then of course I took my own
decision – to work for the religion.

'His Holiness knows my character. I know him. He said I am
the only man in his life who knows what he is doing. Let him
say anything, I know from where he speaks. And what he
means. And what it will result in. So naturally we developed a
link. There are certain policies where we may differ. Because
he is in that lineage, he has to see that something should happen
from that point of view. I don't obstruct his Holiness in that
whatever he wants, he chooses, he is free to do, but I have got
my own convictions . . . I'm not very political, but I would wish
that if I can lead even one man, this is quite enough. This is how
I interpret it.'

The four or five devotees who followed us down have been
listening intently. Now, one puts a rupee on the bed, another
bends to Swamiji's feet for a blessing. We go off into the raucous
streets again.

Then it is a morning, a pale blue day set in crystal, melting
slowly as the sun climbs. Vultures and kites float, rising with the
warmth. A green parrot flits by, calling, and doves fly in pairs, as
tradition demands. Below me stands a small temple, its priest

sitting on the step, reading a newspaper. In the small forecourt, flowers left by devoted women lie around the single tree. A red prayer flag flies lankly from a pole. Beyond it, washing flaps on the roof of the Canadian High Commissioner's house.

Nearby is the Institute of Psychic and Spiritual Research, where Janadan Swami pursues his study of *Dhwani* yoga. This is concerned with the identity of breath as vital essence; not breath alone, but also the sounds breath gives rise to. There are four basic sounds, H. A. U. M: thus the mystic syllable OM is formed, and vibrating beyond that is *akshar*, the primordial and eternal unheard sound which is itself the First Cause of the universe. The first vibration, says the Swami, was *ha-kar*, which then unfolds into forty-nine different vibrations, all of them basic and inherent in men and matter. These are represented by the forty-nine letters of the Sanskrit alphabet. Evolution was the consequence of a polarity between attraction and repulsion, and this is expressed in human breathing through which we remain alive; inhalation equals attraction, exhalation repulsion. That this is so is partly because of the sounds associated with breathing in and out; 'aa-ha' if we breathe through the mouth, 'um-hum' if we breathe through the nose. If we learn to breathe properly, to retain and develop the right sound, the basic 'ha-kar', we shall live longer and come nearer to realizing out psychic and physical potential. Self-realization comes when the opposing forces of exhalation and inhalation, attraction and repulsion, have been stabilized.

Janadan Swami is a frail looking but vigorous man in his eighties. When he smiles, great yellow teeth show clustered on the left of his mouth. He has long, stringy grey hair that hangs loosely about his ears and down his slightly stooped back. His beard straggles, grey and almost pointed, from his chin and throat. He has a delicate nose, well shaped lips; he may have been beautiful as a young man. Now his dark eyes stare at me, their expression inscrutable, almost sinister, as the lenses of his glasses exaggerate his right eye until it seems about to balloon down his lean cheek. He wears a thin ochre vest and an ochre robe. As he speaks, in his high, slightly rasping voice, he gesticulates, his thin arms with their withered skin waving in the air. When he talks of dirt, he picks dust from the floor, spreads it on my arm; his eyes seem to flare when he mentions mesmerism. He moves quickly about the room, unconscious of his movements; he walks like a young man, not taking the care the old often do over the very fact of walking. While he talks, he smokes; the servant brings his cigarettes as I sit down. He seems dreadfully thin as he stands looking down at me; he has eaten nothing for the last two days, someone says. But he still has tomorrows to come, he looks forward to vindication, to a wide acceptance of his theories, to a pilgrimage to his Institute by Western scientists. His optimism is total.

'As soon as a shishya comes and sits before a Guru, he sees the vibrations that emit from the shishya, and because he is more powerful he knows what type of a shishya he is. Attraction and repulsion. I see those attractions and repulsions and I can understand what he is and what you are. There is one desire, a sort of intensive desire in a shishya when he comes to a Guru, and the Guru understands this by his intuition.

'The attraction and repulsion that we find in the breath, in the process of inhalation or exhalation, is common to all beings. Even to the subtlest part of Nature, that is the atom, that power of attraction and repulsion is all pervading. So if we want to know the real nature of that power which is also pulsating in ourselves, we must know the power within us. If we can understand that power of attraction and repulsion we can understand you, this, that, everybody; and we can even attract anyone whenever we like because it is the same power of attraction and repulsion which is pulsating. So the power within must be known.

'In the relation between Guru and shishya, the process is wordless, invisible. It cannot be expressed in words. It can be experienced. Language is nothing; it is conditioned. And if you want to go higher than this you must leave this conditioning. That is experience, pure and simple. That is intuition.

'The commands of the Guru, their physical embodiment, lead to an action. If the shishya obeys his order he develops the power of Guru within, and that is the real grace of the Guru which he can know by uplifting his own vibration to the Guru level. As for me personally, I was a boy when my father died and I left home. I was very much shocked by the death of my father and I wanted to know where he had gone. But I could not find out. Then when I was older I became an anarchist and I was very active. I joined Congress. But in 1925, when the anarchist leader died, I left Congress; the same vibrations that shocked me after the death of my father struck me again.

'I had devoted a great deal of time in anarchist activities, but then I found there was nothing in it. I left. With the same shocked vibrations again in my mind, I went in search of something: what was the cause of all this pain and this suffering? So I travelled all over the place in search of knowledge, in many temples and various places. I even went to a Muslim saint; he said, "Do this sadhana under this tree, this mango tree, and you will get some siddhis [powers]." I did, but later I went on because even that didn't satisfy me. Finally I met the man who was to be my Guru; I met him accidentally and took initiation from him. He told me the technique of Hansa Mantra, of the sound which is inherent in us. And I began to practise this technique continuously. But I asked my Guru, "Is this all you are going to give me, or is there more?" My Guru said, "No, that is all. If you do it yourself, you will reach a state which will itself guide you. And in that way you will develop." So I went on with this sadhana while I wandered all over India.

'As soon as I had taken initiation, my Guru ordered, "Go to

Rangpur (in East Bengal – now Bangladesh) and establish an ashram." So I went there; I stayed in Rangpur for twelve years. Up to then I'd been like a hippie, wandering here and there [laughs]. But in Rangpur I stayed, that was the order I'd received from my Guru. But after the partition of India and Pakistan, I went back to the Guru's own ashram. I only stayed there for a short period, and then left again – there were some differences among the shishyas, so . . .

'Once more I practised the sadhana while I wandered across the country. I had many experiences during that sadhana. I was very much determined that either I would die or I would do it, and I got results, so that after a prolonged period I began to understand. My Guru predicted about this sadhana, that scientists from all over the world would come to me some time or the other during my lifetime and study this technique, this sadhana, and learn to arouse or develop the same power which I have found. This is what he wanted.

'I spent only a very short time with my Guru. When I went to him I was an anarchist and you know what type of mentality an anarchist has – do or die; he wants immediate results. So I went to Guruji in the same manner. I said, "Guruji, you are giving sadhana, no doubt, but can the sadhana reveal the mysteries of the whole universe? If it can, then it's all right. Otherwise, you know my character." I said that openly to my Guru. Guruji said, "Oh, you do it and you will find yourself." Now, how did my Guru help me? How did I receive his grace? Through the *shabda* (sound) which he gave me at initiation. He gave me that in my initiation, and his work was finished. The whole development of my Guru was transferred to me in that way.

'During the periods of sadhana I have had many mysterious experiences. I have developed certain siddhis and so on; I have seen revealed so many miraculous things. That is why I can take shishyas. If one has not developed or understood all these stages intermediary in the process of realization, one cannot understand

91

that while advancing on this path one will come across many experiences of this kind. It is through one's own sadhana, by raising oneself up, that one can understand what power the Guru has, the disembodied Guru. One must come level with him to understand his power. It is not a thing to show; what is shown is a sort of mesmerism, nothing else. But sometimes the Guru shows you that you too can develop this power.

'He shows the miraculous power to the shishya, but at the same time he gives him pain, suffering. This is a very important factor among the sadhus. You may be all right, but the Guru will give you some pain, some difficulties; he will create some sort of a vibration around you that will make you rather perplexed. Then he can test the calibre of the shishya; whether he can overpower those difficulties or whether he will drown in them.

'A long time ago, my Guru gave me physical pain, torture. I had broken my spinal column – it's still broken. See! [He bends abruptly, shows me a bony lump in mid-back.] The Guru wanted to see what his shishya could do; but I was very confident in my Guru. My temperature went up to 102, 104. They put me in hospital, but I left. I thought, "What's the point of lying in hospital? If the Guru has power, let us verify it, let us see whether he can cure me or not." Now the ashram at Kalipur is a thousand feet higher than the hospital. So I walked like that [demonstrates what is in fact crawling] and climbed up to the ashram and stayed there. As soon as I reached the ashram, instead of asking about my condition, my Guru said, "Oh, you have come; now you can prepare my food." Nothing else. He did not ask me any other question, not "How are you?" or "How are you feeling?" or anything like that. Nothing. "Prepare food for me, because I like food from your hands." So, in spite of my temperature running at 102 or 104, I had to prepare food for my Guru. And at the same time he said, "In the morning, you come and massage my legs." But when I massaged his legs, my Guru massaged my back at the same time. This went on for a month, but I realized in just a few days that my Guru would make me all right. There was one shishya who said, "What kind of *gurukripa* [Guru's grace] is that? A Guru cannot cure him." But when I was cured the Guru said, "Come, you wanted to know the power of the Guru? By the grace of the Guru, you can do anything." Which means that the Guru can make the impossible possible. And after that he gave me the power of initiating others. But you see – the Guru gives physical torture, too.

'One more important thing: don't keep a duality between Guru and shishya. If you keep some dualism, if there is separation between Guru and shishya in this physical embodiment too, then you cannot understand anything. And that is why I always say that I make Gurus, rather than shishyas.'

His disciple and assistant, Ramesh Khandelwal, has been interpreting for us. He is a big man, thirty years old, chubby, strong shouldered, wearing white shirt and dark trousers. He smiles often, a confident, big toothed smile, and he laughs; he is outgoing. On his cheeks and large, rather stubborn chin, the slight stubble is smooth and even, it adds no roughness to the curves of his face. He is very fair skinned, and through glasses with slightly winged and upturned frames his grey eyes gleam ingenuously at the world. Under a cap of astrakhan or lamb's-wool which gleams in the light with a faint blue sheen, his dark hair is cropped close, perhaps growing again after being shaved. His big, deep chest is beginning to slip into meditator's stomach; out of it, his voice comes incongruously high and loud, edged sometimes with a sort of hysteria. He thrusts theory at me as fact with the self-satisfaction of the fanatic. But it is impossible to be offended by him; he is a pleasant and generous man.

He sits behind his glass topped desk, waits for my questions. Down the room, other desks stand unoccupied. Behind him, books and propaganda for the Institute line the shelves. A picture of Janadan Swami and of his Guru hang on the wall. From the ceiling four fans are still now in the cool of the morning. In the one above Khandelwal's head, susurrating sparrows build a nest. As we talk, they scream and chatter, flitting busily in and out through the open door.

'When I started sadhana, I was just sitting in the normal manner, when I felt that my body had become very huge. I was rather thrilled; I looked at my body, but it was all right. So I felt that something peculiar had happened to me. This was the first experience, and I was rather fascinated.

'Then I practised the sadhana because it was so easy – a sort of breathing in a different way. After some time some lights appeared – then I had some experience of a sound audible to me. This was within a period of one or two months. I was so interested in these peculiar things that I concentrated even more; and one day I had the experience that I heard an intensive sound, and at the same time saw a very bright light. So I told these things to Guruji and he said, "Concentrate only on the sound. When the sound comes inside you, just try to hear it." Next time I did that; I heard the sound vanish and then I found that a peculiar sort of vibration emerged in me that seemed to want to take me as if it wanted to lift me. It was lifting me up like anything! I felt very much as if I would die. I told this feeling to Guruji, and he said, "No, no, you will not die. You try to go upward, you also intensely desire to go upward." The next time, when this repeated again, I felt the same vibration – invisible. I don't know ... What I felt was as if somebody was dragging me upward very powerfully. I do not know what type of realization I made at that time, but after some time I reached a state ... I don't know even what kind of state it was. But I realized. And when I came back out of that state – I don't know how long it lasted – I found there was peace absolute, such as I have never experienced in any other thing, even in sexual

94

experiences. This sort of experience developed in me a great interest to know more, to be peaceful all the time.

'But this position was not stabilized. I found various difficulties. As Guruji told me, "During the sadhana you will come across many difficulties, enormous difficulties," which is a test of a Guru; I found many difficulties. Some came from my age. I will tell you very frankly now ... It was the age of seventeen – teenage. I was interested in somebody. The sort of vibration that always attracted me. I said to Guruji this was the sort of feeling that the devil makes.

'He said, "No. Do the sadhana intensively."

'So it happened for a long period, say for four years, four or five years ... the unconscious level in which these urges exist, they come up to this conscious level; and they wanted to create a conflict in the personality. And this is a very important fact of sadhana itself: it is the process through which a Guru discovers whether you can overcome these difficulties or not. But for four or five years at least, the sadhana could not develop. There was a chaos. Then afterwards, I regained some power and that conflict was over.

'There came another difficulty, due to family circumstances. Tremendous difficulties I came across because my father said, "You have to do service (i.e. go to work)."

'I said, "No, I will be a businessman rather than a serviceman." But he said no; the sort of will power that had developed in me said like this, "No – if Guru has power, let us try it now." Because I had no money and for business you must have some money otherwise you cannot start, I went to the ashram, stayed there for two months and did sadhana. Guruji blessed me, I don't know in what way, I do not understand at all; but he said, "Go, and you will achieve whatever you want."

'I went to Kanpur again – and at that same time, somebody offered me 20,000 rupees! This was a surprise to me! And I started a business. He gave me the money unconditionally.

That is the point – unconditionally! I was rather surprised – but it was the grace of the Guru . . .

'Then I left my business (after some financial difficulties) because I saw it is nothing compared with the Guru's grace. This time I stayed with him. In the meantime there were so many experiences of supernatural things; I saw something happening and it happened in due course. I saw it in a dream, as you see a black-and-white film. Something comes and goes, and again comes and goes – like that. But still I could not find the source from where such things take place. Still I am not finding. But now I am confident I can distinguish between a dream which has no real value in practical life and the dreams which I have of the supernatural kind about some happening. I am in search of a real method, a methodology, so I can distinguish the dream state and this state.

'The most important thing that I saw during the last few months happened before the death of my father. I dreamt that he died and his clothes were wet, very wet. He was lying on a cot and at the same time a boy was lying under the cot. He died in the same way – he put himself in the well. He was brought back. He was rather wet. And he died two hours after that. And the boy I saw means that he got a new life in the form of a man. I dreamt another dream. He was sitting in a chair and he was determined, he was very aggressive inside. This is the sort of feeling that I developed when I saw him during my dream. And he said "Oh, I want to do something to die." Because he was very much disturbed by the type of suffering he had during his last times. He suffered from some ailment, but the doctors could not find out what type of ailment it was.

'You cannot have faith which has no background. It must be supported by something real. If I have faith that my Guru can do this, it is my faith, not the Guru's; but the Guru is in me and that is the faith of my Guru in me. From that I can push, a will-power develops in a man that attracts him to do whatever

... this is the sort of faith that is needed, not the sort of empty faith. Empty faith cannot support anything.'

Afterwards, chatting, Khandelwal talks of his Guru's powers. When Janadan Swami's Guru was very ill and finally given up, Janadan Swami went into samadhi. Khandelwal said, 'I touched him and he was very hot. And then suddenly – here, at the top of the head – there was a bubble! A bubble! Two or three of us were there. A bubble, here on the top of the head! I was very much terrified. Then after fifteen minutes or half an hour it went away and he woke up – "It's all right – Guruji won't die."'

Nor did he until two years later; when he lay very ill again, Janadan Swami refused to stay but went off into the mountains. One day, seeing a calling crow, he knew the old man had died and hurried back to the ashram to prepare the Guru's resting place with a certainty that came from his 'having been told' what the old man had wanted.

Khandelwal stops suddenly. 'Ha! I'm talking on the day! I mean it was today thirteen years ago my Guruji's Guru died. Yes – today or tomorrow. That is a strange chance!'

Later, setting and witness change. My new informant is a Westerner, the place we meet at is one of Delhi's best hotels – a pale cliff face of windows stuck tentatively here and there with decorations and peering disdainfully out over the utilitarian red brick façade of the British High Commission. He is well known in religious circles: Baron von Blomberg, despite his name and occasional thick accent, is a United States citizen and describes himself as, 'an old Yankee, practical, feet on the ground'.

He wears a dark green silk shirt, a green jacket, light trousers, bright black shoes. He is not very tall, but trim, despite a thickening waistline. He has a steel bracelet on his right wrist, a gold watch on his left, a silver ring on the third finger of his left hand, its stone elaborately set. His mouth is small, down turned, he has pale grey, serious eyes, and cared-for grey hair thinning a little at the front. Reading glasses hang on a black cord round his neck.

Beyond a green curtain a long table is being set for a banquet; as we talk, waiters laugh, cutlery clashes like swords. Von Blomberg talks quietly, evenly, as a man does out of knowledge acquired with difficulty and tempered by intelligent self-scrutiny. He seems like someone who knows that much of what he says and feels will appear weird to the untutored, but who does not care, who cannot say or feel otherwise: indeed, one sometimes gets the impression that he holds some of his beliefs almost despite himself, that only the personal experience corroborating them protects them from a scepticism otherwise natural to him.

Once a Christian evangelist, of the fiercest Protestant variety, he first came to India to help arrange the tour programme of a clutch of faith-healers. On that visit, India offered him nothing and he returned to the West when the tour ended. He has, however, been a lifelong searcher after spiritual certainty and realization; 'although my mind was always open, yet always wanting to know why – a battle between reason and the spirit'. But he remains a seeker, 'after forty years in over a hundred countries, with Voodoo, with Pokhomaniacs, with Dukhobors, with Druzes, with Zoroastrians, and with every possible holy man, not only in India, but in Asia and everywhere else that I could find'. The way in which the seriousness of that is wrapped up in the slightest tissue of self-deprecation seems to me typical of him.

'I came to India not as a seeker, but as a suddenly appointed co-president of this World Fellowship of Religions. I came as a disciple of Sant Kirpal Singh. I saw him for some years inwardly, which no one has been able to explain to me – including Sant Kirpal Singh. If there is an explanation for everything, it could be dreams, but I saw this man ... You know how Kirpal Singh looks with the beard and the turban and the unexplainable eyes which pierce through you and which don't seem to be of this world. I saw him for at least ten years before I met him. I had no idea who he was and didn't give much thought to it, except out of curiosity. How exactly I saw him I don't know – I saw him inwardly and it didn't seem like dreams. Certainly it sometimes occurred when I was awake – but not awake and running around or appearing at functions, no. I might be sitting quietly, and then suddenly ...

'I was still, at that time, on my Christian tours; I was speaking at San Francisco and suddenly saw the picture in the newspaper of this man I had been seeing for years, and I went. And as I came into the hall, he turned to me and smiled – we knew each other at once. He told me that his Master, Sant Baba Singh, had told him about me. He knew that this man – and he gave my full description – would take him, Kirpal Singh, to world leaders to meet them, which I did; and would be his co-worker in bringing together all the religious leaders of the world.

'So I invited him to my home in Boston; and in Boston with some fear ... quite a lot of fear, was initiated by him. Because I thought, "What will this initiation do? Will it change me entirely?" I knew nothing about it.

'The initiation takes the form of the Master giving you the ability to see here, a light here [he taps the centre of his forehead], to see him, to talk with him, to see others – of which you must be cautious; you must give the powerful words which you are taught, and if that face remains he is all right, if it disappears he isn't ... In other words, the light, the beautiful diamond light, and the sound which I get immediately when most people don't. Most people have to sit for hours, but in a way it's their fault because they stew about it in their tents, and they're willing it, whereas the secret is complete tranquillity and relaxation. That also for me is not the ultimate.

'I have met hundreds of Gurus and Masters and about four that I would consider – and others consider – great Masters. I think great Masters are very few – very, very limited. I have been in the caves in the Himalayas; I have talked to those who are turned to stone from years of just sitting without food or water but they exist and they talk. And they give radiance, they give ... I'm thinking of one now who's about 114 years old, near Rishikesh, and almost turned to stone; but still he talks and sits in his cave. How he exists without food or water I don't know; but he does give off an energy and probably contributes a good deal spiritually.

'The quality of a great Master is something you feel. It's not only something you feel but you know others do because of the great number of followers. Their followers are in the hundreds of thousands, I'd say. And you get a sensitivity and you just know – you just know that that is really a great Master. After a time you can pick out these gradations – and when it's been your whole life you'd be a fool not to be able to. There are things that I wonder about. For instance one of the teachings of Kirpal Singh is that from time to time he disappears from here to join the other great Masters who sit in conclave above on matters of great world importance. There have been in my long experience with him – and I'm still with him because he is the most sincere that I've gotten to know – times when I've been informed that a particular question is of such importance that he will join and ask above ... and apparently he does. Now, there are many things like that which I could not explain to a normal person. And that's what I mean when I say that so much happens which I'm incapable of putting into words.

'He, more than anyone, gives me what I need. But still not enough, still not enough ... That may be partly my fault; I'm a rebel and I also have to know why. "Why, Master, must I give up eggs – I see no reason. All right, I can see where I should not eat those with life in them, but those without life, what harm is there in my eating them?" Now, his other disciples wouldn't dare ask – or it just wouldn't occur to them. I don't like any fanaticism, anything which goes too far.

'Between my Master and myself there need be no words and there are very few. Another phase of it is that he often asks me, "Baron, is your telephone still in order?" – which means the talking here [indicates his forehead], whether I am in Boston, Hamburg or . . . doesn't matter; and I answer, "It is in order." The silence between us is one of the most blissful things of all, and something which gives you confidence, complete confidence. But I wouldn't know how to put it in words. How generally it exists between Guru and disciple I don't know.

'What sometimes happens is that, with our work together for the World Fellowship of Religions, something often happens which has to be decided at once. It can't wait for the weeks and days it takes for correspondence. Then I go inwardly and I get the answer almost at once, and I do that. Then, in the next letter – maybe two weeks later – that's always mentioned. But he doesn't know about it, which surprises me. I say to him, "But, Master, you told me to do that."

'"Did I? Then it's all right."

'But how could a Master with thousands of followers know every answer he gives? The answer that I get isn't, of course, a specific form of words; it's just that I know what to do. And again, there's an explanation for it. Of course I believe in miracles, but this may not be one. There's telepathy . . . There's so much we don't know, it's really tremendous.

'I can't accept the Guru as God, but certainly I can accept him as having his god-like powers developed to a tremendous degree, and far more than any other person I know. That I can accept, but I can say too that you or I have like powers, but they are certainly not developed and we haven't spent a lifetime on development as they have. He tells me, "I am a man like you – except that I've learned at the feet of my Master." And so he did, the same as I did – but solely that, you see. Yes, I would say he is God if you are and I am and he is . . . But if one meets Sant Kirpal Singh one is apt to feel something. He is a simple man, the simplest possible – yet there is a divineness there, tremendous power; tremendous love which is the key to everything and which we don't practise. That could open every door there is if we understood it and practised it.

'A real Guru generates a love and the whole world is seeking love as never before. That's what they're really seeking although they don't know it. And physical love and the myriad other kinds of love don't satisfy. But if we follow the reality, the real love, we could have anything we wanted, we could win everyone we wanted, but we don't do that.

'We have a proverb: "Fortunate is he who finds his Guru." Many can go to Kirpal Singh and get nothing, or to Meher Baba or to any of these people. "His own Guru" – the one who is for you at that time. It varies according to each of us. There's just as much variation between Gurus as there is between any other people. You may go to the most enlightened one there is but you may not be ready. Therefore what he gives you will be way above you. You may be ready ten years from now, or an hour from now. But not at that moment. Therefore you go again until you find one who will satisfy you. It may be a very simple one.

'If I went to another Guru, it wouldn't be a question of changing Gurus exactly. Kirpal Singh was what I needed at that time, ten years ago. Now, we have become more than master and disciple, very warm and close friends, co-workers; and in that sense, no. But he tells me, which every great Master will do, "Go, try them all. If you find someone better, take it. Tell me about it." I haven't found anything better. I've learned from others. What I've learned . . . I don't know, it may be something, it may be nothing. It may be that suddenly through observation, and through listening, there's one point that I hadn't gotten. And that's not always intellectual; it can come in another way, in a flash. Even with a Guru with whom one doesn't have the rapport one does with one's own Guru there can be one point ... and most unexpectedly, too.

'There's a Guru completely different from Kirpal Singh. I don't understand one single word he says – never. He gets, he says, messages direct from God, and he claims that Jesus touched him on the foot when he was a soldier years ago in Italy. And his message is, in fact, a sort of high-pitched babbling, going on for hours; four and a half hours. And yet I got something from him. But I never said a word to him, or he to me. I got a further light on my seeking, a further explanation of one or two points that I hadn't, somehow, grasped before. And they came to me in the course of four and a half boring hours, very uncomfortable hours of sitting. I don't know if that came through him, or whether it was just that I was there, half dreaming; but it did.

'And I've learned from everyone I've ever touched. Everyone. And I would tomorrow.'

Then Delhi, wrapped in haze, lies elsewhere. The Fokker Friendship lifts and brown India drops away. Wells like anguished eyes stare darkly up; tiny figures reap infinitesimal crops. The squared-off land lies level to the four horizons; its fields are green and brown, and all the hues of each. We swing over a river in which small, brown boats sit immobile, as if in syrup. On a mudflat, water birds stand in long flocks, dots like hundreds and thousands dusted over the riverbank. The whole world now is the same sand colour – a grey-brown, a pale purple with which the earth seems shot.

VARANASI

The English called it Benares. After Independence, it became Banares, then Varanasi. But for the holy men who live or make their pilgrimage here in their hundreds of thousands it has always been Kashi. The tubby Indian Airlines bus rackets and bounces towards it. Camels, two in a row, then one alone, lie prone. A donkey rolls in the dust beside the road; children run, shouting – it is Saturday, which means freedom from school here too. Sewing machines stand in shop doorways – India's primary automation. Cycle rickshaws, cycle repair shops, cycles. Outside a shoe shop, rounds of leather, embryo shoes. Sweetmeats on display, chai shops, fabrics like shadow-dulled rainbows at the back of emporia like grottoes.

Later, bedlam at Ganges side. People press, rush from their coaches, walk in relentless files towards the steep steps of the *ghats* and the holy currents lapping their feet. And among them passes a rabble of touts of all ages and descriptions, indescribably reptilian, their betel-stained mouths gaping in smiles more horrible than beggars.

'I am not guide, I am temple priest. I show you ...' 'Just take my card, there is no obligation to buy, I am showing you only ...' 'Ivories, very precious ... not a shop, sahib, a museum only ...' 'Boat, sahib?' 'Silks, brocades – at my factory, sahib, here is address ...' '*Baksheesh*, sahib!' 'Sahib!' Pipes are played about me, drums tickled, plastic toys displayed. Beggars sit in their prescribed, morose rows; in shadow, barbers clip the hair of pilgrims. A party of Tibetans, monk led, marches towards the river.

And there, at the foot of those worn, vertiginous steps, it lies, the flat, greenish Ganges, lined by temples, red or yellow-ochre, and platforms on which sit the cross-legged, expounding *pandits*, while behind them ash grey, paint marked Nagas parade alongside the sluggish water.

I clamber, sweating, from the river. Along the filthy road, market women beguile servants and watchful wives with tomatoes, straggling cabbages, spinach. Cycle rickshaws jangle past in straining packs. Seventeen flushed Americans climb into a canary-yellow coach, their jutting cameras the genitals with which they rape the world. Dark lenses cover their eyes as if to save them for ever from the infection carried in a human glance.

Later, I follow my guide down narrow lanes overhung by jutting upper terraces and lined by black, narrow shops, caves decked with poverty's luxuries. Withered women sell raddled fruit from wide, unravelling baskets. These lanes of Varanasi, crowded with beggars, children, sadhus, pilgrims, tourists, calling pedlars, hippies, widows in white, cows, donkeys, goats and dogs. We pass under an arch, walk between high, white-washed walls. A gap on the right shows steps plunging to the Ganges, at their foot a slow, nosing cow, a tethered boat, green water.

At the monastery, we are met by the mahant elect, Swami Padmanabhand Saraswati, a man in his late sixties. He has a long, narrow, curved nose, faded brown eyes sunken under thin eyebrows, grey stubble on his cheeks. His head is covered in an ochre scarf so that he looks like some cowled Inquisitor. But his eyes, although suspicious, are quite kind. He leads us upward past the scaffolding where, in the centre of the math, workmen are building a new temple. On an upper floor old monks crouch in ochre robes. They watch us almost without comprehension, draw up bony knees, fold long hands about their shins, let their mouths hang open; Kashi is a place to die. In a small cell, a fat monk lies on the floor, half naked, his legs spread.

We come out on the roof at last. In the soft haze of dusk, the Ganges curves away to the right and the clutter of towers, roofs and steps follows it, dimming with distance. Across the river lies a deep sandbank, like a grey-brown cloth spread over the land. Small figures move beside the water, washing gleams in the evening light. A tree overhangs the roof, green parrots scream, a cow calls. The white pillars of a balcony near by seem to recede as the light fades; the children's heads on the roof behind us, peering cautiously over the parapet, flatten and darken into silhouette. The lamps come on, giving the curved river a new outline. I sit on a bed, the Swami on another at right angles to it. He speaks very quickly, out of an almost toothless mouth, and although he is fluent in English his words are heavily accented and slurred. I bend forward, straining to hear.

'This math was established some 510 years back. The founder, whom we believe to be an avatar of the Lord, came here then and took sanyas diksha at this place, Kashi, on the Mani-karnika Ghat. After taking sannyas he wanted to establish a math and he founded this place here, this very place, which is called the Dattrya Math. Now, our mahant is the forty-fourth mahant of this place – a continuity of mahants. Now there are five of us here, three are sannyasis and two brahmacharyas. We are sadhus and to maintain ourselves we go from door to door. We go in the morning to three houses and beg there and whatever they give us we take; we have only one meal a day, at twelve o'clock.

'We come here because a person who has some religious ideas thinks that Kashi is the only place where a man should go and give his last time to the Ganges. So our life should be passed in such a way that we must end our life on Manikarnika Ghat. We leave everything – our wife and household and every-thing is left and we come here. Once we come here, then naturally we have got certain religious rules. Under those rules, we are controlled by the authority of him we call Guru. Now the Guru gives us the idea of what we have to do in the world, why we have come into the world. Then if he is satisfied he allows you to stay in the math. Not everybody is allowed to stay. You have to take training for it; I stayed here for three years and when the mahant was satisfied that my whole idea is to spend my life for God only, not for the ordinary things of the world, when he was satisfied of that, then he gave me sannyas. So this is the procedure. And if he expels me tomorrow, I will have to go out into the world.

'How one selects a Guru depends on generations, generations. We don't think that we have only this life, we come from lives together. We think that a Guru knows us three or four lives back; he sees where you were, where you are and where you are likely to be before your death. Knowing all these things, then he can guide the shishya. Because we believe that if we are to come to God, we do not know the exact path – but if the Guru knows that we have to take the long path, he will guide us along the long path, and if we are more suited to the short path, he will guide us to a short path.

'There is always a very close connection between Guru and shishya. And I'll tell you one thing that is in the Hindu religion and is in no other religion, and that is that the Guru makes the shishya a Guru himself. In other faiths what happens is that a Guru may very well make a shishya a god, but here a Guru makes a shishya a god and then worships him himself. Before giving him the final mantra, the Guru himself worships the man, he tells him everything and he tells him, "Now you have become a spiritual god, and now I am worshipping you." So a Guru worships a shishya, which you will never find in any other religion. And if the man who has acquired the mantra from the Guru is a pure man, if he has perfectly acquired the full sense from the Guru, then he will never leave him.

'Then a time comes, after some sadhana has been perfectly done, when the Guru has only to sit before him for the shishya to get knowledge. He does not have to talk. Only by seeing each other, and not talking, the shishya will get the sense, will get jnan [knowledge].

'And if I am the Guru and you are sitting by me, whatever I say, you are sure to take up. Suppose you are not my shishya and he over there is, and I am talking, then he will take from what I say that which he wants. You will not be able to get it. The words will be the same for both of you, but only he will be able to take it up; they'll mean something different to him than they will to you. So everything depends upon the person hearing it; if he has enough power to catch up the meaning, he will catch it up.

'What happens is that the Guru first tests the shishya, he'll test him for ten days, fifteen days, one month, a year, seven years, ten years – in the *Upanishads*, thirty-three years, thirty-three years again, thirty-three years ... Hundred thousand years the shishya is tested! Then he will say, "Yes, now I am satisfied." Then he gives him power. It is not so easy; I could not make you a shishya today, that is not possible.

'Guru-shishya *parampara* [the continuing connection] is not just a question of mantra and knowledge, or like a schoolteacher who will allow any student to come to him and will give him his ideas – no, no, not that. Even a carpenter will ask a new man to sharpen his tools; only then will he allow him to touch the wood. Similarly, the shishya is first tested. The Guru must ask, "Do you have full faith in me or not? If I find you have full faith in me, then we can go on." The Guru parampara is not for a day or two; step-by-step, step-by-step he takes the shishya up.

'Once in Nagpur there was a Guru, and one of his shishyas had some doubt about him. This shishya thought to himself, "Oh, this Guru does not have so much power." The Guru understood that the shishya had his doubts about him. So he said to the shishya, "I have a pain in this leg, so I can't talk to you today. You come tomorrow."

'But the other one said, "No, Guruji, I want that mantra today."

'The Guru said, "No, I can't give it you today – you come tomorrow. I have too much pain."

'But the shishya argued so the Guru said, "Well, if you are so keen about it, come after one hour." After an hour, the shishya came and the Guru was actually weeping. He said to the shishya,

"This pain is very bad, and I don't think it will be removed unless you put your mouth here and take out all the pus."

'But the shishya thought, "How can I put my mouth on that sore place – it is not possible, not possible." So in his place the Guru called a lady who was sitting there – "Oh, lady, put your mouth here and take out all the pus." And she was a real devotee, she thought that the Guru would not ask her such a thing unless ... So she did it. And within five minutes she found that there was nothing but a good mango there! She took out all the juice and then he told that shishya, "You had no faith. She had full faith. I will give the mantra to her and not to you." So you must have full faith in the Guru, then you can progress.

'I was a believer in God right from the beginning. My mother and father also believed in God, so naturally I copied them. After that, I was taught in a missionary school and I was taught the Bible. And while teaching us the Bible, the teacher talked some nonsense about our religion. So I said to him, "I will read our Gita and then I will talk to you after one year."

'Then I read the Gita and a commentary of about a thousand pages. I went through that thrice. So then I went to him and said, "What are you talking about Krishna and Gita and so on – your ideas are all nonsense and wrong; you should not talk such things." And I was very glad when ten years later I found that teacher had become Hindu! I was very glad for him. He remembered my name; he says that he was teaching one of the students in a school at Nagpur and, "He spoke about Sri Krishna and since then I have been reading about what Sri Krishna is and those words about Sri Krishna sound in my ear and now I know what the Hindu religion is."

'Thus I came in contact with some sannyasis and they gave me some idea of my religion. Then I passed some ten years on the holy river Narmada in Madhya Pradesh and began to study; but my Guru told me, "Because you are in Government service and so have got this other duty, your mind is such that it can't stay in one place for two or three years. So you will do a penance for that." And that penance I did for three years; I sat at one place for three years and I was very surprised that the calmness in the mind was there.

'Then I came to Kashi. And here I heard lectures of the Arya Samaj and all these people; because if we listen to different persons, we can form our own ideas. In this way, I found my own ideas about this. Then I went to one of my Gurus whom I thought proper. I learned the whole life of that man, I knew that from the time when he was a child of seven or eight years old he had got very high ideas of religion. Now he is still there in Madhya Pradesh – he is now wandering there. So I made him my Guru – he is Swami Swarupananda Saraswati – and he brought me in his line for ten years. And after that, I took sannyas. In sannyasi I find that the real idea, which I was hankering after, I can attain. So, in short, the whole life of the mind is controlled by Gurus.

'As to how I came to my Guru; in our religion it is not the shishya who goes to the Guru, but the Guru who comes to the shishya. God sends that Guru to a shishya to take him up. The shishya has to make his own sadhana; then, if he has full awareness of religion, God himself will send a Guru to him. That is exactly what happened here. Once – I shouldn't be telling you, but I will tell you – once I did not believe in these sadhus much, in the beginning. Because I studied in the British language and with British teachers, I had no faith in religion much, no faith in Gurus, no faith in sadhus. But I told you, after these foreigners had created such a disbelief in my own religion, I went to the books. But after that I got some shocks, various sorts of difficulties, some deaths and some other things. So once I was in my house and I was thinking, "How shall I get complete peace?" I returned to the religious books and so I got peace. Then, while I was reading the books, I found some difficulty.

Spiritual difficulty. So I wanted to be restored by some spiritual authority.

'And what happened was that, as I was sitting, a friend came to me and said, "Oh, some sadhu is coming today." I told him that I did not believe in sadhus much, but if he arrived I would go to my friend's place and just hear what he said.

'He said, "Come on, we will ask him these questions."

'I said, "Yes, I am prepared for that."

'I went to him, and to my great surprise . . . he was sent by God to me! I never knew that, but when I came into contact with him I bowed down and I told him about my difficulty. He said, "Oh, you have a difficulty? But I have one difficulty about you." So I asked "What?" He said, "Well, I want to come to your house today."

'At first I refused that order, but my friend who had brought me to him said, "No, no, he's a good man – you allow him." I said, "Very well, on your account I'll allow him."

'Anyhow, this spiritual man came to my house; he stayed in my bungalow. For two or three days he stayed there. One night, at two o'clock in the night, I got some doubt whether he was a real sadhu or some *badmash* man. So I decided to go at that time to see. So I went at two o'clock to him, and to my great surprise I found that he was in samadhi. And the second surprise was that, when I went and bowed down, he said my name and said, "Oh, you have come here at midnight – have you got another difficulty?" Then I told him that all my difficulties had been solved now – "I had difficulty about you, who you are, but now I have solved it."

'After that he said to me, "You wait for one more year. After that I will call you." For one year I waited; then I got the idea that I would just go and see him. And to my third surprise, I took a ticket to Mathura and when I got there, I found him on the station! "Oh, you have come," he said.

'"Yes, I have come."

'In this way, the Guru can come in contact with the shishya. That was Swami Swarupananda Saraswati, and he gave me the full spiritual idea of what is God, what is man. I stayed with him then for fifteen days; I was still in Government service and I had come on leave. Then he came to me and he was with me for two months. Then every year he used to come to me. Fourteen years went on in this way and ultimately he asked me to take *danda** and he sent me here. He comes here from time to time.'

When we walk back through the lanes, we find them dim with the smoke of cooking fires. Soon we are among people again, above the river, in amongst the circling, screaming, vulpine, staring and demanding crowd, in a place of a hundred lights and colours, of fruit, chai, barbers, Coca-Cola, flutes and beggars.

Another day, a boatman takes us through noon heat almost as solid as walls, leaving behind on the shore the stretcher poles, the shrivelled garlands, the ash and the black, corrupted wood of last night's funerals. Washing, like the organized flags of a political demonstration, is draped high on the bank; below it, *dhobi* men twist their backs and wrists, and crack coiled laundry expertly against the stones: shirts, trousers, saris, sheets, swing and fall like flails. The steps rise mountainous on the right; Swami Keshavpuri says, 'They were built by rajas in olden times – no one can think of such a great construction work now.' High on a balcony a woman hangs bright clothes, as if in celebration or welcome, their colours crackling in the sunlight; she tugs at her shining hair, walks off into shadow. A few

* This is the staff a sannyasi gets upon initiation. Patanjali, who lived one or two hundred years before the time of Jesus, wrote in his *Mahabashya*, 'Just as on seeing smoke issuing from a particular place, one infers that there is fire there, so on seeing a staff one infers an ascetic.'

midday bathers dip, dip again, lift the water, let it fall back, carry it high so that it drops on their heads; they watch it as it shines, as it drops flashing back into the river, the mother, this endlessly accepting Ganges; they pray. Two boys swim and shout at us, and the boatman, draped in beads, smiling, his grey moustache heavily impressive, shouts back.

In Varanasi, Swami Keshavpuri has been my guide. He is a scholar, he runs a Sanskrit school which is caged in a litter of lanes and reached by a tunnel which dips under the buildings, a toy shop on the left, cheap jewellery on the right, make-up opposite; a welter of shops, so quickly left behind. Within, all is ochre, green, blue; square pillars decorated with blue outlines of gods, Saraswati, goddess of learning, the most prominent; galleries above, with drying ochre washing; in a central block, classrooms, their walls green grilles so that they seem like cages, rising in three storeys. Below these, three large plants stand in pots.

Swami Keshavpuri is quite young, about forty; he has beautiful features – narrow nose, high cheek-bones, and his hair hangs down to his shoulders in tight ringlets. His beard is without ferocity, his eyes are gentle, happy, though a little vague, as are the small, abrupt gestures he makes from time to time. When he smiles, one can see that his teeth are betel stained, and it mars him. One senses a tremendous gentleness in him, an unpretentious unworldliness, which is not absence of vanity, and certainly not of self-interest – he is ambitious to do more scholarly work – but lies in the sense that, whatever he may be doing, he is really getting on with something much more important which makes the present transactions peripheral. Yet he spends time on showing me places and introducing me to the people in them, he leads me from monastery to monastery, he neglects his own work to help me do mine.

His monastery stands back, up a narrow lane on the right side of which there is a chai shop; in racks against the wall lie rows of earthenware cups, to be used once, then broken. Beyond a turning stands an arch; on the right, a small temple, then a row of houses. Steps run magnificently up to a terrace; huge doors lead into the house. I leave my sandals at the foot, follow the Swami up. Guarding the door, a near naked man, servant or sadhu, sits splay-legged on a chair. From time to time he belches, covering the sound, as holy men do, with the powerful syllable, 'Om!' He varies these with deep sighs of boredom – 'Ram, Ram, Hari Ram!'

The room within the doors is gigantic. I guess that it is fifty feet long, twenty-five feet high, twenty-five wide. Ancient beams hold up the distant ceiling, the faces of moustached great men of the past chin themselves on the picture rail and peer down through gloom and varnish. A huge chandelier hangs from the centre of the ceiling, its cut-glass patterning picked out by dirt. A dozen, twenty, glass lampshades hang from that ceiling or curl out from the stupendous walls – but the light comes from a neon tube above one of the three arched doors that lead to the building's dark interior. In the distance, brass gleams mysteriously like the dull reflection with which genius might light the background of a Dutch masterpiece. On a bench, beyond the right-hand door, papers are piled in low, brown edged towers. There is dust, a sense of age, perhaps disuse. A great carved desk stands out from the wall on my right, a great carved chair behind it. On the wall, three gigantic mirrors brighten the dimness; another on my left faces them, reflects and diffuses the faint light. Beside it, a charpoy leans against the wall and a rolled mattress lies on a long, wooden steamer chair. But these few pieces leave the room a desert; we are like survivors within the high walls left by a civilization which, one might think, we can hardly understand.

Swami Keshavpuri sits on a mat, I on a piece of sacking on the stone floor. When he speaks his voice echoes. He makes his abrupt gestures, his soft movements, as if almost to disclaim what he is saying. 'This math was founded in 864. It has had sixty Gurus. Do you want their names?' I shake my head and he nods, perhaps a little disappointed. It is this kind of monastic history that he has been working on. He begins to talk in his soft, high voice. From time to time, a bird, invisible in the darkness under the distant ceiling, punctuates what he tells me with raucous screams.

'My order is called "Puri" and that is included in my name. The differences between orders are not doctrinal, they are outward – whether they live in math buildings or whether they wander, this sort of difference. I am an idle man, very lazy, about practices etc. I stay awake long in the night and read and write up to twelve, one, or if I have some serious work I stay up until two o'clock in the night. On certain occasions I have desired to make some worship; now, these practices should be performed in a lonely place and a pious place. If there is a temple, if there is the bank of a river; a calm and peaceful atmosphere is far more helpful for such worship. I prefer night in my activities generally; my Guru also instructed me to perform my duties in the night. So I tried to sit down beside the little temple down there of the goddess Durga; but you see, when I try to control my breathing, to carry it in and throw it out, I am very much tired and puzzled because the latrine and urinal are just beside the temple. And at night there is no cleanliness and so many people stay here, and the bad wind – this just touches the mind as if somebody is striking a hammer! So I pray the blessed goddess that I am not getting any harm; otherwise it may be harmful for me. Because I take in and throw out air, and the bad air destroys the mind. And if I am not careful at that time it can lead to much harm. This is the system of yoga; these are the distractions of yoga.

'I myself had no proper Guru. In my early life I was staying and studying with my relatives. Heaven knows how the idea

arose in my mind that I should learn Sanskrit. Nobody insti-
gated me, but all of a sudden the idea arose in my heart. I
passed the middle examinations first and during that time the
idea arose in my mind. I didn't have the facility for Sanskrit
there; my relatives got me admitted to a Sanskrit school, but
that was a small school and no attention was paid to the students
by the teaching staff. My relatives were dissatisfied with the
system of study and they withdrew my name.

'One day, I left my home and wandered here and there. I
went to Allahabad as the first step towards studying – I was
perhaps eighteen then. I stayed in a monastery there; at that
time I was only desirous to study. No other idea was stuck in
my mind at the time. But by and by, as I began to study . . . I
can say that it was fate which led me towards this religious life.
"Man proposes, God disposes" – according to that rule; I
believe in that. [He laughs.] I stayed there, and then went to
another monastery and then to another ashram – all that was
also for my studies. One year I stayed in Allahabad and passed
my examinations, and then I was sent to the other monastery;
but there I got nothing – there were no facilities for studying –
and thereafter I went from there to the next monastery. In this
way I wandered during my studies; and in this way a long time
passed. And now, I am learning as my fate is leading me.

'According to the definition of a Guru, I did not have one.
Because they are institutions. And there are rules and regula-
tions according to modern times, and in the monasteries the
ancient ideas are vanishing day by day. These ideas are being
destroyed, are vanishing. The real thing is hard, very hard. To
find such a spiritual and pious man, therefore, is very hard. I
feel myself fortunate to have met a person whom I accepted as
my real Guru, from whom I took my sannyas diksha. Though
to me I treat it as a custom – I don't give it more importance.

'Later on, in my wanderings . . . The Swamiji told you that
the Guru finds the shishya – I was searching for a man I had

heard about and I went to him. He asked nothing about me. Before, I had seen him in another city and then when he saw me he was pleased to see me. So I think it was the instigation of God, the instigation of faith, that led me towards him. He told me things which he knew and which he had experienced; he told me without any return and without any examination. Only a few hours passed. He said, "Pick up your pen and write this down." He was speaking and I wrote down what he said. He ordered me to do things according to his way. And I have faith in him. As for the Gurus in the monasteries and so on, I obey and I respect according to custom. But faith is another thing.'

I take a taxi to the airfield. My driver is the one who has, over the past few days, whirled me through the jams of cycle rickshaws or led me, on foot, through the narrow lanes. He says, 'You people, English, American, you speak to us like all equal. Now, I driver, I do service; but afterwards, all same. But these people here, in India, they do not speak to poor peoples, they do not sit with them . . .'

Again I float above this endless India which passes below me, brown, grey, white, pale green, green, dark green, black. Water shines, glittering like a desperate signal. The sun runs its light along meandering ditches as though tracing them for some purpose, as though searching for something it has lost. Pale towns lie marked with shadows; from here they seem like intellectual abstractions put together by some frowning, absorbed artist. Rivers lash about the plain like whips. Here and there, sand fans across fields where floods have left it. Above Lucknow, a vulture sails beneath us, its dark, rigid wings braced with white.

POONA

The railway through these mountains is a trophy won by engineers in a wrestling match with nature. First there were the plains, at hot sea-level, where everything looked burnt and brown and the trees so tired they seemed less a part of the landscape than the tall electric pylons which marched away in every direction like the patrols of a conquering army. Down there, the stations whirled by, each in its own miasmic dust and stench of urine.

But up here, we rumble among mountains, hazy now in the heat but in the morning clear and pink. Precipitous valleys fall away from the edge of the track into a hidden, idyllic beauty of streams and trees, cowherds and their beasts, brown villages in snug clusters under protective hillsides. The stations come and go as we labour up, the tunnels wipe out one vista after another, the mountains creep closer.

It is over four hours before the train reaches Poona, and evening is coming in on a cluster of cloud; there is a cool wind and the smell of recent rain. The ashram lies above Poona itself, beyond a long ridge. It is at the edge of the town, houses are few, roads have outstripped their surfaces, the way is difficult to follow. Once my taxi rolls out on the dark, open hillside and the driver, laughing, pulls us round again in a wide, bumping circle. At the gate a young man is waiting for me and behind him, in white, Swami Amar Jyoti.

The Swami is of average height by Indian standards, stocky, his long hair in oiled ringlets, his beard slightly frizzy and not really thick so that a round, stubborn chin shows through. His cheeks are pouched, his mouth wide and mobile, his earnest eyes dark. His reticence seems deliberate, his control conscious. He is about forty and bears some resemblance to the Mahesh

Yogi, the so-called Maharishi; in twenty years he will look even more like him.

I drink tea, I eat, I am given pills for my cold ('Bio-Plasgen', made by Dr Wilhelm Schwabe, in Karlsruhe). We talk of Swamiji's travels – of London: 'I felt familiar there, I had memories. The Trafalgar Square – well, of course one has heard of that. But I walked there, I seemed to know ...' Of his lectures: 'I spoke of the Universal Religion in England, in Greece, in America – as far as I know I was not disliked. Yes, someone once objected because he thought I looked like Jesus' – he laughs, tosses back his hair – 'but they gave me so many titles ... I did not reject them – why should I?'

I get the sense that his lack of wide fame irks him in a quiet way; having consolidated his base he is anxious to get at the world. In a month or so, he is going on an all India tour. This ashram, called Ananda Niketan, has a school attached to it; it organizes activities in a local village, such as a dispensary where medicines are given free, a garden where the children can play and where they are given a snack; it runs a lending library; it holds devotional meetings every Sunday.

Swami Amar Jyoti shows me the blue-walled Assembly Hall, its three large windows each covered by an ornate metal grille. On three sides stand low, glass fronted bookcases: Aurobindo, Vivekananda, Sivananda, Isherwood, Huxley, Brunton, Alan Watts, Churchill's collected speeches ... Outside, beyond a low ridge, one can see the brightness in the sky which marks the lights of Poona, five hundred feet below us in a shallow valley. We walk to a long lawn which is stepped into two levels, with a wall all around.

'We used to put plays on here. I think I can say they were unique! That area there' – he points to the higher part of the lawn – 'we could use all of it, 120 feet! We did anything – a burning village, herds of sheep, a horse, a rider ... If we needed someone ploughing, we'd put a man up there with an ox and he'd plough it up! We had lights, reflectors – we had to repeat it six times.'

He shows me his own room, bare but beautiful. Gold coloured curtains cover the wide, low windows, about the bed there stands an elegant frame for mosquito netting, a white statuette overlooks the bed, a light shines down on the frilled pillow. The Swami looks about, his attitude curiously reverential, rather like a guide, objective, but impressed by what he is displaying. He says, 'In this room, intense meditation has gone on, some experiences of the astral body, very deep thoughts about God ... Eight years God has sent me this deep quiet, as much as I have wanted ...'

He takes me into his own office – a small desk, two chairs, a box file, a roll of coconut matting. He speaks in a quiet, even voice, but I feel all the time that his stillness is not central. When he talks of God, there is a hint of the proprietorial in his voice. I get the faint feeling that he thinks I might be useful to him. Yet I like him and find him intelligent, easy to get on with, delightfully free of any nonsensical formality. Perhaps my cold blurs my sensibilities and I do him injustice.

'Initiation is generally of three kinds; one is through the eyes, by sight; one is by touch; the third is by the mantra, through the ear, mantra being perhaps lowest. Lowest doesn't really mean low in that sense but that of the three it is the least one. Highest would be by the eyesight, touch is second. But there are yogis and there are responsive disciples who could get it from a distance. You can be initiated in a dream also. But all this would be categorized in these three, so supposing there is a gathering where a Guru meets you and you are attracted to him and he gives you something true mentally, that also is initiation. And you may accept him as your Guru without words, without any agreements – this is informal.

'Between Guru and shishya, respect is not autocratic, far from

it, because they are the humblest possible persons; but then it
all depends upon the relationship. He won't necessarily agree
to be your Guru, even supposing you gave him your money or
respect or whatever. The essential relationship between Guru
and disciple is not really dogmatic and is not really autocratic.
The thing is, he should be pleased with the disciple, to impart or
communicate what he wants to. It is not like salesmanship or
professional at all in the real sense of the term – unless he is a
professional Guru.

'Now, if I can put it in my language what I mean by the
professional and the non-professional. Generally, by professional we mean when a Guru is ... greedy may be a very
strong word – but when he is conscious of making disciples.
Not necessarily to give them benefit, as is his first and foremost
duty, but to be happy with more disciples, a name and fame
kind of thing. Or if the presents and the gifts are what he is
happy about, then he stands to be a professional. So if you bring
more things to him or if you bring him a great name and fame
then he is more happy. But then there are non-professionals
whom we would call selfless Gurus, those who don't bother
about their establishments; they don't bother whether they
have an establishment, even, they don't bother if they have two
disciples or one *lakh* [a hundred thousand]. But they see the
merit of their disciples, they see the acceptability of them.
Whether you call them "Guruji" or not doesn't matter; call
them God, even, they don't mind; call them friend, they don't
mind. They may sit with you on an equal level, they will be selfless persons. Those who consider name and fame or the increase
of the number of disciples and establishments make, as it were,
a government by itself in a miniature way; if you feed your disciple then more attention comes your way, and if somebody
comes who isn't your disciple then you don't bother with him.

'But here we have another pitfall. Sometimes our own understanding, a disciple's own understanding, may also be mistaken.

For example, supposing the Guru has never drunk water in his life and he preaches to disciples that they can drink water if they like. An apparent contradiction is there; because he doesn't drink, perhaps he should not say the others should drink or that they are free to drink. But there are certain natural phenomena by which his body may be conditioned to certain things and he will preach something else which he may not be doing. We have to see whether his own bodily functions are conditioned. Supposing he is smoking and he makes the general statement that nobody should smoke, it's a bad thing. The disciple may say, "If he is not able to give it up, then what about his powers?" Now, how are we going to judge these things? All these are there, certain minor and major things which we have to see from many different angles, not in a merely human way. We can't make this judgement in a dictionary way; it is between Guru and disciple. We may judge him by certain things today, and one year later a disciple may understand the *lila* [play] of the Guru in a different light.

'And suppose ten disciples are there; they are hearing and seeing the same movements, the same talks, same habits. Each one will understand the significance for himself. And that process is exactly how the disciples fight amongst themselves over the same aphorism, over the same saying of the Guru, over the meaning of a certain movement or habit. That the significance is there is certain; the meaning is there. But to understand that significance is different!

'One thing is very common – that within himself he is "same-sighted". He has no high and low, no near and dear; but in actions and behaviour and relationships there will be differences. There is an aphorism in the *Vedas* which says that we have to achieve "same-sightedness", but not the same behaviour. If we induce same behaviour, which is called uniformity – as a law of nature it can never be – the very attempt may be dangerous or harmful. Suppose I was to consider my wife, mother, daughter and sister all as one, and to do anything with anyone? In behaviour we have to see the differentiation. This is exactly the case with the disciples; according to each one's capacity and response we have a difference of behaviour. And the Guru may bewilder one sometimes, he may rebuke someone beyond all limits and with someone else he may be very forgiving. But then, supposing a doubt arises – and this is very common – a doubt arises in a disciple's mind. His foremost duty must be to go to the Guru to get it explained before forming any decision about the Guru. Supposing you chose the wrong Guru . . . I won't say the wrong Guru, but not a suitable Guru. Then, whose fault is that? People think that the Guru is responsible, but we would think – not because we are Gurus – that if people choose an unsuitable Guru it is their own mistake, too. Their own incapacity, their own ignorance, is no excuse. The choice of the Guru is equally the responsibility of the disciple.

'If the disciple wants a higher Guru he has to be free to find one. But pitfalls are there for the disciple if he has already chosen a Guru. There are other Gurus who may be more attractive, but in a spiritual sense may not be higher; perhaps may be lower. And suppose the disciple simply goes for the glittering gold which is not gold at all. Now these pitfalls are there for the disciple; that which glitters may not be gold and certain Gurus may not be glittering but may be really spiritual, and others may be very glittering but, in a spiritual sense, lesser . . .

'But if one talks about breaking one's conditioning, that's a method by itself. If one wants to do that, without a Guru, then one is one's own Guru. One becomes one's own Guru and so one may be satisfied that one is free from the exploitation of an outer Guru – presuming that all Gurus are exploiters, which is not the case. It is a fact that one can exploit oneself also; with marijuana and hashish and things one can exploit oneself; there is no Guru there. Myself, I have taken LSD once in America. In my

own opinion, without mentioning names like hippies or beat-
niks and so on, let us take a man going through experiences by
taking LSD. Taken in a very well calculated dosage, once or
twice, it is quite all right. The difficulty is that afterwards he
forgets that he has to rely upon his own conduct. Supposing
that, in the normal sense of the term, he is leading an impure
life, then LSD has no meaning. He has to follow the course,
follow it. He took the help of LSD, well and good, there is
nothing wrong in that. I am not against it – provided you can
follow it up with a certain life outside . . .

'LSD will give you a pick-up, no doubt, but it will not
necessarily remain with you. Supposing in the next birth the
same person is born without LSD? Think, he will then be a
thoroughly ordinary man. What about his own experience and
the development of consciousness? The most important thing is
that his own level of consciousness should go up . . .

'As to how I set out on the spiritual path, that is all very
natural, because we inherit something from previous births;
that alone explains many things. But to give you a surface reply:
up to the age of nineteen I was called a "good boy", but still, I
never went to a saint or to a holy gathering, and I seldom went to
temple. I wouldn't say I was atheist, no; but nobody led me into
this life, nor I think did I read any significant books on spiritual
life up to the age of eighteen. I was simply in college as a normal
boy, active with studies, with play, with sports, I was not
atheist, but I was not very God fearing. Respect for my parents
and elders was there, as taught. And then at the age of nineteen when a proposal for marriage came as is the tradition in our
home – unless it was a love marriage, which was not the case –
my inner mind said, "No". Not that I hated girls, nor that I
hated romance, nor that I did not know what love is. Some
emphatic "No!" was coming. Some time before, my parents had
given their promise to a certain girl's parents and they wanted
me to see her, which I ignored. And in between this had

come Partition, the division of the country. I came to Bombay in
'48 and my ideas underwent many changes. I realized that
pressure for the marriage was all based on the girl's family
which was poor; they needed someone to take care of her.

'In this one year my ideas came to a certain finalization. Not
that I had had women, not that way; but then, one of the things
was not to get bound with one certain, limited thing, and the
inner urge was to serve humanity; the country, as such, also. In
other words, to move in a vaster domain. At that time, whether I
wanted to realize God or not was not uppermost. We can call
this urge "dispassion", perhaps. This led me to leave the whole
thing, and for twelve years I was not known to my people. Then
naturally in a few months my real aspiration of realizing myself
became clearer.

'First I began with serving the people in a certain section of
Bengal. For one year I was among the selfless workers there,
helping people, living like a beggar, giving aid to certain refu-
gees who had come from Pakistan.

'Then one day an inner voice said, "If you don't know yourself, then how are you going to help others?" And this led me to
a further search. I went to other parts of India as a wandering
monk; to the Himalayas, to many ashrams and Gurus as well.
Now, don't ask me who my Guru is because that will open up
endless stories. You see, it was not usual for me to have a Guru.
It is not usual. The sort of man, by which one means a Guru . . .
I did not take a Guru in that way. My own standard of Guru is
different.

'The informal sannyasi is one who may not be initiated for-
mally by anyone, but in whom the inner urge opens up in such a
natural way that he feels no passion for the world. He sees
nothing attractive in the world and he goes off on his search,
naturally. This is exactly what happened with me. So that I
cannot say who is my Guru in that particular way. But help, yes,
I got from some, especially two. I don't like to name them

because one is always in the Himalayas, never comes down and nobody knows him. And the other Guru who helped me, he never asserts himself as a Guru because, "in a spiritual sense nobody is disciple or Guru." He talks in those terms. "If anybody has a feeling about me that I am his Guru, then, yes, I am; but I am nobody's Guru: I am of service." Now language used that way will contradict me if I say "So-and-so is my Guru." Suppose you go and ask him, "Is So-and-so your disciple?" and he says, "I have no disciple. I am not a Guru." If you are an understanding man, you will take it rightly; if you are not, then you'll feel some slight. Even in America I have stopped years ago giving the name of the Guru, because it is not really understood.

'I went to the Himalayas on my own; it could be that my last journey was with myself. Let us say I am my own Guru. Even this I say very rarely because it does not mean that one should have no Guru. Some may need it, others may not need it. I have needed one for a short time, for example; others may need one for a longer time, or even not at all.

'My past births drove me from within and showed me the path to follow which allowed me to arrive at something which is within me. It was just natural. For many years I went like that. I am explaining why there is Guru in everybody. We don't deny that fact. But when it is not opened up and manifested we say, "Let's have a Guru outside, so the inner Guru can be opened."

'We have to be so vigilant, even with our own consciousness: an effort, a strict effort. And then comes a certain level from which it doesn't come down; there's an establishment there, a fixture. LSD cannot do that. Nor can the outer Guru do that. Then the genuine term for it is "awakening"; yes. As we awaken from dreams into this outer world, this outer world is like a dream in relation to that consciousness.'

In the morning I walk from Ananda Niketan, over a long

hillside, a rock encrusted, khaki coloured waste. Goats bleat and roll like quicksilver across the land – as the goatherd pushes here, so they escape him, squeezing away in another direction. The low walls of the ashram seem to be keeping this burnt and unappetizing wilderness at bay. In fact some of the neighbouring plots have already been bought, and in time retired industrialists will build their villas all over this crisp ridge. Ananda Niketan seems like the outpost of an oasis, its young trees flourishing, though a little straggly yet despite their froth of flowers. Above my head, kites wheel and scream, their curved wings rigid on the wind.

In daylight I can see that there is a wide area of flagstones beside the windows of the Assembly Hall and before the entrance. Behind the main building stands another, stone pillars marking the extremities of a terrace and holding up a red tiled roof. This is the Swami's own abode, where the night before he told me of his successful meditation. Trees surround it – guava, mango – and it faces the long, jutting stretch of garden where vegetables are grown. Two small bungalows stand farther on, shelter for the faithful, with beside them a little ablutions block. Chipmunks scatter as I walk back around the house, past the raised 'stage' and to the wide steps that lead to the entrance.

Swami Amar Jyoti sits with me: 'We have not made objective experiments. The yogi has no aparatus like the scientist. His laboratory is the mind. Only to another yogi can he show, and a little sometimes to a student or someone serious come to learn. But the main difference is that the scientist wants to show what he has learned, the yogi to conceal. If he does show, it will not be to demonstrate, but to teach . . . Now, see, they have gone to the moon. When they go to Mars and Venus and so on, then sooner or later they will realize that there is so much there, so much outside . . . And then perhaps they will realize that they cannot look for happiness outside, but only within. After all, who is less harmful than the ascetic? He wants little so he need not struggle for riches. He has found peace so he radiates peace. He has conquered aggression so he will harm no one. Practical people say he is useless ... but who has really achieved more than the man who has done what he set out to do?'

The Swami is sad that I have missed the weekly meeting; some twenty people come every Sunday and there are always another dozen or more who are casual. An American who has been living on the ashram for five years has just left to travel round the world on a scooter; now there are two men here, one with a curious, unbroken voice, and a young Nepalese servant. The young man who met me at the gate as I arrived is one of the most constant and devoted visitors; as I finish my lunch he appears again, ready to do what may be asked of him.

He is an engineering student, it turns out. He has thick, black hair, a short, straight nose and a firm mouth and chin; he is very dark, and pock-marked. Occasionally a strange expression comes into his eyes, a sideways, sliding glance, an obliqueness which I cannot quite decide is neurotic – perhaps the same pox which marked his face damaged his sight. He is Swamiji's convinced follower.

'Exactly in English to put down what is my relationship with Swamiji would be to just say "disciple". Once we have a relationship with Swamiji, you can say disciple, and you can say personal God also.

'I am an engineering student. My mother is quite religious. My father is usually abroad; he comes here every three years, two and a half years, two years – he's in Manila, he works there – but he was in Colombo quite a few years. We have been staying here in Poona for seventeen years or even more than that.

'I have not come across any conflict up to now between religion and my engineering studies. It will come after this if it comes, because now I have to decide whether I want to renounce everything or become a householder and do my duties. In the end, I don't think that there'll be any conflict. But I'll have to think around the whole problem by myself – it's very difficult to say. Sometimes one wants to do one thing, sometimes the other. Swamiji says it will happen automatically; there is no need to plan ahead for it. When it happens, I will know it. Actually, I wanted to leave before graduation but he said, "At least finish your graduation."

'The things he's taught me – you just can't put into words what he has done for me or what I feel. But there are little incidents which I can realize . . . First I used to try and hide little things here and there; I don't do that any more. I am absolutely frank with myself and can say, "Here there is something wrong with me."

'All problems that concern me now, any problem that comes to my mind, I'll discuss with Swamiji. Anything personal about me. Questions about sex and all, I used to feel nervous a little bit; but now no more. To him and to others I talk, though that depends how close I am to them. In India it's usually like that since there are no psychoanalysts here.

'If I renounce, I'll come and live here at the ashram; but Swamiji has not given me a diksha yet. Even if I become a householder, I will keep up the connection – that is definite. Most probably, though, I won't become a householder.

'I don't think that, if one continued as an engineer, the scientific way of thinking would bring one into conflict with this way of thinking in the spiritual life. I don't think so, provided one was brought up like that. That means you can carry on being an engineer, provided it satisfies you. What's happening now is that's not sufficient; being an engineer. What I want to know is exactly what it is – as they say, truth. That is why I feel that I may renounce. It might have been helpful to me that Swamiji knows something of modern ideas, scientific ideas.

'I don't mind serving my Guru in any way. But even if I say that I give my will up to the will of my Guru, it's not that. It's got to come from within. And that has not happened yet. If that had happened I wouldn't still be in the Engineering College. But that will come automatically as you advance.'

The Indian Airlines bus roars and, bouncing heavily, turns out into the traffic, leaving the Dreamland Hotel behind. We roll past the flaking terraces of Mabo's Hotel and a hectic roadside stall selling multi-coloured cycle seat covers. Sheds flick by, tiny establishments set up by endless mini-capitalists; the Chopda Cycle Mart, the Nepali Stores. The buildings thin out, fall away. A brown, unpleasant plain stretches dry and dull to a nearby horizon. Clouds lollop up as though summoned by the evening. Then long lines of huts, barbed wire, basket-ball courts – Poona is a military town. Painted and beflagged, a cluster of buildings: 'Air Mens Mess No 5', a sign reads. Finally the camouflaged hangars, the windsock, the long concrete – Poona Airport. We sit or stroll about the wooden shack, are finally called to our Viscount. Clambering across the sky, we butt into evening. Below us, the rumpled mountains disappear as if behind endless layers of dark muslin.

KANHERI CAVES

We sit in Borivali National Park, eat oranges and bananas, slowly fall silent. Birds call: on the far and distant bank of the lake cranes stand, then slowly flap in laborious circles before coming down at the point from which they started. Above them, the steep green slope flings all its colour to the lake where it shakes and spreads across the water. Butterflies are everywhere, some drifting like bright yellow scraps of paper, celestial confetti, others blue trimmed or large and purple-black.

At the caves, we clamber up stone steps towards the sombre, dark brown rock which curves like a helmet over the hilltop.

Carved into this are long-abandoned temples of the Buddhists, relics of their ancient ascendency. Buddhas stand or sit, pitted by the years and surrounded by smaller figures, souls or adherents. On the rock names are carved: N. Christian, 47th Reg. 1810 and H. Barton, 4th Reg. 1819 – tourists in their day recording their passing and so becoming curiosities in their turn.

We clamber round the hill, pleased with the cunningly placed steps, the ingenuity which ran the rainwater from level to level in so directed a way. We wake echoes, the ghosts of a long dead devotion. Here, too, other men have left a mark – we see more dates: 1706, 1710, 1735 ... Men passed by, saw what we see, attempted to leave a record, then went away.

We walk down into the valley beyond – palm trees, rice, many flowers. There is a snapping sound on the left, a cow in underbrush tearing at a juicy branch. Stakes across the path mark some limit, steps a little farther on, another. A small notice says, 'Please Remove Shoes'.

Barefoot, we move on, past a small temple like a white, stunted telephone kiosk. We wait on a terrace; one side of it is made of galvanized iron set in a frame that stands against the rock face before us, snuggling under its overhang. What is behind it? The far end of the terrace is the wall of a stubby hut; the other two sides are open and supported by rough wooden struts. A smiling, moustached ancient ties a calf to one of these, then soothes its nervousness. The sadhus are at food and we sit cross-legged on a strip of garish linoleum and wait for them to finish.

The holy man here, Swami Lomashgiri, is one of those who has set himself a programme of specific austerities. *Tapas* means 'heat' or 'ardour' and suggests how positive the drive is to asceticism in the Hindu religion. By its means, one gathers up one's psychic energy, one both proves and refuels one's determination and ability to succeed in one's spiritual endeavour. It is by the means of tapas that power is obtained; in a curious way, such power depends on the ascetic practice more than on the religious faith – even demons have acquired powers through tapas and the energy finally generated in this way by the ancient rishis frightened the gods themselves, or so the legends say.

There are many kinds of *tapasvin*: those who remain in one place for year after year; those who never sleep except in the hardest, most uncomfortable place; those who spend weeks partly immersed in water; those who mutilate or cut themselves; those who stare at the sun until they go blind or hold their arms up until they wither; those who clench their fists until the nails drive into their flesh; those who keep their heads to the sky until the muscles fix in that position; those who hang head down, suspended by their feet; those, too, famous in Western joke and story, who lie on beds of nails. Any pain or restriction from which humanity can suffer has been used by the tapasvins; the one we have come to see today is a *khadashri*, one who lives standing, never lying down. In twelve years, I have been told, he has only once been prone and that was when a severe swelling of the ankles forced him to hospital. The Swami never speaks, has said no word for many years. If we want words they will have to come from his disciple.

Moving briskly, belching slightly, Swami Lomashgiri emerges, a tall figure in ochre robes, *tilak* mark on forehead, a black beard, a long, lined face with an expression benign, but distant, like a headmaster prepared to be tolerant of children but not to share their preoccupations. He moves vigorously, stopping patiently as someone touches his feet, yet giving the impression that he is anxious to be on his way.

With a crash he throws back those panels of galvanized iron to reveal that beyond them lies his cave. In the centre of this stands a swing; dark, polished wooden uprights support a wooden bar, from which the swing itself hangs, some four feet or so from the ground. It is padded with pieces of old blanket and a strip of cast-off carpet. The Guru hurries to it, turns to look out at us, then leans on it resting upon his folded arms; it is in this way that he has been standing, awake or asleep, these dozen years. Before him, there is a narrow vase of flowers; a commercial calender decorated with a garish devotional picture hangs beside him.

An attendant carries his table out of the eating hut. It is at least four feet tall, made especially for this upright Swami. There is something slightly ludicrous about its size as the servant begins to wash it. From the hut, too, comes a visiting sadhu, a red tilak on his forehead, grey hair on his chest, full grey beard, white dhoti. He has a face of total ordinariness, anyone's uncle with a towel round his middle. When he needs to see anything close to, as when he takes my hand to read the palm – a skill he displays despite the disdain of the Guru's principal chela – he puts on round, wire rimmed glasses. In a red, wrap around wallet he carries a mirror, perhaps six inches by three; one can imagine him doubled over his roadside toilet, observing with delight his iron grey beard, the false hair at his holy crown, the precise placing of the tilak.

The chela is a model of handsome vigour, someone who might have posed, turning a strong neck to look over his shoulder, for the bottom left-hand corner of some legendary scene by the hand of a Renaissance master. He laughs almost as soon as he is in daylight; he is sturdy in his mustard coloured robes, his hair curls long and thick, his beard lies in loose ringlets, and when he laughs he shows strong teeth bent inwards with an unexpected woolfishness. His lips are rather thick, his dark eyes gleam happily. His skin shines and stretches with health. He sits on his rush mat, smiles all round. His name is Swami Puroshattam Giri and he seems carved out of contentment. As he speaks, the calf roars a disapproving counterpoint.

'I spent two years wandering all over India before I found my Guru. I met sadhus and visited places of pilgrimage; I was in

Vrindaban, Mathura, Chandigarh and so on. To find your Guru you must spend a long time with sadhus and *mahatmas*. That teaches you about the personal qualities of a Guru and gives you an image of him. You should serve the sadhus and listen to their lectures and discourses. It is not difficult to learn if a Guru is really untouched by worldly desires and all that. Besides, if you have made some spiritual progress, that will guide you in the matter of finding your Guru. Then, when you discover the Guru whom you will follow, you will know it because the inner voice will tell you. When you find your Guru you find peace of mind.

'I was given the sacred thread when I was eight and then I spent five years or so being educated in the sacred writings. I am a follower of Vedanta, of the doctrines of Shankaracharya, who pushed Buddhism out of India when it threatened the very existence of Hinduism.

'After I had been wandering for about two years, I just happened to come to Bombay. I stayed in a small cave near here and so I came to know that there was a sadhu living here. I came here to see him, and the first time I saw him it was as though I had been thirsty all that time and now the thirst had left me. I felt very peaceful. That is how I knew I had met my Guru.

'After that, there came the test period, which always happens in order that the shishya can prove his fitness and devotion and to discover how well he and the Guru match. I served the Guru and I begged for him. Then after eight years I was accepted by him as shishya. That was four years ago – I have been here twelve years altogether.

'The roof here was built very recently. Before that, it was all bush. Even to get here was quite a struggle. There were no people. It was really a wilderness. The road to the caves was built only a few years ago; before that there were never any people here.

'We get up at five thirty in the morning and have our bath. Our temple is there so then we do our puja, our morning devotions – and until twelve we have no visitors. The whole of that time we sit in meditation. Then from noon until five people can come here and visit the ashram. At five we eat a meal and we sit down, and then we may meditate until three in the morning. This pattern may vary a little according to the season and what we feel like. Sometimes we might be more awake during the day, at others we might rest in the day. It depends. But really, this question should not be asked of a sadhu – there is no reason why I should not answer but it is one of the questions one does not ask.'

A few years ago, the government wanted to move the sadhus out because they were living in a National Park. The holy men brought a High Court action and won it on a claim that sadhus had lived there for over four centuries; thus English Common Law continues to protect the humble in what was once the Empire. I look round the small yard before leaving – mattresses air in the sun, the doors of outhouses stand open, flies strum on the heavy air. The calf pisses, then licks itself. Against a wall, tubing stands and near it a pump, an incongruous twentieth-century artifact. An umbrella hangs by its handle in the sun like something put there to dry and keep for harder times. Someone tries to give the calf milk from a bottle with no teat; the struggle shows no winner, milk flies about the yard. The chela straddles the small beast, rams the bottle down its throat, laughs as it begins to drink.

We walk away past fruit trees and rising palms (a general fertility marks a Guru's virtue), until at the stakes that mark the ashram limits we look back. I am startled at the happiness and calm of this place when I consider that the Swami's actions of standing up for a dozen years, keeping silent as long, seem in a normal context to have about them something of desperation, something almost hysterical, the last exhibitionist fling of a God-maddened man determined to be noticed by the Almighty.

It does not seem so when face-to-face with this anchorite. It is rather as if, having conceived of the Absolute, of Godhead, he had decided to give it a present. The renunciation he has made, the discomfort and even pain he suffers, are peripheral to the central process of meditation, of attempting to merge with Brahman. Such sacrifice is not demanded of the chela. Nor, one is certain, is it felt as sacrifice.

BOMBAY

Maharashtra, the state in which Bombay stands, has a tradition of householder saints, of men who live ordinary lives, work for their rent like anybody else, but act as holy men at the same time. In that tradition is Sri Sadguru Nisagadatta Maharaj. Once a businessman, although always interested in religion, he was initiated by Siddharameshwar Maharaj, a Guru who accepted the belief that religion transcends caste and is too important to be followed as a career. Within a year, Nisagadatta Maharaj was holding meetings and giving religious discourses. When his Guru died, he went out into India for six months 'without giving thought even for a moment to those who were dependent on him', as the introduction to his *Self-Knowledge and Self-Realization* tells us rather smugly.

He dislikes miracles, which he considers hinder spiritual progress. He will not recognize distinctions of class or caste or race or even religion. He lets no one serve him or offer him gifts. His basic belief is that our sense of self, summed up in 'I am', is our 'point of contact with reality'; consciousness is the world process within us – that is, it is contained by our perceptions and is thus necessarily inward not external. We must observe our own undirected mental processes; later, we can increase our awareness of our consciousness, the continuing condition of being, summed up in that simple 'I am'. Containing as that consciousness does the whole of reality, it is a short and even a necessary step from one's total awareness of it to a final, overwhelming certainty that one is essentially divine, that divinity is and has always been within one, and is thus within everyone. So overwhelming is this certainty, in fact, that it will capsize awareness itself, leaving one in a state of timeless self-realization, a constant, blissful present. (How that certainty exploded within him Nisagatta Mahawaj has explained in a passage which I quoted in the first section of this book.)

We stop in a narrow lane bustling with children, bicycles, women with loads on their heads, men with handcarts. We go through a narrow doorway and leave our sandals in a side room where silent women stand to watch the unknown 'white-skin'. A narrow, metal stair, very steep, leads up to the first floor. Here there is a long room, the darshan hall of the Guru. On the left stands the garlanded picture of his Guru; before it stand silver lions, a silver elephant, silver cups and lamps. Garlands hang from the dark green ceiling. To the right of the picture stands the cushioned *gadi*, the low throne of the Guru, raised up on the dais level with the picture and the silver animals. The walls are a pale green, with the usual array of gods and the saintly dead; on the photographs, the tilak has been marked in red, a round mark in the centre of each forehead like a holy wound.

Opposite the dais there is a barred and wire meshed window. On a wine coloured cushion beside it, leaning against another flowered cushion, sits a man who might be old or only in late middle-age. He is toothless and his grey hair is thin, but he is vigorous and his dark, almost black, almond shaped eyes snap with life. He is happy, he smiles a great deal; in the introduction to his books, his birth date is given as 1897. Above his partly collapsed mouth his strong, vigorous nose is almost too blunt and positive for his neat, round skull. He wears a white shirt over a white dhoti with a thin green band, and a dark green, short sleeved pullover. When I meet his eyes and have the courage not to look away, I seem to feel a strong, wordless connection between us. It is meaningless, no more than the kind of sympathy one sometimes has with strangers, it translates into no conclusions; but it seems to me it is there.

When he speaks, his voice is high, a little rough, almost raucous. He makes his points with extravagant gestures, raising his hands in the air, the arms stretched, then bringing them down abruptly to clap his hands together, thus underlining some telling word. To vary this, he sometimes slaps the top of the oval table beside him. With a large lighter, of which I get the feeling he is rather proud, he lights a stick of incense and later, incessantly, little brown cigarettes.

Before I can collect myself, he asks me whether it is the two persons in the Guru-shishya relationship which interest me, or the relationship itself. I say it is the relationship. So he asks me what it is. I ponder, or pretend to, and he suggests it might be a meeting of minds. I am not sure I like the light in his eyes; I reply that I am uncertain what he means by 'mind'. He smiles, but gives me up. He launches out into a disquisition.

'See, the Guru and the shishya are like two kernels in one jack-fruit, one raw, the other ripe. The raw one wants to be ripe; the ripe one is ripe and wants nothing more. While the raw one feels different it will continue to demand, to want something. But there is no difference – it is all jack-fruit, all the same stuff. The difference is only felt by the unripe. When I met my Guru, I experienced the ripeness in him. Now that ripeness is in myself, I am one with my Guru. There is no separation, everything that I am is my Guru. At the start, I used to ask myself "What is Guru?", "What is shishya?" But now I no longer ask myself such questions because they are meaningless. There is no separation so there can be no answers, no explanation – there is only being.

138

'As a writer, you watch, you go away with an idea, you write it down. The Guru-shishya relationship is organic – they are one. But you will take away the idea of their being separate people because you want to write about it. But the actual relationship, the organism, the Guru-shishya – that continues unchanged after you have gone!

'Once the book is written, everything is as before. Therefore, once it is written, forget it! There is no writer, there is only the writing of the book. If you think yourself "the writer", then there will be no way to let the book go, you will concern yourself with the reader, you will suffer from criticism. Yet at the time at which you are writing the book you are not differentiated from it – you are not English, you are not Indian, you are not African: you are the writing of the book. It is consciousness which creates the book and in the creative state you are conscious of yourself only as the writing of the book. Consciousness is writing the book, you are within consciousness and consciousness is within you. So you are not the writer, but the writing, the process by which the book is being written.

'Everything occurs within your consciousness; when you travel, remember that things move in you, not you in them. You even exist because you are within your consciousness, so you are within Consciousness, *Cit*, in the absolute sense. In the end, you must say to yourself, "I am everything and so I do not need to change." You must reach that point of realization.'

No one else, I think to myself, has used my craft as the metaphor which will make the most sense to me – for 'book' substitute 'life', perhaps. We begin to prepare to leave. While he has been speaking, some twenty people have come quietly and one by one up the narrow steps, prostrated themselves before the picture or the gadi, then settled down. There are more men than women now, sitting cross-legged on the floor. As we go down the stairs, someone lights a candle before the picture, perhaps getting ready for *arati*. As we move out into the noisy evening, I remember the Guru's face as what he said was being translated – his smile was that of a man who has told a good joke and knows he will get his listeners' laughter as soon as they have understood it: a conspiratorial smile, a glee he could hardly contain as he bent through the thin coils of incense to take another pull at his cigarette.

*

Throughout the second half of the nineteenth century, the most famous holy man within reach of Bombay was Sai Baba, one of those saints whose great goodness is witnessed by the fact that both Hindus and Muslims claim him as their own. He wore Muslim clothes – but the caste marks of the Hindu. His birth was mysterious, no one knows his parents. He settled at Shirdi, (where he had first appeared when he was sixteen as a guest at a wedding party), from where he had disappeared after three years, and to which he had returned after four more. There he performed the miracles which ensure that his portrait decorates the cabs of pious Hindu taxi drivers more than fifty years after his death. He fed wick lamps with water and lit them. He heard the thoughts of men many thousands of miles away. He cured the sick, he revived the dying. He is supposed to have done no sadhana; not that he had found a short cut to spiritual perfection, but that he had done all the work necessary in previous incarnations – or, as others claim, that he was an *avatar*, the embodiment of God. He is supposed to have known the scriptures better than the learned, yet never to have studied, to have understood everything intuitively, innately. All his life he lived simply, although his proximity to a great mercantile city meant that vast wealth was his for the asking. He always wore a loose robe, a *kufni*, which would be in rags before he took another, and a ragged scarf around his head. That is the picture of him that is everywhere to be seen; seated, leaning a little sideways, looking out at us from time and certainty; he has the appearance of someone very poor who has learned to be patient with his lot. When he died, there was great lamentation; but devotees had visions of him, miracles continued, and the sense developed that he was still watching over those who loved him.

A disciple of his, Sri Upasani Baba, eventually set up an ashram nearby in Sakori which is near Nasik, a holy city not far from the source of the sacred river Godavari. There he took women as his disciples; their initiation was a ceremonial marriage to him as their Guru. As a result, his successor, two Guru generations on from Sai Baba, was a woman.

She is the daughter of a Brahmin; her grandfather was a very pious man, the devotee of a Guru named Gajanana Maharaj. Once, when the old man was dejected because all his children had died except for one son, the Guru is supposed to have said, 'Don't worry, you will have one son and through him I shall take birth again in your family and lead hundreds of pure souls like you to Liberation.'

He died in 1910; a grand-daughter was born to the old man four years later. She was pure, hard working, avid for the teaching of holy men, devout. She came to Sakori, she became the devotee of Upasani Babi. After his death, she took charge of the ashram, of the *kanyas* or nuns who lived there. She is Godavari Mata, the present Guru.

All this information comes from a book written by one of her most devoted followers, Mani Sahukar. Mrs Sahukar lives with her husband in an Edwardian, pale green house with a decorated façade and stained-glass conservatories. She has grey hair drawn back, pleasant dark eyes, a welcoming smile; her lower lip juts slightly in a signal of determination. When I arrive to speak with her, she ushers me into her living-room, sits down opposite me, folds her arms, watches me placidly. She wears a light brown sari with an ornate border; a pin hangs loosely in her back hair.

The room has pale green walls; hangings cover the doorways.

The black and white tiled floor is warmed by a red carpet. An old-fashioned radio stands on a table in the corner. Beyond, a walled-in terrace gleams in sunshine. Against a lampstand leans a large picture of Sai Baba. Godavari Mata and Upasani Baba and Mrs Sahukar's mother are others whose portraits hang for remembrance. Dominating them all, however, is the almost androgynous profile of an ethereal girl, her perfect pre-Raphaelite features shining within the folds of a bright red coif: Fabbiola. Another reproduction of this painting hangs in the dining-room. In the twin-bedded room between, Sai Baba stands in many poses.

Mrs Sahukar sips tea, then begins to talk. She speaks English quickly with a Parsi accent and in a clear, youthful voice. Her clarity is a tribute to her education; she graduated in philosophy from Bombay University. Her manner is matter of fact, she laughs easily, she describes a reality as solid to her as the road on which she lives.

'At Mataji's ashram there are thirty-five kanyas being trained. It is like an order of nunhood but with a very vital difference: there is not that rigidity and severity and the renunciation is not so much physical as of the mind and the spirit. It is not that you have got to put on ugly clothes and all that sort of thing, that you should not talk to this one or that one. Not that idea of external renunciation – except of course celibacy is a must. These girls are taken at a very, very tender young age. They come themselves and then it is up to the Mother either to accept or reject. She does not test them, one glance is enough for her. Then they have a period of initiation, which is a very, very rigorous training for twelve years sometimes. They come very early, sometimes they even come at five or six years old. They come with their parents, but then the child herself shows an inclination for this kind of life.

'There have been, in all, only three failures in a period of more than twenty years; no, actual dropout has been only one. Two have gone before they have been initiated, so that doesn't matter. But one girl, after she became a confirmed kanya, couldn't bear that sort of life; but instead of being honest and telling her Guru that she wanted to leave the ashram and become an ordinary householder, she played a trick. She said she was going on leave somewhere and they allowed leave, and then she got married! She did not come back. Because she did this . . . I don't know why she did it after so many years in that ashram. That was many years back when Upasani Baba was alive. She then after some time lost her husband and she suffered terribly which is no part of their doing – but nature also takes revenge. That she should have played such a trick with her Guru was in itself something which the laws of nature cannot tolerate. So then she wanted to come back but of course they wouldn't accept her.

'Upasani Baba has built a temple for the kanyas there and this temple is one of the most aesthetic things I have ever seen. It is very beautiful. Upasani Baba was really a paradox. He was very, very orthodox and in his way of living he hated anything elegant or dainty and yet at the same time the ashram that he built is full of beauty. In his time the kanyas were allowed only to wear very coarse saris and they were given very, very simple food. But Mataji has changed the whole thing completely and Upasani Baba expected that and accepted it also. He said, "She will change everything that I am doing now." He believed that she was greater than he was. He really believed that.

'Diksha, initiation, is a wonderful ceremony where Mataji actually accepts the girl after twelve years or more of rigorous training. Then that girl is supposed to be married to her, married to the Guru. And there is this very special ceremony performed; it takes hours and hours. So full of aesthetic beauty. You see, there is a great emphasis, where Mother is concerned, on aestheticism. That is why she likes rituals; it gives great opportunity for expressing things beautifully, that is what she says.

'I started myself by being a devotee of Sai Baba who initiated me in a vision. First, you see, when I was a student in college I had taken philosophy as my subject. In those days no Indian philosophy was taught and I was very dissatisfied. It didn't seem to satisfy any urge in me so I began to wonder what to do about this. So then I started studying, of course through translation, the Gita first and from that I found that this was my cup of tea. So I went deeper and deeper, always through translations; unfortunately, I don't know Sanskrit. But I was intellectually a little arrogant perhaps; I had that tendency, so bhakti didn't appeal to me – not the least bit. I thought it was sentimental, something which had to be for people of inferior mental calibre. So in that condition, I had a paying guest staying with my mother and he once told me that there was a great disciple of Sai Baba's here in Bombay – should he bring him to me? So at that time I was going through some mental crisis, so I said, "What for? I am not interested."

'He said, "Don't be so foolish, he's a great man. There is no harm if you meet him."

'I said, "All right."

'So in that mood I met him. He came there to my mother's house; we were a group of about seven people. And this man, very venerable looking, beard and all that, kept looking at me, you see, in a very peculiar way. Then he took me aside and he asked me, "What is it that is worrying you?" So I told him my problems.

'Then he said, "Well, don't worry. Why don't you believe in Sai Baba?"

'I asked, "Who is Sai Baba?"

'So he said, "Well, he was a very big avatar; and I have brought you books written by me." You see the peculiar way he talked, as if he'd come prepared!

'So I said, very foolishly, "Will you give me what I want?"'
'He said, "Don't ask such questions, just read the books. And I have also brought a picture for you."'

'So he put his packet in my hand but it made no impression on me at all. I put the whole packet away somewhere, I didn't even open it. Now tell me, these things can't be accidental! My husband, you see, took down the packet and he started reading these books and he said, "He seems to me a great avatar; why don't you read about it?" So I said, "If you want to, go ahead. Why should I? I don't feel the need." He didn't say anything, but I felt contrite that I should have spoken to my husband like that.

'So in order to please him, I took the picture and I had an old frame, so instead of buying a new frame for the picture I folded it and crushed it into this frame. That is why the legs are not visible and the hands are not visible, only the bust is visible. I just put it there, in front, because my husband sleeps on this outer bed.

'Then, one afternoon, as I was just dozing I got a vision. Now the quality of a dream and the quality of a vision, these are two very different things; only those who have experienced it can know what the vital difference is. So I dreamt that this picture became lit up and there was a beautiful smile on his face, and the hand, which isn't visible, came out and beckoned to me. All this was dream; and I saw myself jumping off the bed and going to him and then he put his hand on my head. I never felt such ecstasy in my life! But, with that, I got up.

'Naturally I was very much moved and perturbed so I told my husband that this had happened. He said, "In the books I have been reading it says, when Sai Baba liked somebody, he had the habit of beckoning them in this fashion." I hadn't seen the books then. So I was of course more impressed; but, you see, that seed was sown. My mind would say, "It is only a dream; there's nothing to be so flustered about." But then something inside me wouldn't leave me alone. I decided I would visit his *samah* [tomb]. So that is how I started going to Shirdi [where Sai Baba's ashram was]. In those days it was an awful place, there were no amenities and I was not used to any discomfort; it used to disturb me terribly but, you know, I would just keep on going. Every time I would come back swearing that I would never go again. Then I would go again and that's the way he trained me, and all my arrogance and everything started disappearing.

'Now miracle after miracle came to me, such as ordinary people would think incredible. To give you one example. I am a student of music, vocal music, and something went wrong with my throat – I couldn't sing. I visited many doctors and they could neither diagnose it nor cure it. I was very upset and so I went there, near the tomb. There I just prostrated myself – by that time I had completely changed and bhakti began to seem very vital – and I just prayed to him: "Why should this happen since I am not interested in ordinary society and music is so dear to me?"

'After saying that prayer I went to a friend who stays there. I talked to her and then went to the room which was allotted to me. When I reached it, there was nothing there except my bag and bedding; I thought I would remove my sari and be comfortable. I was loosening the pin when something rustled in the folds and a packet fell from my sari. Of course I was stunned, I didn't know what to do; I looked here and there. I picked it up, it was very neatly folded, so I put back my sari and ran off to my friend. I told her, "What is this? Something very peculiar has happened."

'Of course she joked, "Oh, you must have brought it with you from Bombay."

'I said, "Don't be absurd. I have been sitting with you for half an hour and I just wanted to take off my sari and something fell!"

'"Nobody was there?"

'I said, "No, just my bag and my bedding."

'I opened the packet. It contained six or seven little pellets. So she said, "Now what are you going to do? Don't you know this is Sai Baba's miracle?" She'd had experience of it.

'I said, "Yes, I realize that." So I took the pellets all together. At the time I didn't connect this miracle with my prayer or my wish. I just took them. When I came back to Bombay, at my very first lesson, my voice was perfectly all right! Then I knew what it was. But this is his method of drawing people. Once I was absolutely established in him, the miracles ceased, as much as to say, "Now you don't need them." But this is his shock tactics, if I may call it so.

'This is why I went to Sai Baba. And for years, of course, my devotion deepened. Then people began telling me, "There is a lovely ashram just next door, three miles away; why don't you go?"

'I said, "Why should I? I am quite satisfied with Baba." But in my heart there was a hankering for some living manifestation also. I didn't go, but somebody opened an ashram here in Bombay and Godavari Mata was called to do the opening ceremony. I was sitting there with all the others and in my lap was the book I had written on Sai Baba.

'Somebody said, "Oh, Mataji has come." I just turned around to see and at that very moment something in me . . . I don't know, I can't explain that experience; something sort of . . . I just surrendered. She was at that time very beautiful, even physically. Now she looks aged, but she had immense lustre, physical lustre. I thought, "This is Mataji!"

'Really, I can't explain what had happened to me. I was like one in a dream. She was sitting on the platform and we were all queuing up for her darshan and I had that book in my hand and so spontaneously I said, "Oh, Mother, I have written this book on Sai Baba and I give it to you."

147

'She looked at me and said, "So you've come at last."

'This is the very peculiar thing she said. "So you've come at last," she said! There was nothing that I could say.

'Then I started going to her and there came a time when I was so much in love with her that I began to be disturbed. I felt, "Am I being disloyal to my Guru? What is happening to me?" And it became very awkward, a confusion in my mind. "What am I to do?" I said to myself. "The best thing is to ask Mother herself." That was my reaction. Why talk to anyone else?

'She was sitting alone and I just frankly told her my whole problem. I said, "Ever since you have come, I dream about you; my own Guru, Sai Baba, seems to fade away. What is this that you are doing to me?"

'She listened patiently to everything; then she said, "Sai Baba and I are not different. Don't be confused." The minute she said that all my misery and contradictions disappeared. She took off a locket she was wearing and showed it to me. She said, "Whose picture is this?"

'I said, "Sai Baba."

'"So don't have these doubts but, in your prayers, you keep on saying his name." After that I was absolutely free from doubt.

'I asked her one day, "Mother, will you give me a mantra?" and she said immediately, "Yes." Of course, I was a little nervous. It seems that there are many ceremonies: one has to take a coconut and do puja at her feet and so on, and I am not able to do all these things. So I was telling my friend, "What am I going to do, I don't know how to do all these things?" She said, "Don't worry, I will tell you later, because Mother said she will initiate me the day after next." So I was waiting, biding my time. But the next morning when I went for Mataji's darshan she said to me, "You want a mantra; here it is!" You see, she gave me no chance to worry about it. I was absolutely stunned but overjoyed. I didn't have to go through all that – she knows exactly what you are, you see, and she adapts the sadhana to the devotee.

'Godavari Mata never preaches. She never preaches. Her method is very silent. She helps you through a silent projection of her grace, but if you ask her questions she replies. But you will find that when you become very intimate you see the answers without anybody actually uttering them.

'I have no children. And if I had had children I would never have persuaded them or forced them to do what we are doing. I never once in my life told my husband to believe what I was believing. Indeed, as I went deeper into it he became indifferent. But one darshan from Mother completely changed him.

'I had a very powerful background in my mother. You see, she was not educated in the ordinary sense but she was a very intellectual woman. She was a natural intellectual and self taught; she taught herself English. She had a fascination for the language and she would read books. She couldn't speak it but she could read and understand everything, even philosophy. So it happened in a very peculiar way; one day she was walking down the street and there was a person who sells all kinds of old things. He had some volumes and mother went to see what they were and they were Swami Vivekananda's volumes. She was attracted; she said, "What are these?" He said, "Oh, some books they are." She bought the whole lot and she started reading them. Of course there was an opening there already, you see. As she began to start reading she began to get more and more immersed, absorbed, and in the same way that I was initiated by Sai Baba, she was initiated by no less a person than Ramakrishna Paramahansa. It was a wonderful experience she had: she was initiated by him in a vision. She had a very, very powerful mind and she started studying raja yoga on her own from Vivekananda's books and she acquired tremendous siddhis.

'She passed away six years ago. So this tradition was there but she never once told us, "Read this" or "Do that". Then she started her sadhana and she was very much advanced when Godavari Mata saw her. The very first day Mataji said, "She has done a lot of yoga." Just by the look of her Mataji said that. And very graciously she got up and she took a morsel from her plate and put it in my mother's mouth. Actually put it in my mother's mouth. So that background was there and I have got two brothers who are similarly inclined and a sister. My father died very early; but he was very materialistic in the sense that he was not interested in religion or spirituality although he was a brilliant doctor. But he passed away very early. We got everything from my mother in a subtle way.

'I still definitely consider myself a Parsi, though. There is no question of my leaving my religion or having a ceremony performed or being converted. Because at a certain level there is neither this religion nor that religion.'

Mrs Sahukar follows me to the landing, invites me back, asks me to see the ashram. I doubt if I will have the time to travel again but I agree to go if I can. I do this to please her – her intelligence and sincerity charm one into wanting to do so. She seems in some way good, not self-deluded, properly certain. I walk out into the battering sunlight. Dust rises from the bare roadway. In a few strides I am again in danger of being cut down by Bombay's black and yellow taxis slipping like unnaturally aggressive dolphins through these turbulent oceans of traffic.

*

We sit in a long room, I on a black plastic-covered couch; three doorways lead to a wide, balustraded terrace, their blue hangings flapping as the fan overhead stirs the heavy air. In the house of one of his richer supporters we are waiting to speak with Acharya Rajnish, a teacher, a travelling preacher, a man who numbers hundreds and even thousands in his audiences when he speaks on Bombay *maidan* or in the other centres at which he pauses to spread his ideas on God and man. A mirror surrounded by a deep, carved framework stands against one wall of the room so that ghostly figures – we ourselves gathered here in ones and twos to see the *acharya* – stare strangely out; it is as if we were separated from our reflections by a trellised arbour. Beside the mirror hangs an overcoloured picture of Mahatma Gandhi; a little lower down hangs a certificate from the Imperial Society of Knights Bachelor. On it, in fading copperplate, the name of some member of the family once of service to the King-Emperor. Against the opposite wall stands a glass cabinet filled with tarnished silver: on one shelf lies the insignia of that Imperial approval, now as much a part of history as the Moghul ascendancy or the Aryan invasion.

Later, shoeless, I am led past a pale blue, patterned curtain to where, beyond it, Acharya Rajnishji sits on a bed, caught in light as if for a performance. I approach, others crowding behind me. The acharya, haloed by the scent of sandalwood, taps the foot of the bed and smiles. At his nod I sit down. The rest press closer, stand beside him, sit on the floor about my feet, lean in over the end of the bed. They look expectant – a stranger has come to interrogate their sage.

He sits cross-legged, his plump and hairy stomach slightly creased as his shoulders droop forward. He holds a blue towel across his lap; from the waist down he is wrapped in a fine white robe. His hair has receded, leaving a smooth, pale brown skull, now gleaming with sandalwood oil, and a fringe of long, grey hair which hangs down behind his ears to his shoulders. His beard is long, its black, oiled ringlets almost dividing so that it looks forked. Half-hidden in this is his small and smiling mouth. As I settle myself, he fixes me with a rolling, slightly goatish, light brown eye.

When he speaks, it is fluently in a high, youthful voice; one can believe that he was a good lecturer at the university where he once taught. He does not falter, even when the microphones of the faithful tumble, or quarrelling voices shout under the window, or, beyond them, someone lets off a late *Diwali* fire cracker. As he speaks, he emphasizes his points with elegant, long fingered gestures resembling those which Indians have codified in their dances. He watches me with great intensity as he answers my questions, his eyes fixed on mine. I look into them, then past him through the small window at the dark trees, and at the high lights of an apartment block sending out their interrupted beams like signals as the breeze pumps the branches to and fro.

'As far as I am concerned, that type of relationship which has been in existence between Guru and shishya – to me it all seems immature. In a spiritual relationship, nothing like this can exist. There is no possibility of it. But it has been in existence and that has been the rock on which the whole of Indian spirituality has been based. It has been the foundation stone – but the wrong foundation stone. Because of it we seem to be spiritual and we are not. There should be disciples, there must be disciples – but no Gurus. But in this life there are Gurus and no disciples; there is no attitude of learning. Because that attitude demands an attitude of ignorance. A person who thinks, "I do not know" can become a disciple, but in this day no one thinks like that: everyone knows only. So there are Gurus; a Guru means a person who says, "I have known" and to me this very assertion is absurd. Because life is not such a thing that you can say, "I have known". There never comes a moment when you have reached and nothing remains further to travel. It is always travelling, it is always a reaching but never a reached point. The very concept of a Guru is basically irreligious and un-spiritual.

'Whosoever claims to have reached the end of that road, the very claim negates them. The claim comes not from knowing but from ignorance. The Guru also comes not from knowledge but from ignorance. Because to be in a situation of knowing, one is bound to know simultaneously that life is endless; there is a beginning but there is no end. The same people who claim to have known, claim too that God is in everything, that God is in you. They say, too, that God cannot be defined. They say, too, that the truth is infinite. If the truth is infinite then you can never be a knower as they claim – you cannot be. A religious man is a man who is not claiming knowledge but is claiming on the contrary the mysteriousness of life. If you claim knowledge then life becomes not a mystery but an open secret; then even God is not a mystery.

'A person can be aware of the mysterious, of the *mysterium*, one can be one with it, one can live with and love it, until he himself becomes mysterious; his very presence becomes something mysterious. And in his presence, something can happen, but that is something like infection not teaching. His presence can become infectious and something may happen within one in his presence; his presence may work but that is not teaching. And if he begins to teach directly, then that happening will be hindered, that happening then becomes impossible. When I become a teacher, then your mind is not concerned with my presence, then you are concerned with my teachings . . . If one is to become infectious it is better to be silent and live with somebody; it may happen at any moment, no one can predict it – it may happen! And there is more possibility of its happening if the person is silent. When the person is not silent then there is a direct effort to teach; the mind of the teacher becomes tense and the mind of the pupil too becomes tense; then there is only a verbal communication. But we need a deeper mingling; no deeper participation than that participation is possible.

'When one effort comes to failure then you begin another effort; when one Guru fails then you go to another; when one method fails then another and another and another . . . And this can go on for lives together. But when you come to the point when everything has become a failure and you know that no Guru can help you, no method can become a process, then you have come to the absolute failure – only then is the "I" dissolved because there is no question of its being in existence: it has gone. It lives in the hope of achievement in the future and it gathers its strength from its hope in the future. Sometimes nothing can be achieved, just as it happened to Buddha when he was in total failure and he left everything; sadhana, yoga, the practice, everything, the meditation . . . everything was left and he was in a total vacuum about what to do. Because everything had proved nonsense and he had come to a point of no return; there was no question of going to another method again. There was no possibility of any dream now – not only of worldly dreams, but the spiritual dream too had failed. And in that total vacuum, in that night, the happening took place and he was not present any more. So Buddha could say, "It is not that I have achieved it, I could not achieve it. When I became a total failure, this came. I have not brought it, it has come to me."

'So you cannot prepare for it although the mind longs for preparation, it longs for method, technique, and that is why the mind can be prepared for everything. In a scientific experiment there must be preparation; in our worldly living there must be preparation. But the unknown cannot come to your prepared mind; it must be an effortless achievement.

'But in another way it can be meaningful: the relationship of a disciple with a Guru from the standpoint of the disciple can be meaningful; but not from the standpoint of the Guru. For the disciple, if he feels reverence towards somebody . . . Another thing – a Guru expects reverence and says that a Guru must be respected and reverenced; but to me, when you feel reverence towards someone, that is the relationship. Not that the Guru is to be revered but when you feel reverence towards anyone then you may feel the relationship of a disciple towards the Guru. But that is totally the standpoint of the disciple; there is no

Guru as far as the Guru is concerned. He feels reverence – well, he can feel it, but it must not be demanded. And if it comes without any demand, then it has got meaning because to feel reverence towards somebody is to become open to their selves. When someone demands love then the mind towards which the demand is made becomes closed. Whenever the mind feels insecurity it becomes closed, and whenever there is a demand it feels insecurity.

'And one thing more; when the Guru becomes the centre the relationship becomes one to one and the Guru demands that, "This reverence that you pay to me must not be paid to any others." When a wife demands, "This love must be towards me and not anyone else," she feels that when it is overflowing towards everybody she is cheated; and the Guru, too, feels he is cheated if this reverence goes to anybody and everybody. So there is also the second demand: "It must be only towards me – I am the Guru and no one else can be your Guru." This too becomes binding and closing. When the disciple is at the centre there is no question of this closing; then there is simply an attitude of learning. He comes to you and learns and feels reverence, then he goes to someone else and learns and feels reverence, then he goes on and goes on ... Then the whole life becomes the teacher, the whole life becomes the Guru. Then God, the very divine, becomes the Guru. And the moment comes when there is nothing which cannot be revered, when everything becomes a point of reverence. This must be; and this can only be when the disciple is at the centre and not the Guru. When the Guru has been at the centre the Guru has failed the disciple; he has not helped him.

'I am reminded of a story: a certain monk was celebrating a particular festival, a festival known as the Day of the Teacher. But no one in his village knew that he had a teacher so everybody asked, "Who is your Teacher? Why are you celebrating this day, a day sacred to one's Teacher, living or dead? Who is your Teacher?" The monk laughed and said, "There was one man who refused to be my Teacher. And because he refused, I learned. And now I am paying my respects to him."

'In the Indian tradition the Guru has been in the centre, and that is why there has come to be a rich tradition but not one rich in spirituality; a long tradition but not one rich in spirituality. And once it is understood that verbal communication is teaching, then the Scriptures too can be felt as Gurus; the Sikhs call their Scripture Guru Granth – the book as teacher. When the verbal communication is teaching there is no need of a living person; verbal teaching can be taught by Scripture, through a computer or through any mechanical device. Once verbal teaching is taken to *be* teaching then a dead tradition is bound to develop. The written tradition can be relevant in everything but religious experience, because the happening cannot be recorded; it is impossible to record it. There is a record of what Krishna said but there is no record of how Krishna became Krishna. And that is the essential point, not what he said.

'There is a very lovely incident in the Buddha's life: one day he comes to teach a gathering; so many people have come, he sits on the dais ... and sits and sits and sits. After some time there are whisperings, "What is going on? We must begin now." But he is silent; half an hour, then one hour passes. And everyone is asking, "What is going on? He must talk to us, he must say something to us." Then Buddha says, "I have said that which could be said; now I was saying that which could not be said. Have you heard?" But no one had heard. It happened that one man, who had never spoken anything, for the first time laughed, laughed uproariously. Buddha was holding a flower in his hand; he called the man and gave him the flower and said to the gathering, "That which could be said, I have said to you; and that which could not be said, I have given to him." So there has grown up a tradition of two thousand years; monks have asked what was transferred to this man, what was said to him?

But nothing was said – not said, but heard! Something was heard in that total silence, someone felt what it is and became aware of some unknown happenings.

'I arrived at these thoughts, not over a long period of thinking, but over a long period of searching. And every search failed. I knocked on every door and every door was a failure. A moment came when I left everything and I was doing nothing for a year – for a whole year, almost nothing, just sitting, just standing, just thinking. Then it came. There was no preparation – then it came. This year was rather a negative process of preparation. Any unconscious effort that may have been made dissolved. Then there was no beginning and there was no going and no reaching and no effort. Then it came.'

Tiny beads of sweat sit for a while on his smooth, young-looking brow, then disappear. Now and then a current of air passes through the crowded room, an intermittent mercy. After fifty minutes or so he leans back; the audience is over. He seems to have been delighted by the very act of speaking, taking pleasure in the play of his own mind, so that sometimes he has made the same point in several different ways for the sheer gratification the turning, interlocking wheels of his intelligence give him.

Now he stands, leaning over the side of the bed, relaxing. He takes my raised hands between his; his palms are warm and dry. He smiles, he is happy, he moves to and fro on the bed like a champion mildly elated after some minor skirmish, an exhibition match. He speaks to favourites, laving them with his enjoyment.

I go away, pick up my shoes, walk with them in my hand to the long room where I first waited. I have a pain in my left temple. I feel very tired.

✳

As a matter of fact, he is rarely in Bombay; he is the most active of four secretaries of an all Indian association of sadhus (the only active one, rumour suggests, because he is too irascible for the others to work with him) and he is based in Delhi. But it was in Bombay that he first burst in on me, the telephone ringing at six in the morning – 'Swami Ananda here!' – and he followed it within the hour, standing ochre robed outside my hotel room door while I gaped at him, still in my pyjamas.

'I don't care about that – it is all the same. You could be naked! I wouldn't mind.'

He sat down, looked at me, his smile quite fierce. I had written to him from London, then from Bombay, we had arranged to meet but then I had fallen ill.

'Where have you been?' he yelled. 'I have been in the mountains, the Himalayas. You could have come. Now . . .'

He is seventy-two, with thinning white hair dragged from his forehead and gathered at the back, a long, pointed beard, spectacles: he looks a sort of Merlin. His voice is loud, his opinions certain, his views in the wildest way reactionary. He led me to many places and people I would otherwise never have seen, he introduced me to Gurus who would otherwise never have seen me; the corollary of this was that he was absolutely autocratic in his decisions about whom it was and whom it was not suitable for me to talk to. He was totally generous, dragging me about at the end of his prodigious energy as if I were a dog on a lead. He was the only man I met who consistently took care that my unfamiliarity with Indian food, furniture and customs would cause me no discomfort. Often I was less unfamiliar and more comfortable than he thought, but the idea that what they were accustomed to might be strange for me was one which occurred to so few Indians that his consideration always touched me.

If I think of India, I think of Swami Ananda, moments cut vividly into a film already slightly blurring in my memory – at Bombay Central Station, adamant about a fifty paise tip as the porter curses him; he is always careful, even tight with money – in Dehra Dun a similar scene unwinds with the driver of a tonga.

Or in our small room at Lonavla, two thousand feet above sea level, where we have gone to a religious meeting; sitting on his bed he says, 'Those Beatles . . . that John Lennon, they do just what they like . . . He left his wife and married that woman who looks just like a monkey, that Japanese. They've all gone sex mad. In a few years, they'll all be impotent. You wait – impotent! And then they'll come to India and ask some yogi to give them an aphrodisiac!' And, later, 'It's all right, I don't snore, yogis don't snore. If they do, they wake up at once,' then going to sleep to snore gently while I read.

I remember him at Rishikesh, coming down the steps towards the young Ganges, waving bread in his right hand. 'Come, I'll show you something. Are you listening? Come on!' He laughed, hurrying past me. Mountains sheltered the last of the blue sky. In the distance, lightning flickered and dark turbulent clouds beat up against the wind. Swami Ananda threw bread. 'Look – fish. Can you see them?' And there they were, great carp, wheeling and leaping, slithering about each other like snakes, snapping at the bread with a ferocity that catapulted it away from them as if in a parable on greed. 'Look, they are fighting! Can you see them?' Swami Ananda laughed, throwing crumbs. The water hissed as the tangled fish cut it into foam. Backs and tails whirled through the waves. He laughed again, threw a last handful, then, the first rain beginning to fall, watched as the fish, a hundred or more of them, slowly began to disperse.

On a train, en route to stay in the maths of the holy: 'You want to smoke a pipe? I know what it is, I used to smoke pipe. You want to smoke one now? Go on! Where we are going, it is not allowed.' But later, as we carve up our vegetarian cutlets: 'I'm not going to have you eat eggs and that thing. You can have that in Bombay!'

Sitting on another train, he read in the *Hindustan Times* an article on the 'new morality in Europe'; it was the Sex Fair in Denmark which most engaged their interest. Swami Ananda marked occasional paragraphs with a pencil. 'Sexual acts in public!' he exclaimed. He laughed, but primly. 'That's a bit too much – how can they do such a thing? No, no – I'm asking! How can they do such a thing? It's like animals – no decency . . . Sexual acts in public!' But his indignation did not hold and he laughed again.

Another time, in Vrindaban, he murmured, 'I usually feel optimistic. You understand? But sometimes when I think of the world . . . *So* much of dirty things in the world now – Europe, everything going down and down . . . But I feel a resignation. Resignation! You understand me? I used to do so much of shouting, passion, all that thing . . .' Then stronger, later, 'This may not be the supreme truth but I believe it: I can't stand a man who tells lies, who lies to himself. You understand? I do not so much condemn a man who commits adultery as a man who tells lies. No, no hear me! A man's first concern is not to tell lies to himself! . . . You know, until two years ago I never used to allow anyone to touch my body. Yes, it's true. This is a thing sadhus believe, that the extremities are very important; the fingers, the toes, the top of the head. If you take an X-ray photograph you can see all that power streaming out – sometimes more power, sometimes less power, but always streaming out . . . and when a sadhu touches you, sometimes you can feel that shock. You understand me? . . . So many diseases are infectious – V.D., smallpox, cholera, so many. But there can be mental infection and spiritual infection also. But why do we always think this is negative? It can be positive also! Then it is transmission, then we call it transmission, but it is infection also . . .'

The stops and emphases of his conversation recall him, vigorous, eager, furious at humbug or stupidity, not above swearing if he feels that it is needed to punch home his meaning, stumping endlessly ahead of me, impatient as I struggle in his wake.

'My family were very religious minded. They were worshippers of Lord Krishna and they belonged to the bhakti cult, the cult of devotion. But I took to the path of advaita vedanta under the Shankara school of thought.

'I had my education in Calcutta University; I studied philosophy. But then I left my career and got in this monastic life because I found I didn't like that way of life, ordinary life. It seemed to me that the common man's life was full of tragedy, the same things repeating and repeating and repeating . . . It was not inspiring to me. So I thought that something quite inspiring, something quite ennobling must be found and I departed. Of course I have a great deal of devotion in me but I wanted to go on that path shown by Shankaracharya and adopted that philosophy. Then I went here and there and met a lot of people and had some connection with the political movement of that time. Not Congress – other things, revolutionary activities . . . But that also I did not like, it did not appeal to me. This was before I left.

'Finally, I left all my connections and I passed as a probationer for about six years and then I was ordained and consecrated as a sanyasi monk and I entered a monastery order proper. Before that I was a novice. Then I became a fully fledged monk. When I was initiated I asked my Guru if I could go out and move throughout the world, throughout the whole of India. I made my first pilgrimage; I went up to the Himalayas and there I got very much attracted. The atmosphere enchanted; it was simply self-assuring and I could gather courage and inspiration from the air and the atmosphere and the winds.

'I found my Guru because I was in search of a person who could guide me the proper way. I met one or two but they did not impress me. Then I suddenly got my own Guru, a very highly qualified person, a man of yoga and philosophy who was also an English educated man. He was very frank and direct. I met him at a festival, a *Kumbhamela** – something like that – he was very kind to me. But then I used to question; generally my fellow disciples did not have so many theories or hold so many talks and discussions with the Guru, but I went on asking and asking and asking. I didn't doubt the Guru's words but I made inquiries: "How is this? How is that? How are those things?" Others say that the Guru should be taken as God; I could not take my Guru as God. I took him as a friend and guide and a man who could help me to reach the aim of my life, self-realization.

'I think that there is divinity in the Guru but I must realize it. Simply saying it doesn't mean anything. If somebody says something I can't expect to understand it if I don't feel it myself. Of course there are things which a lot of people take for granted but in my case I must feel the presence of divinity. Well, a man like me eats and sleeps and laughs and smiles and gets worried and does other physical things – how is that compatible with the idea of divinity?

'But then I was told that it was all through the divine current of thought which flows through the physical channel. So I came to understand. But I differ in this way, that the physical man is not the Guru. The Guru is a power; the *gurushakti* lives in the particular person who, himself at some time, was a disciple of a Guru so that he knows the psychology of a disciple. After becoming a Guru he knows himself that he is fulfilling a certain mission. Having realized something in himself his desire is to help others – willing persons, aspirants – to go that way.

'In that way I had a very fine relationship based on love and respect and reverence; he used to ask me to sit before him and he

* Great gatherings of sadhus and the devout, which are held at regular intervals at some point of pilgrimage on the banks of the Ganges.

would look at me, into my eyes, and he used to say, "Oh, you have a great chance to do such and such things." But I didn't achieve so much as I expected because my Guru passed away some time after. I felt that it was possible, but without the help of a Guru you cannot unfold your inner being.

'I could not get any other person of that stature. I walked about the country but I did not get that feeling of reverence. He did not have a successor either. He was a man who was moving about the country, going here and there; he did not have a particular monastery.

'Another important thing; he gave much stress to obedience, humility, consecration and surrender, complete surrender, self-surrender. He said that you must not have a different existence, you should always think that you are part of, linked with, the Guru. So his advice was always, "You make yourself empty," so that the Guru power may enter into my mind or heart or psychological frame and I may admit it. And purification is necessary. Purification means to shun all desires, ambitions, so all the limited things may not stand in the way. So that's necessary.

'I told my Master, "I put myself at your disposal, please receive me and accept me and guide me and advise me." This was the way. That is a very sublime state of affairs. But for fulfilment, as to how it will happen in the long run, I don't know. Whatever I am now, I am a product of his teaching. I did not have so much thought and so many ideas and so much liberalism; I was very conservative in my life. But now I feel an atmosphere of universal love and brotherhood, and these things might be due to my Guru's guidance. So Guru and shishya, I say, is a spiritual unfolding, the unfolding of a potential divinity. You must have the co-operation, the guidance, the help of a person whom we may call Guru or teacher or preceptor or spiritual guide. This is a wonderful institution in India; but there are very few people who successfully surrender.

'My Guru used to ask me to sit before him from time to time and in silence. No talk. No speech. I would sit, simply, closing my eyes; and sometimes he would touch my forehead also. Then he would also ask me to look at his eyes. This happened many times. Things like that act invisibly – I can't say what the effect on me was. But it might have had an effect in a long slow action, in slow motion . . . sometimes some things take three months, four months, five years to work, but it doesn't matter.

'But it starts with sitting. The seed of the banyan tree is just like the mustard seed; but the mustard seed flowers and blossoms and gives its fruit in three months and dies. The banyan tree takes a long, long time; it develops slowly but it sustains what it does. This is why I feel that whatever I have been doing and thinking must be the teaching of my Guru and that through him something is unfolding in me. I have developed decisiveness, I have got resoluteness. Once I was wavering; I did not know what was good, what was bad, what was not good for me, what was not good for society or for human beings. So in this way there is a new approach to the world.

'As I have faith in the Guru, the Guru also must have faith and confidence in the disciple. This mutual confidence and respect develop something which is a . . . divine relationship, you might call it. Very sublime. Just like relations between wife and husband if there is reciprocity, understanding, respect, no question of doubt at all. "Oh! I cannot doubt my wife, she cannot do it!" This is confidence, self-confidence and the confidence of the man in her chastity and purity. And that reacts also in the wife.

'So also it reacts in the disciple. "Oh, my Guru believes in me – I cannot! Even though I feel something wrong, I cannot. I cannot!" Those things develop some sort of dignity, self-dignity in a man that protects him from outward pressures, from desire and other things also. There are a lot of so-called commercial Gurus; some teach yoga asanas, some teach pranayama, some

164

teach meditation. But the true work of a Guru is to receive the disciple as his confidant and then try to unfold him through guided teachings. Not through shastras, books or scriptures – they are there; it is physical association, mental and physical that is the big thing. And a true Guru will always wish that his disciple becomes higher and higher and greater and greater – but there are a lot of other Gurus who become envious. If his disciple gets good publicity – Oh! He doesn't like that publicity! There are a lot of such Gurus, which I don't like.

'Gurus of a lesser degree are not bad always, they are very sincere also. It is not because a Guru is not highly developed or of the highest order that he is not capable; it does not matter because he has reached upwards so far and he is sincere. But there are other Gurus who want to make material profit out of saying many things but not achieving anything. These are dangerous for society also. In the name of gurudom and of giving knowledge or spirituality, a lot of so-called Gurus, commercial persons, undesirable persons, disturb the atmosphere. There are very few Gurus who really want to realize themselves and who truly want to develop the divine potentiality of their disciples. Very, very few. Very, very few. And these people belong to the whole world, not to a particular country or nation or religion. I believe it. They do not belong to a particular religion, they belong to the whole human race. Their silent service radiated for the wealth of the whole world.

'Just as sitting here we could hear messages over the radio from Moscow or New York, so a Guru who has got a relationship towards the whole mundane earth, towards nature also, feels he can radiate. You put a very fine flower in a room; if you enter some time afterwards you will notice a fragrance. So a Guru or a spiritual man, he also radiates a fragrance, a spiritual fragrance, something which permeates the air and cleanses it – a spiritual deodorant, deodorizing the environment. He is like that. And he reaches the people through sleep, through dreams, through silence: but not until and unless you allow yourself to receive. How? By making the mind vacant, by sitting quiet, by doing meditation; just as with a transistor or a radio you have to find the particular station, so in order to receive the Guru's message you have to fix yourself in certain postures of mind and body.

'When one goes to a sadhu and asks to be his disciple, if the man feels he can accept him, well, "Come on, live with me." He may not do anything formal but will go on living with him. And in living with him he finds that he goes to the latrine, he goes on coughing, he goes on taking food, he goes on smoking *bidis*, the normal things. And he says, "Oh, he's a normal man, he's an ordinary man," and he goes away, he leaves. But if he lives through these day to day incidents and he carries on and lives with him and feels some attraction, then the Guru feels, "The boy has got some integrity, some perseverance, some sincerity." Then he will start teaching him about yoga asanas and other things to purify his body. To purify his body and mind so that whenever that energy is given it may not get displaced.

'You never know, sometimes it happens, when a man has some impurity in his character or in his being and the divine power is transferred, the man becomes dumb, the man becomes mad. This happens. So it is necessary to prepare him, to make him a probationer. Otherwise it can be too much. Some evil man becomes a Guru, boasting, "Oh, what have we here! We have become a Guru!" and jumps and shouts and goes away ... This, we say, is when the instrumentality is not correct, not perfect. The instrument was not well chosen or not quite purified to receive that high potential, you see. The current that wire can carry is 220 volts. But this particular cable cannot withstand the impact of, say, 6,000 volts – it burns out. So likewise there are some persons whose capacity for understanding, whose possibility to receive, is limited; the chela may therefore get derailed.

'Realization does not mean that you went up to the realization point and stopped there. It is a continual process from point to point, point to point. But there is definitely great danger in being too successful as a Guru with a big ashram and so on. There is a great danger, first from the ego, second from sex – and it is finished. This has happened before my eyes to so many disciples; the Guru decries them, they become annoyed because he becomes a big man and they go. The Guru may also not like the chela to go ahead and get fame and name and his photograph in the newspapers and ladies and money and all those things. They are stuck, they cannot progress to a higher position. It is checked there. Devotees come and they give garlands, they give fruit and, "Oh, maharaj! Oh, maharaj!" – and the ego is inflated and a new sort of worldliness is built up.

'You see, there is a likelihood of getting immersed in desire and name and fame and attachment, and they can't proceed further. By hook and by crook, some people go on developing until they reach the level of a Guru, but they are very unusual, I tell you this, very unusual. You see, I have got certain things in me. I don't find a man to whom I could go and discuss and ask his advice. I am a man who knows a lot of people here, but in the whole of India I don't know anyone I feel I can ask. I actually asked two or three persons, but . . . I don't mean to say I have achieved a very high degree but my conception is clear, clean and clear: I want to be a divine person. For that, whether I have the capacity, capability, potentiality, that God knows. But by doing this, by going that way, one may accomplish . . . I have come to journey's end so far as the physical goes. I am at journey's end now and so I have no possibility. Now I feel, really speaking, to be a true Guru or to be true disciple is very, very difficult.'

A scattering of last instructions, a soft handgrip (I remember his words – 'I allowed no one to touch my body'), then he is marching away to his rickshaw and oblivion. Left in the Vrinda-ban roadway, I feel like weeping, as if he were someone I had known for a long time and now shall never see again. He is so strange a mixture – a questor, an executive, a shy man ('I could never laugh or dance or these things,' he says. 'Now I can, the last two years I can embrace people; but before that . . .'); an honest man, often irascible, yet gentle, humorous and kindly. A life-long celibate, he remains intrigued by sex; totally loyal to the concepts of his philosophy, he is yet delighted to have them observed and discussed by objective outsiders. He is vain, noisy, hectoring, overbearing, demanding – yet a thinker who has not gone flaccid under the weight of dogma, one who takes little for granted. As a result, he feels himself alone in a world of accep-tors; being lonely, he is delighted to be recognized ('so *many* people know me'), yet is quietly contemptuous of most of those who do so. He knows that their narrowness makes their opinions worthless, their ignorance leaves them without standing.

The rickshaw rattles round the corner, out of sight; he has not looked back. The small cloud of dust its wheels have raised settles slowly. High in the blue sky, three vultures wheel; they have the world in scrutiny, like gods. I walk slowly back to the ashram . . .

4

The Godmen's Flock

HEREDITARY GURUS: THE VALLABHACHARYAS

ALTHOUGH in a religion as eclectic as Hinduism divisions tend to blur and labels to become meaningless, two main streams may be said to run through it. The first is the Shaivite, devoted to Shiva, the tenor of which is ascetic and self-mortifying. Those sadhus who distort and sometimes cripple their bodies with austerities of the most extreme kind are nearly all Shaivites. The second stream, that of the Vaishnavites, lays no such stress on self-torture. Worshipping Vishnu in his incarnation as Krishna, they prefer that happy god's lightness of heart, his emphasis on the pleasures of the senses as a metaphor for the pleasures of the spirit. They are bhaktas, followers of the way of love and devotion and tend to be anti-Brahminical, to disbelieve in the total merging of the individual soul with Brahman, to use vernacular languages rather than Sanskrit, to focus their faith through idols, to delight in ritual. Madhva was one of their philosophers, and in his monasteries only the mahant himself is expected to remain celibate. This relaxed attitude to sexual relations, at least in the religious context, is partly based on the complex involvement of Krishna with the gopis, and particularly with Rahda, thought of as his consort and perhaps, like Eve from Adam, created out of his left side; yet, according to the *Puranas*, she was the wife of a cowherd. Apologists sometimes point out that, at the time when he sported with her in Vrindaban, Krishna was only a child, and they offer this fact as the basis for their assertion that the Krishna–Rahda relationship has been most unpleasantly misunderstood. If this is so, it is a misunderstanding shared by most Vaishnavites, and one which has had a great deal of both ritualistic and artistic consequence.

One of the main Vaishnavite sects is that founded by the philosopher and teacher Vallabha. He lived from 1479 to 1531. As is usual in these cases, he is supposed to have been a child of prodigious ability; he began learning the four *Vedas*, the six great systems of philosophy and the eighteen Puranas (part of the non-Vedic scriptures) at the age of seven, and mastered them all within four months. By the age of twelve, he had formulated his teachings and was able to set out on his travels in order to propagate them. He became chief acharya to the Vaishnavites, settled in Kashi (Benares), and there wrote the seventeen philosophical works which became the foundation of his sect.

Vallabhacharya called his system of beliefs *Suddh Advaita*, or pure nondualism, thus by implication criticizing Shankara's form of advaita. The basis of this criticism was that Shankara's view of the monistic universe depended upon considering the palpable world as illusory – the doctrine of maya. Vallabha, on the other hand, said that the material was real since its creation was willed by God and its substance is not different from his. God, being alone, desired to become many, thus spinning the world out of his very essence, a process which nevertheless effected no change in him. His desire for plurality, based on a kind of cosmic boredom, makes his creation of the world almost a frivolity, something devised for his own pleasure. It is here that there appears a concept often met in Hinduism – lila (sport): the sport of God, the game he plays. This game explains not only the creation of the universe but the inconsistencies which beset the life within it, the appalling absurdities and illogicalities which so often make the human race their victim.

The soul, Vallabha said, is a part of Brahman and eternal; it issues from *Akshara*, a form of Brahman, like a spark from a fire. That is, it is real, it is separate, yet its substance is the substance of that from which it came. What is unreal is the notion of the ego, the idea 'I' and the idea 'mine'. Those who think that this is reality belong to the lowest stream, that of *samsara*. Higher than these are those who follow the *maryada-marg*, the path of Vedic knowledge. The highest, however, follow the *pushti-marg*, the pathway of the love of God. This division of souls into three basic types is very important to the followers of Vallabha who, as bhaktas, naturally set great value on a clamorous, self-submerging devotion. Those who follow this third path may achieve immediate liberation, release at one blow as it were; those who follow the sober way of Vedic knowledge can only advance soberly, step by step.

The gopis of Vrindaban, the dairymaids who tended the cows and sported – in pure or in ambivalent manner, according to the tale you choose – with the young Krishna, are the clearest example of those who follow the pushti-marg. They joined in the lila of God, in his game, his sport, and to do so remains the highest aim of the devotees of Krishna. He is the husband of all souls and every soul aspires to join with him in a divine bliss.

As a result, the enactment of the love games between Krishna and the cow girls becomes a holy rite of great significance. But apart from that, since Krishna represents not only the creator but also the continuing enjoyer of the world, fasting or mortification of the flesh become positively sinful. On the contrary, all enjoyment is permissible, provided that it becomes an offering to God. You offer up your vices to Krishna; if you enjoy food, eat – but eat for Krishna; if you enjoy making love, make love – but do it for Krishna. In the surrounding puritanical gloom, such a doctrine shines out delightfully.

Also of great importance is the worship of the idol. Every devout family in the sect will have an image of Krishna in its home. This brings into prominence another aspect of the god; *Bala-krishna*, Krishna as a young child. Every morning the idol must be awoken, washed, dressed and fed; no meal may be taken without the idol's being offered some of it first (an ordinance which usually makes it impossible for devotees to eat anywhere but at home). The place where it stands must be kept clean, it must be taken out, as Krishna went out into the fields of Vrindaban; in the evenings, it must be undressed and put to bed. Tended like a baby, Krishna in this form seems totally dependent upon the worshipper – a reversal of what is perhaps the actual situation and thus becoming a strange, upside-down metaphor reverberating with meaning.

The tenderness with which this care is lavished is by no means formal. The concern is profound and genuine; the idol is not a representation of the god, it is Krishna himself. The image is given its divinity by the blessing of the Guru, who hands it to the devotee and receives it back again only when the latter becomes unable to look after it properly, or dies. And it is the expectation of the really dedicated that, if their devotion is intense enough, the idol will repay their care by speaking with them – that they will be raised to a level at which its divinity becomes physically clear to them. There are many stories about such rewards; one is of a Brahmin who, finding the floor before the idol dirty, began to sweep it, only for his broom to break. In despair he did the unthinkable and bound it up with his holy thread; it was precisely this sacrilege which proved his devotion, and the idol spoke.

Vallabhacharya had eighty-four disciples who spread his doctrines throughout India. His real successor, however, was his second son, Vittalhnath. All the present Gurus, in the different parts of western India in which their temples stand, are the descendents of Vittalhnath's seven sons. They continue, therefore, the ancient Vedic tradition of the householder Guru who inherits his students or disciples, just as they inherit him. In each of them, the spirit of Vallabhacharya is supposed to live again and all are treated with the most profound reverence from the moment they are born. They have always been given a respect which has at times reached improbable dimensions: what they said was totally obeyed, what they asked for was given them without stint or question. It can easily be seen why, with their basic philosophy, some of the things they asked for tended to shock outside observers. The wives and daughters of devotees were sometimes handed to the Guru, the maharaj; since he and God were interchangeable, this seemed less of an enormity to the devout than to others. Body, mind, and property, called *tan, man, dhan*, were totally made over to the Guru. The water in which he washed his feet was drunk by the disciples, the juice of the *pan* from his mouth, the leavings on his plate, were eaten by them. Not only that, the rituals prescribed that, from time to time, the Gurus should take the part of Rahda in the holy story; thus whispered accusations of homosexuality arose. In 1862 the High Court in Bombay found the then maharaj guilty of gross profligacy; one suspects that, whatever this Guru's actual excesses may or may not have been, no Victorian colonial judge could have been expected to understand the philosophy of worldly delight upon which the Vallabhacharya sect is founded.

Strong today in Bombay, Gujerat and other parts of western India, they seem to have outlived the scandals of a hundred years ago. On the other hand, the hold the Gurus have over some of the peasant villages is said still to be enormously strong. In the cities, where devotion is perhaps limited by a greater sophistication and where all faiths are in any case more on the defensive than in the country, the Vallabhacharyas bring a pleasant leavening to a general puritan rigidity. Nowadays, their conscientious sybaritism probably finds an outlet more in music and dancing than in an indiscriminate, if religious, sexual indulgence.

*

He is often at the café where the writers and the painters gather, the long terrace roofed but open to a lawn; the heavy Victorian extravagances of a museum façade cut off the view beyond.

173

Today he comes towards me down the aisle between the tables.
'Goswami asked me to contact you.' His voice is rich, his
English heavily accented. He has plays to his credit, writing
them in Gujerati, never in English. I have never seen him in
Western clothes.

We climb an iron staircase to the roof, sit there as though
kept afloat by the traffic's cacophony. The green copper domes
of the Museum playfully catch and roll the evening sunlight.
Colour slides from around us – soon stars will mark out the
receding segments of the sky.

He is a short, stocky, heavy necked man; under his flowing
white shirt he is running to fat. His face looks a little as if it has
just been slapped together out of clay; heavy lips, slab cheeks,
an inexpert lump for the chin . . . but when he smiles he is
strong toothed and life transforms his features; his eyes regard
one steadily. He turns towards me and runs a thick-fingered
hand through black hair which is going patchily grey over one
temple. He begins to talk in a loud, slightly throaty tenor voice,
pronouncing each word with great clarity as if afraid I will not
understand it. He speaks slowly with a deep concern for the
simple fact of speech; he enjoys and savours what he says so
much, one feels he has been waiting all his forty-odd years to be
asked to discuss these matters.

'Vallabhacharya's God is the child of your home; you can
worship him as a child. The adoration which we have for a child,
the love and affection we have for a child, if we can give that
same love to Lord Krishna or if we worship Lord Krishna as
our friend, then that's all right, he has got so many friends.
There are even so many fellows worshipping him as their
beloved. We have got so much love for God – for his love, you
see, we can discard our husbands or our elders so that love can
be given to God.

'In the same way, the Guru was regarded in former days as

Lord also. The Guru is greater than God; Guru is greater than God because the Guru is the man who will show you the real path, or he will lead you to the path by which you can know the God. But whether it might be Vallabhacharya or Vallabhacharya's Guru, that path is forged, or used to be forged, by that individual fellow. It is a personal God – you have to find it out within your own self; you can't find it outside your own body or outside your own mind – it is within you, you have to persevere.

'Now, I am a disciple of Vallabhacharya, I belong to that sect. I was born in the sect. From my youth I was always thinking why the Guru was given so much importance and I had long discussions with Shyam Baba and other Gurus. So they told me very friendlily that I could worship God in whatever way I liked; he can be one's friend, if you like, he can be one's father, he can be one's child. "We are coming in no way between you and God. The only thing between you and us is that you look to us as the incarnation of Vallabha. Due to our mistakes, you have got some doubts or suspicions that we are not the incarnations of Vallabhacharya. But you are free to take your *kanthi** and touch the feet of Vallabhacharyas's portrait, we do not want to come between you and Vallabhacharya."

'You see, from 1941 to 1951 I was a member of the Communist Party and so many of my Communist friends used to come to my house in those days. And my wife used to perform her worship, sprinkling colours on her idol and so on. My Communist friends, in a very mocking tone, said to her, "Why are you doing this nonsense? As if God were yours only and not others' – God is everybody's, so how can God play Holi, the spring festival, only with you? Why not with us?"

'So she replied, "But *my* God will play at the spring festival or join in my joy that it is spring only with me, not with you."

* A bead necklace of religious significance.

175

'"Why only with you? Why not with us? Do you deny that he is almighty, that he is the Lord of all the universe?"

'"I accept that God might be the Lord of the universe, I even accept that he is everyone's. But my relationship with my God is not of that kind. My God is just like a child, he is a baby, he is my personal child. Just like a judge or the president of a state has also got some personal relations – his wife might be there, his children might be there, his friends might be there – so I have got this family relationship with my God. Because I never regard him as almighty; this child-God, how will he help me in my calamity? I will help him in his calamity."

'He was her personal God – that was her experience. It was an absurd answer according to modern theory, but to that absurd answer my friends hadn't got any reply.

'My wife told them, "If you are near God, this democracy and socialism is not correct. Daily I am reading in the newspapers their misuse. My God never created concentration camps. My God never invented those modern, scientific ways to torture a particular human being. Or put some innocent fellows to death because they are not actually obeying their orders in the name of socialism and democracy. I am not harming you. If you don't want, or if you hate, my way, have no connection with me. Let me do my work; you do your work."

'When they expelled me from the Communist Party in '51, I started preparing flower garlands for her God. I started that in '48, about three years before they expelled me. I did it to begin with only to appease my wife. I had no belief in that faith, but . . . I prepared these for her for about four years; after that, what happened to me I don't know, but it is my experience that if, due to some work, I could not prepare that day's garlands, I felt a kind of uneasiness as if I had not slept for two days or had not eaten food or something – some sort of emptiness within me as if my preparing these garlands for her god had something to do . . . I don't know . . .

'It was also said by one of my Gurus that, "You are reading all these books and those thoughts are torturing you, so I advise you to prepare garlands for her god if you can't do the worship – it will only take half an hour. Buy flowers for fifty paisas and prepare two or three garlands for her god." I was going to the Guru because of my wife.

'I can tell you that the very centre of this religion is to establish a human relationship with that idol . . . The relationship can be that of child and mother or that of friends – with the Guru and with the idol. The followers of the Gurus call them child – "Baba" means child. They even call a fellow of twenty or twenty-five or fifty – Baba. Shyam Baba is my Guru's son. His name means, "Shyam Baba who is a child." His father is my Guru; that is, he gave me diksha as a child. But Shyam Baba is my friend and it is to him that I would be more likely to go if I had a question. For about four or five years, actually, I have not been going to the father and I ask all my questions of Shyam Baba. First he is my Guru, but I am also free to see my Guru as a child, or as a Lord, or as my beloved, even, or my father or my child, so I have chosen this way. I give him all my respect and all the marks of respect that are due to him; but still he is my friend.

'If we are going on a journey and we will not be able to perform all the rites during our travelling period, I will ask the Guru in what way we should take the god with us, how we should manage that, since our god must be looked after during the travelling period as if we were taking our own child with us. So he will suggest a certain way of doing it, perhaps to take a box, make some holes in it, put some mattresses in it, so that the god can travel. These are the things my wife used to ask, practical questions. I don't know about other sects but, you see, we have a lot of improvisation in the way we should worship. Suppose it is summer, a summer day, we will prepare a small pool and then we will put a small boat on it; then we will put our idol in that boat, only because in summer that's a nice way to . . . But it is our improvisation. Sometimes we are worried whether that kind of improvisation will be suitable for our god or not, and then we go to the Gurus. And he might say, "Whatever you are improvising is all right," or he advises, "Why are you taking so much trouble – why are you not just spreading the scent of roses instead of all this?"

'Concerning our personal affairs, too, we might ask. Guru was regarded not only as Guru, but the custom is maintained in certain Gujerati as well as other families that he is regarded as a member of the family. This relationship is established so we can have no hesitation in discussing our personal problems. But business problems are of a different nature; they were not of very much importance in former days, though nowadays when we are living in an industrialized, commercial society these things are becoming more important day by day. But formerly it was not a very important problem. In no way can God help you materially . . .

'When we first meet the Guru, it may cross our mind to think that he is a man and yet is more than a man – that may cross our mind for a moment. When we greet him and bow to him, it will be in our minds. After that, he will put his hand on my shoulder – "Oh, Nandu, you've come after so many days . . ."

'At the beginning, I even found accepting the Guru difficult. For a long time, I could not actually accept this habit of touching their feet. I used to just go there; but I found that they had no prejudices. Even in Christianity you will find that the Father will say that the Jew is a bad fellow. At least I found out that these fellows are free from such nonsense.

'So when I first went to them, I had reservations about them. I thought like that, that they would be splendid and important . . . But when God is a human being, then he must act like a human being. When God is actually acting in a human way, like Sita or Ram or . . . Why should the Guru not be a human being?'

Another member of the flock, very different from the first: we meet on the top, seventh floor of a wide windowed block of flats. The doorways are littered with the abandoned sandals of those within, corridors are full of servants, wives, daughters, sons-in-law, sons, grandsons, great-grandsons. The man I have come to meet is wealthy, one who has owned a business and retired from it. Now he is seventy-eight years old and holding respected court through his declining years. He is stout, with fine white hair, in a shirt of embroidered lawn and a crisp white dhoti. Beyond his spectacles he has one blind, wall eye; the other is fading as a cataract descends.

He is eager to teach and preach, to deliver those endless homilies, those moralizing generalities, which seem to make the old and rich so happy, particularly in India where every ortho-dox ancient is expected to develop some of the signs of sanctity.

The room to which he takes me overlooks roofs and the sea, leaden today under slow and thickening clouds. He sits grate-fully in the one well upholstered chair, smiles faintly at the advantages of age. Coffee is brought in by a silent servant in vest and khaki shorts. The old man sips, nods at me, asks me about myself; there is no point, he says, in talking seriously until he knows whom he is talking to. Finally, perhaps satisfied about my intellectual, if not my spiritual, *bona fides*, he settles to exposi-tion.

'In the sect to which I belong, the Guru must belong to a par-ticular family. But, you know, what person of that particular family should be accepted by me is open to me. I can pick any-one I like. And why is it traditionally so? Because these Gurus are expected to live a particular holy life all the time and for generations together. They have to understand their own religion, they have to understand their own philosophy;

therefore, through their powers they can give a push to those that they accept. If I make a bad choice, well, I make a bad choice; but after the push, I can continue in my own way. I can evolve in my own way. Now, the selection of a Guru is also very difficult. But, you know, we have to take certain chances also in the case of our marriage.

'When I was a young man, I had certain doubts and then I slowly came to realize . . . But I never consulted the Guru. I was accepted in Rajasthan by one Guru whom I didn't meet at all later on, who didn't take any particular special care of me to see what life I was living; the religious ideas were put, the religious way of thinking was put, but I could get talks only from the talks of other Gurus who were there belonging to the family. One of them is the one whose photograph is there [he indicates it]. He wasn't my Guru, I didn't take my . . . But he belonged to the same family. In his life, you know, I came more in touch and I could understand more, without his, you know, preaching about it: from his life, from the life that he was leading, from the lives of his followers. You see, that was the position; they don't help everybody, you know, but they give something so that people who have faith in the words of the Guru can follow their lives like that. And then they evolve and they get much out of it and they understand much of the philosophy of the religion.

'We take two dikshas. The first means that I'm a Vaishnavite belonging to a particular class. Then I take the higher diksha (*brahman-samand*) in which my contact with my Lord, with my Guru, with my God, you may call it, with the High Spirit, call him Brahman – has been established by my Guru. He has helped me to establish that and in his presence I dedicate myself completely to my Lord. That is the diksha. And now I can say that I belong to him – I have the right claim over my Lord. I can serve him. And I can say, "Look here, don't look at me, look at your Guru. Your Guru is your representation

here, and because he has accepted me, you cannot reject me."
That I may claim from my Lord however bad I may be.

'Although I accepted the Guru who gave me diksha in
Rajasthan as my Guru, I never revered him as my Guru. I think
of him as my Guru; but all the other Gurus, that whole family
of those Gurus born of Vallabhacharya, whenever I see them I
give my reverence to them. And when the Guru gives me that
diksha, *he* does not give it, he says, "In the name of my ancestor,
I am here requesting God to accept your soul who has come to
you."

'When I go to any Guru, say any member of the Vallabhacharya family, I usually bow down to him though he may be a
child . . . I shouldn't feel ashamed of it at all because I don't
respect him for knowledge, I respect him for the root-person; I
may even call him my prophet. So that's what I'm expected to
do. More than that is not expected from me unless I want to
have a closer contact. That's a different thing, if I want it. But
they never expect anything from me. They expect that we are to
go our own way; "We have accepted you, and you go by that
way and find your own way." If you have doubts, you go to
them and they will show you the right way; and they might show
you the way that will suit you.

'Usually, one would not take a problem in ordinary life to
them because very often we don't give them the credit of having
worldly knowledge, you know. All my difficulties from the spiritual point of view I can put before them and they can give me a
reply. But the relationship between Guru and shishya in the
Vallabhacharya is very educative. Mind, they are not sannyasis –
they are living the life of a family so they know more about it.
And they have their own temples. And they also give you an idol
to worship so that you can keep yourself in complete touch all
the time with the divinity. If I am prepared to give my life to
God, then I will serve that idol.

'Well, I'm an idolater . . . You know, usually to explain to an outsider we say it's a symbol on which we concentrate and see the spiritual beyond. But if you were to ask me I'd say that, no, I don't consider it a symbol. I consider it my God. The moment the idol seems symbol, the godliness in him goes out. I never think of what material it's made. When I am meditating, when I look at it, I am looking at my Lord and I see it in a different way than you see it. I will not think of anything else. And I and my idol, or my God, we are in tune with each other, we love each other. And this sect teaches your love and your relationship towards God. When I bow down, I am thinking completely that I am bowing down to my God. I am not bowing down to an idol. I am in complete touch with him, losing, within a fraction of a second, myself. And when I lose myself, with whom am I in touch but him? This is the yogic side of this, or the samadhi side of it.

'We have to meditate on our God. We have to think of him all the time. And, automatically we are thinking, "This is the time when my God wants this". I'm always thinking of him. And I must reserve some time to meditate over it. Not meditate with a view to getting knowledge, not to go into samadhi and to find out something about . . . But to meditate on my love. And who does not meditate if you are in love with somebody? All the time you will be thinking what she may be doing. Or all the time she may be thinking what you are doing, and that's how you are in touch with each other. And the person who lives all his life for his God until the end of his life, thinking of him as the nearest person, the nearest relation, would he not reach a state which would be very high?'

Goswami Sri Shyam Manoharji is, as he will tell me, of the sixteenth generation in direct descent from Vallabhacharya. He is a Guru, lifelong and inescapable, divine because his ancestors were divine. He is a bulky man in his thirties, six feet or more in height, wrapped in the white muslin coils, rice-paper thin, of a

South Indian dhoti, its end draped across his pale, fleshy shoulders. His heavy cheeks are covered, when we first meet, with four or five days' growth of beard, his hair is fairly long and looks unkempt; it is a deep black but just touched with grey above his ears and at the nape of his neck. His eyes are slightly bulbous with heavy lids and strange, spiky lashes, but they gleam with the expectation of friendship. His nose is strong, a little hooked, his lips thick and slightly pushed out by his pointed and protuberant incisors. His chin is set rather back from his mouth, is small and round, in some way hinting at possible weakness yet stubborn at the same time. On his wrist he wears a steel faced, steel braceleted watch, on his feet *chappals*, or sandals, of tooled leather. "Baba" means child, baby, and because he is the young Guru, with a father and an uncle still active in his branch of the family, he is called Shyam Baba.

His manner is at times exuberant, at times reflective. He smiles a great deal, now and then laughs, yet gives the impression of a sincere man deeply troubled by the role he must play; a little like a prince unsure of the value of royalty. He has been under pressure to wear Western clothes but, perhaps precisely because of his inner uncertainties, he refuses to do so.

He clings to the clothes tradition prescribes, I feel, because he is afraid that, should he ever change into the Western shirt and trousers, it will be for good. Each time he wears them they indicate his conscious choice to be what he was born to be. If and when he takes them off, it will be only once, and what he exchanges them for will indicate new decisions, another lifestyle. He is too honest, too simple, perhaps in some ways too good a man to camouflage himself or move through his city under false colours. Should the time ever come when he buys a Western suit, that will be for him a proclamation of freedom and of abdication. I sense at the same time, perhaps, a subtle, willed martyrdom. The ridicule he excites on occasion emphasizes the incongruity of his role in the modern world and the absurdity of the clothes that symbolize it; it may seem to him that, though he is its focus, it is really directed at all the dead generations for whom he wears these robes.

In the Vallabhacharya tradition, the sect's temple is within the walls of his family's home. At first sight this building seems enormous, a place of ancient courtyards and passages, an Indian Gormenghast – all stone floors, carved balustrades black with age and dirt, sudden, wooden-ceilinged corridors. Then, opening like a shout, a hall, a silver Guru's throne in it faced by three upholstered chairs. And Shyam Baba stands in the doorway, looks uncertainly around.

'Here my grandfather used to preach. Now . . .' He peers helplessly about him; his eyes look almost dazed behind their spiky lashes. 'We don't know . . . We don't use it for anything.'

To reach the Gurus' building, one passes under an archway which pierces a high wall, then crosses a large forecourt surrounded by other houses and fed by alleyways and smaller yards. Trees and creepers cover these façades. At the head of a narrow wooden stairway runs a gallery and beyond that the enormous, gloomy audience hall. Around its walls hang portraits, stylized and hieratically stiff, of Vallabhacharya and Vittalhnath and the early Gurus. A young lad passes us, moving from one garlanded picture to another, touching each one then kissing his fingertips. A young woman in a dark sari comes up to Shyam Baba, bends, touches his feet and moves away.

It is odd to watch this, a gesture of devotion so common in India. Later and elsewhere it will be done to me several times, probably on the safety first principle that someone so much in the company of sadhus must have been pollinated by their virtue, despite the unlikelihood and total lack of evidence that this is so. Some sadhus bless, lift up those saluting, murmur almost as if embarrassed. Shyam Baba keeps still, looks away; it is as if his feet have momentarily developed a quality over which he has no control but which provokes an endless, mildly astonishing devotion from all these people. It is as if for that moment his feet are not his own, as one's finger is not when one offers it to a baby for a plaything.

Then on into the building – unexpected turnings, panelled walls, sudden grilles and doors, glimpses of rough, tiled roofs, galleries, then stairs of ancient wood, each step striated with age, powdering into dust. Rooms are bare, often enormous, but with no more furniture than a great wardrobe, perhaps, and a folding chair; or a worn carpet, a shelf or two, and on the wall a picture of blue-faced Krishna. Here and there, people sit or stand; or hurry, whispering, down some long gallery and out of sight.

We overlook at last the central courtyard, where the green painted temple stands open for the faithful. On its wall the painted figures in shallow relief of tense lions watchfully wait to prevent the idol of Lord Krishna from leaving, Shyam Baba says. On a roofed balcony, framed by thin, gracefully carved columns, a man stands with his left leg crossed over the right and its ankle resting on the rail; without speech or movement he watches us go by. Another, an old man whose lined face has the fierceness of a mountain brigand, turns suddenly from conversation and the small curved dagger at his side swings with the movement. Below, huddled women sing a raucous devotional song while others, men amongst them, crowd for the darshan of the god. Shyam Baba stands beside me, shrugs.

'They are here; but in our sect they should worship at home . . .'

I am taken to a small room, ducking under a curtain to go in. To the right of the door is a bed with two mattresses on it. Behind that, a window covered with brown paper. In the back of the room stand two fans, not needed now in Bombay's December. Against the wall opposite the bed stands an enormous white refrigerator.

On the bed half sits, half lies a round, old man, his head almost completely bald. This is Goswami Sri Dixitji Maharaj, the father of Goswami Shyam. The old man has been very ill for a number of years and spends most of his time here. He sits up now, crosses his legs, holds a cushion between knees and belly for comfort. Beside the door, an attendant in shirt and trousers waits.

'Ask my father questions,' Shyam Baba says, preparing to translate.

We begin to talk; now and then the father laughs, turning his head towards the young man at the door; when he does so his lips form a circle and his whole, almost featureless face, seems to converge upon this small, sudden opening, so that he seems all mouth. At other times, he looks round as if for approval as he explains some doctrinal point. While we talk, an old man then two women come in, touch his feet, tuck money or a gift under the cloth he sits on. He hands them a *prasad* (literally 'grace', an indication of the Guru's favour) of *pan*, the little green package of betel leaf and spices. The visitors touch the feet of his son then go out. No one makes any move to pick up the money; the attendant will do that later. Goswami Dixitji looks at me almost slyly as the first of these devotees leaves: 'There you see the practical side of the Guru-chela relationship,' he says. The little mouth rounds and gapes, the high laughter takes over the room. But later, he loses his patience with me; he wants to discuss doctrine, philosophy, metaphysics, history, not the mundane facts of Guru existence which is what I want to hear first.

'Ideally, the Guru exists in order to pass the divine on to the chela. He opens the way to the divine. How that differs from what happens in practice it is better not to ask! [He laughs and nods about him.] It was different in my father's time. Then there were people who believed, who wanted to learn. Now! . . .

186

Too much love of pleasure, too much greed for money. Now people don't have time for these things.

'A true devotee or a true follower would expect today the same as would have been expected ages ago. And a true Guru would help him as far as his powers allow him to help him. But the majority, ninety-five per cent, are not to be taken as an ideal example of this relationship. What I saw in the time of my father I can't see nowadays in the devotion of people and in the ideal life of Gurus. Ultimately, a follower would expect to realize the truth of God and of divinity – that is what a shishya may expect from the Guru – but this expectation has become mistaken in the present circumstances. I don't mean to say that there is a total absence, you might find one or two examples of this, but the rest . . .

'I confess that I can only pass on the knowledge of the true principles of religion; I have no other ability. [He laughs.] And whatever I know of the means to remove our heredity, remove that misery, I help them to remove, both in a practical and in a spiritual way. There are some sorts of misery which can only be removed in a spiritual way. Sometimes, too, someone with a practical difficulty, something wrong with their marriage or something, comes to me for advice. First I try to understand the circumstances, and then I try to help.

'People from other castes and creeds can come here as disciples. It does happen. I personally know four or five examples of Europeans and Christians and Parsis . . . a Muslim boy . . . In that way we are quite open hearted.

'I have been lying on a bed for seven or ten years. But whenever I feel well I give discourses regularly in the evening, in that big hall. People come and have a glimpse at the Guru and show their reverence. As a matter of fact, in our sect particularly, the religious duties ought not to be performed in our house, but under our guidance they have to perform their religious duties in their own homes. That's our tradition. So, as a matter of fact, that sort of . . . as you have in churches, that sort of thing is not here. Of course, people do not observe those religious duties in their own homes. Instead of performing those duties in their own homes they come here and have the darshan of the deities that we serve and which we worship, but that is not an ideal solution. We allow it because of our own lack of conviction and they come because of a lack of conviction in them. But that is not ideal, they must worship God in their own home as if God were their own child. That was the ideal way of worshipping, but nowadays people do not observe this.

'Teaching is imparted . . . As a matter of fact, teaching should be imparted because our ideal solution was that we should remain busy always in the worship of God, and when we are not worshipping in the intervals, we should teach our . . . or preach to our followers. That was the ideal of teaching. But you see, what happens now is that even when we do not worship all day as we ought to, we generally preach to them in the evening which was the normal time of preaching. Teaching exists only in that way.

'With certain limitations, the Guru is worshipped as a means of reaching divinity itself. In action and behaviour one would know the Guru is not divine but emotionally this is not the case. Emotionally you should have the sentiment that the Guru is an absolutely divine being, but in behaviour and in action you must behave as if the Guru is not divine . . . and is divine also. That means to a certain extent the Guru is a human being and to a certain extent the Guru has some divine personality, too. You behave in such a way. But emotionally, you must feel such emotion that the Guru is absolutely divine.

'We don't have meditation, we have only worship, a worship full of, so to say, earthly love towards God. After all, there must be some spark of divinity in that love also; but apparently it is a most earthly love towards God.

'Just by a contact to induce a divine sentiment in the disciple, that is the privilege of the founder acharya, Vallabhacharya, and his sons and his grandsons; and some of the others. It is a rare gift. If God gives us such a gift we also can do it, not otherwise. Either from God – or from the founder acharya.

'In our practice, however, we do not have people who renounce the world. Some commentators say that, because we don't have this apparent renunciation, therefore we are some sort of "drink, eat and enjoy" sect. This is not the actual situation. You have to give up everything at the level of emotion, and not at the level of outward behaviour and action. Because if you know the essential meaning of our diksha, in that diksha we say that we are emotionally renouncing everything to the lotus feet of God, and that we are the servants of God. So it is there sentimentally; emotional renunciation is there and must be there because it is said that unless you have that sort of emotion, unless you renounce the worldly emotion, you can't have the emotion of God in you. All your natural tendencies should be sublimated to the level of divinity. If you are erotic, be erotic for God. If you are greedy, make some sort of contact between your greed and God. That sort of psychology we have.

'The first step, if you are a shishya, is that you should come with all curiosity about the divinity. And then you should be a disciple and you should follow the path as the Guru preaches it to you. How you come to it and how you search is immaterial – the main thing is that you should follow his preaching and you should practise it. If you have any sort of doubts or any inconvenience in this religious practice, then you can come and iron it out. But the responsibility to make real contact between Guru and shishya is to some extent divided half and half. The Guru makes an effort to have contact, close contact, with the shishyas. And to a certain extent the shishyas should make an effort to have close contact with the Guru.'

When I leave, Sri Dixitji Maharaj reaches out both hands,

lays them on my head. Bending, I smile, sweat, feel nothing but a faint embarrassment. Nevertheless I am grateful for the kindliness of the gesture – I had thought him irritated with me. I back out of the room, past the grinning attendant.

Goswami Shyam's own room is not large but narrow, rather dark; as one walks in, ancient wood seems to enfold one. At the far end of the room there is a long window with dark-rimmed panes each decorated with a pale, chased design. From the crackling and industrious lane below there rise the sounds of radios, street criers, gossip, craftsmen at work, bargains being struck. On the wall to the left of the window hangs a picture of Shyam Baba's great-grandfather doing puja on his birthday. Above and beside the window hangs another picture – an idealized and haloed version of Vallabhacharya himself. The picture slopes out from the wall; the tiny, real garland round the Master's neck, blue and red and yellow, hangs vertically into the room. In the light from the window stands a large drum. It is obvious that the Goswami uses it as a work table – there are books and manuscripts spread on it and a blue, metal folding chair behind it. A half partition divides the room; beside it are two metal chests covered with books and more books stand in piles beside them. More books still, in Hindi and Sanskrit and English, make neat rows on the shelves of five glass fronted cabinets. In the front of one of these stands a volume of Bertrand Russell's autobiography, his picture on the jacket incongruously gleaming from the shadows. Over a line strung across the room, a white dhoti hangs, drying. On the floor not far from the door is a strip of comfortable carpet, a pillow at one end – the Goswami's bed. Above it hangs a picture of Krishna and Rahda; a copy of one of the royal nudes from the Ajunta Caves leans against the wall.

He talks of these paintings, shows me a book in which more are reproduced. 'Oh, they are very nice, they are charming. Look at this line, how powerful. And look, the royal personages are all nude. Only the servants have clothes on.'

We discuss the rise of science and scientism in the West. He laughs. 'You know, you have Galileo – so we also have Galileo. About a thousand years ago we have a scholar who produces this idea of the heliocentric universe, but nobody takes any notice! They say, "There is no mention of it in the Scriptures so it cannot be true." They think him a good scholar . . . but a little mistaken only. They have made no trouble; it is just not written in the Scriptures so it cannot be true.'

We settle cross-legged on the floor. A young man puts his head through the door and asks a question; there is to be a concert in the inner courtyard this evening and preparations have to be made. The young man makes that swift to and fro gesture of the head that means acquiescence in India, and withdraws. Goswami Sri Shyam Manoharji turns, smiling, back to me.

'Generally in the Hindu tradition we think that any person who teaches or preaches anything is to be considered as Guru. Nowadays in some cases the idea of Guru involves the idea of his divinity, the idea of worship of the Guru. When we consider Guru, sometimes all these sorts of hyperbole will be there . . . But actually, Guru also knows that he is not God or the exclusive representative of God . . . Sometimes, some persons have some sort of revelation in themselves and then they declare themselves and claim for themselves that they are . . . represent themselves as divinity. But otherwise, you see, Guru knows he's not representative of God and shishya also knows; but even then in the *Upanishads*, you know, we have a symbolic worship, so that morning is God and star is God. You know quite well that star is not God or morning is not God but even so you have to concentrate upon morning as if it were God. You don't have symbolic worship in the West. We have a very long tradition of symbolic worship so we can actually grasp the idea of how to symbolize.

'In our sect we are direct descendents of Vallabhacharya and

191

I'm the sixteenth generation from him. We are born acharyas, so to say; we don't have to qualify ourselves in any way. The moment we are born we become acharyas. But even then, Vallabhacharya has clearly laid down some of the qualifications of Guru, particularly for our sect, and there is the consideration of all our qualifications; we must be from the secular point of view a just man, and from the scriptural point of view a righteous man; and from our sectarial point of view Vallabhacharya actually lays down three conditions to be a Guru: he says that he must be a staunch worshipper of Krishna, he must not be a hypocrite in this worshipping and he must know the essential doctrine of the message of *Bhagwan* [God]; these are the three conditions of a sectarian Guru. That does not deny the other qualifications, that he must follow the scriptures thoroughly or that he must be a just man from the worldly point of view also, but from the sect point of view these are the qualifications. So these are our obligations. We are supposed to take training in all these matters but because we are born acharyas sometimes we take and sometimes we do not take. You see, from childhood people treat you as somehow extraordinary.

'In our sect, it is a point of dispute whether other persons can become a Guru or acharya or not. But as the tradition exists there is only one outside case: the son of Vallabhacharya adopted an outsider and asked him to preach and teach our sect; they are not direct descendants of Vallabhacharya but they are Gurus in our sect. Otherwise all the Gurus in our sect are descendants of Vallabhacharya. We have no qualification to make you a Guru in our sect. But this is a disputed point, let me tell you. You see, Vallabhacharya lays down the condition that if you do not find your sad-Guru then you should make your effort your own self because God is always there – he will help you . . . So it is not strictly true that Vallabhacharya only is Guru, but all the commentators have put great emphasis on the conception that Vallabhacharya is the Guru in our sect and that we are the door to the Guru as Vallabhacharya is the door to the God; so we consider Vallabhacharya is the sole Guru.

'Actually, it is there in the history of our sect that Vallabhacharya was not ready to marry; he was to lead this celibate life. And then God actually told him, "You marry so that your descendants may propagate your sect," so then later on he married. So it is considered for the propagation of his own sect that he married and not for the other consideration of life; because his intention was simply to live a life of celibacy.

'Being born into this family there is a compulsion, so to say, to propagate this doctrine. But there is argument nowadays that if a Guru is not involved in such matters why should we consider him as a Guru although he is born into the family of Vallabhacharya. If he is not propagating the sect or if he is not taking any interest in our sect, why should we consider him as a Guru? Because that was the sole purpose of the marriage of Vallabhacharya. That sort of discussion is going on in our sect, you see. It started quite a long time ago, fifty or a hundred years ago, but still it is going on.

'My shishya will be anybody who is attracted toward me and who is traditionally following our sect. Now, for instance, the shishya of my father, the son of the shishya of my father will be a shishya of mine. He will naturally say, "As I am the shishya of the father, my son will be shishya of . . ." It makes no difference. First they receive diksha from us. We have actually two dikshas in our sect. We give them the first diksha at a very early age, infant age, even, at just one month or two months. Later on, when he becomes able to utter, he decides he will take the second diksha. In the first diksha we only utter our diksha mantra in the ear of the infant three times. At the second diksha we put the *tulsi* plant in the hand and then we make him utter our diksha mantra and then that tulsi is offered at the feet of the Lord; that is how we give them dikshas. And after that he will consider me as his Guru. We go through it too. My uncle gave me that diksha. So he's my Guru, not my father. But as I told you, I am of the opinion that nowadays we should put more emphasis on Vallabhacharya so I don't consider my uncle as a Guru although I considered him Guru for five or six years. But the last five or six years I have come to the opinion that I don't consider him as my Guru. I haven't declared to him. "I don't consider you as my Guru," but I have developed the idea that he is not my Guru. My Guru is Vallabhacharya. And for those five or six years I have not given diksha to anyone . . . for some other reasons. Second diksha – I'm giving first diksha but I'm not giving second diksha to anyone. There are so many reasons. If you want to know them that will require a special discussion. [He laughs.]

'Nowadays it has become merely a mode of practice so we just give them diksha in a purely verbal way and they just take it in a verbal way and afterwards they just start coming in temple and touching our feet or this and that . . . And the real source of spirituality is not there. Spiritual feeling is not there. Spiritual intimacy is not there.

'Theoretically, the duty to teach must be there. Because Vallabhacharya was going once on a journey and there was a serpent lying at the roadside and the ants were biting him. So Vallabhacharya said, "This is a Guru who wasn't actually able to liberate his followers so he has become a serpent and the ants are his followers – so they are now punishing him because he could not liberate them from the world." So you can know what Vallabhacharya wanted to suggest by this symbolic narration.

'But that is liberation in our sectarian sense which is a total intimacy with God. We don't believe in merging into God but we believe in total intimacy, such intimacy that God becomes as friendly to us as you and I are talking with each other. That sort of intimacy with God should be developed. And we have so many forms of intimacy – lover and beloved, mother and child, two friends. This means that the emotions must also be attached to the intimacy between God and us.

'In our sect I'm not so optimistic, as a matter of fact, as to think there is really any way of reviving the real function of the Guru. After considering all the realities of the present age I think that the reins have gone out of our hands. I don't know what will happen in the future. I am agnostic in that sense. [He laughs.] I think that it will never come again in our hands.

'As a matter of fact, we have what you might call a Pope in our sect and we also have Cardinals. But these posts are not so potent in the sense of authority. They are posts really for the sake of posts and nothing else – authority is not there. All the descendants of Vallabhacharya have the same authority for interpretation or for anything else in our sect. Of all the priests of our sect I think my father is the most learned man. By that he has a special respect and status. I don't think that I will be having that status or respect. [He laughs a little.] Because I am neither working in that direction nor at present have any clear defined goal before me.

'You see, the responsibilities that are upon me – I may refuse them. But I am not so optimistic when I find that things are not going as they should go. I think . . . why should I be involved in that? That is . . . I don't know what will happen. I am just struggling in my own way and I don't know what will be the future. Because, you see, I have come to realize that everyone in our sect is a walking ghost. This makes me afraid, all are walking ghosts. So . . . I don't know what can be the future or walking ghosts. [He laughs.] Ghosts are as eternal as death. You can destroy a living man but you can't destroy a ghost.

'At present I am doing M.A. in philosophy. I am specializing in the philosophy of Vallabhacharya (that is our own philosophy) and Bertrand Russell . . . [At my surprise at the spectrum this covers, he laughs.] But I love Russell very much. I don't accept his ideas at my sectarian level because I take that level as the most personal thing. After reading Russell I was changing only my belief but not my faith. I think that my faith is permanent, as it were, but of course Russell has changed many of the beliefs.

'No, even in mythology you'll find so many characters who challenge God. They were atheist. And even in *Rig Veda* you find a very nice statement and it says, "Who knows from where this process of the world comes and who knows where it goes? Does he who directs it know it or not?" So the *Veda* is doubtful whether the Lord is omniscient. [He laughs.] "Whether he knows it or not"; a very beautiful idea is there. And even in the *Mahabharata* you'll find so many characters who challenge God. It's all the sense that he is God omnipotent and they are jealous . . . We also say, "If you are dependent on God it is a mere shallow worship, but if God depends on you it is a true worship."

'You see, we have a story: a logician who was famous for his arguments proving the existence of God – very similar arguments are given by Thomas Aquinas in the ninth or eighth century – once went to the temple and the temple doors were closed. And then he abused God, saying, "You are too proud of yourself. I came to have a glimpse of you and your doors are closed. What do you think of yourself? Your existence is dependent on my argument!" [He laughs.] And it is said that then the doors opened!

'If you look at the life of Vallabhacharya you will find many disciples living with him alone all the time who have different sorts of experiences. And that depends on the personal relationship between Guru and shishya, you know; not the official or institutional relationship. If some of my disciples agree with my personality they can come and live with me, if I am able to allow them to . . . As a matter of fact, in our sect, we have too much intimacy but that intimacy has no formality. Ceremonial formality is not there. When they get married we are invited, we go and we bless them, and that's meaningless in this context. Or every day they come and have a glimpse of our idol and then they touch our feet and we bless them and . . . it's meaningless. You can theoretically do without it. Now, the second son of Vallabhacharya had some lady from the harem of Akbar the Great and she was never allowed to go outside the harem but yet she was following – I don't know how she managed it – but she was following our path.

'If you go to the other side there are so many formal . . . so much ceremonial formality between Guru and shishya. That sort of ceremonial formality is not there between us and our disciples, but intimacy you'll find to a great extent, which has its own good and bad side. Some time ago this intimacy had a bad result on some of the illiterate tribal areas where we have our followers. They considered the Guru himself as the Lord and so many . . . bad relations between the female followers and the Gurus were there. That sort of thing is due particularly to that sentiment.

'There has also been one case: the Maharaj libel case, if you have come across it; the Maharaja was charged that, "When you give the second diksha you actually have sexual relations with the ladies." But that was not right; it was a misunderstanding about our sect. Of course it existed and it existed even then, but that exists only when Gurus are not conscious or when shishyas are not conscious. This sentiment has some good advantages as well as bad advantages.

'It's a danger only because we say it is not a good way to achieve divine sexuality, so to say; this sexuality is also to be sublimated to the level of divinity. So if you always get some of this sex, the worldly sex, you are bound to lose some of the divine sexuality. I am not using the proper word but I can convey some idea by the word, "divine sexuality". So you have to make your sexuality also divine and when you are using the worldly sexuality it may disturb your mood, that is why it is prohibited, prohibited in the sense that you have to sublimate and let it loose in worldly affairs. Neither do you have to destroy it, you need not destroy your sexuality but you have to sublimate it. Be sexual towards God, in a sense. That is what we think, so if you just remain in the worldly sexuality it may be a hindrance to making your sexuality divine. That's why it's prohibited and when it's prohibited that has to be followed. That prohibition has to be followed. So that's why there is danger. Otherwise, sex itself is not so much danger. But a limit is put there and when that limit is transgressed you are doing something wrong.

'In a word, I can tell you this: Vallabhacharya says that whatever you like, whatever temperament you have, just with a little sense of the divinity of the idol, you can divert all your tendencies and temperament towards the idol and then you will be divine. Whatever attracts you, whatever enchants you, just try and sublimate it at the level of God. Suppose you like painting, try to paint how God might have . . . These are all examples of that tendency. Have you seen all the paintings there are of Krishna? I will show you. You might be shocked . . . We never think that this is sex. There was a European critic who borrowed these paintings and the next day he returned them and said, "These are nothing but sex." Then our old pandit was perplexed and said, "You can't understand us and we can't understand you because we don't have the notion that God is always omnipotent and omniscient and we are always sinful. We sometimes have a sexual relationship with God, we sometimes have . . . We can have all sorts of relationships with God so we don't think in the terms that you are thinking – that there is nothing but sex. We see there is everything."

'All the mode of worship is arranged in that way only, that your passion will grow step by step. In such a way only, the mode of worship is arranged. The different sentimental poems are recited with sentimental songs and *ragas* and melodies, the particular melodies which may suit to the season and the time of the day and to narrating the events of Krishna's life; while in the act of singing we have to worship God so that our passion

grows step by step, to that level that you must become a . . .
Romeo . . . You must become a Romeo of God! And when you
become the Romeo of God, that is the highest level. Then you
don't care for anything. For worldly thing or scripture. You
don't care even for . . . You reach to that height, to such an
extreme sentiment of love with God; that is the highest state
and we call it . . . intoxication. That is the highest thing. When
you reach to the intoxication level of love, you are God, Vallabhacharya says. You have done whatever you can do. That's
where you have to reach. And any sentiment, any passion,
which may help you in reaching that stage, that should be
taken.'

In the silver throned hall, bare and dusty, the metal speckled
by corrosion, I am introduced to a bald uncle, tall, his lips
scarlet with betel juice. We talk about artists, since the uncle
paints, and about the house, built by Shyam Baba's great-great-
grandfather, a pearl merchant, owner of five vessels, a rupee
millionaire who is said to have lent large sums to the British (a
claim often made by today's generation for a wealthy ancestor,
as if wealth had nothing more ostentatious in its repertoire than
lending to the lords of all – which is probably the case). In the
father's sick room, a light is on, gleaming behind closed doors. I
hurry on, retrieve my sandals, walk out into the seething city.
The small shops are lit and crowded on a Friday evening; at the
tailor's, men work late, framed by children's clothes which hang
about them like red and yellow climbing plants. I pass a dyer's,
a seller of oil stoves, a shop filled with sheets of aluminium,
another garish with plastic buckets.

'Ghee and Butter – Imported Goods', says a sign. I look in
at the barber's where three men sit in a row, each leaning
patiently to the left to accommodate the razor. In the chemist's,
small glass jars gleam yellow, ochre, aquamarine, cobalt; while
across the road, spices lie in white and brown and yellow heaps.

At the street corner, a boy holds a tray supported by one wooden strut; he sells plastic toys displayed in racks and from these racks, tugging at their strings, balloons lift to beguile children with their round, reflected light.

THE SECTARIAN GURU: THE SWAMINARAYANAS

It was in the year 1800 that the great Guru, Swami Ramananda, a follower of the philosopher Ramanuja (who, he claimed, had initiated him in a dream), stepped aside to let his place be taken by a nineteen year old. 'I have only been clearing the way for him,' he is supposed to have said after their first meeting. 'He is to be the principal hero of the Lord's drama, for whose arrival I was waiting.' He followed the logic of this, some two years later, by ceding his position to the young man who was henceforth known as Swami Sahajanand.

In this dramatic way the first and founding Guru of the Swaminarayana sect stepped into the religious limelight. He seems to have been a man of compelling spiritual qualities; certainly, Swami Ramananda's followers appear to have had no serious doubts about the fitness of their new leader. Swami Sahajanand made reform his objective, a reform directed principally against the excesses, as he saw them, of the Vallabhacharya Gurus. He created a band of five hundred devotees, the founding saints of his continuing order of monks. They gave themselves up to a life of total austerity, yet at the same time managed to go outward to the needy, building almshouses, digging wells and doing charitable work.

His precepts, collected into a little book called *Shikshapatri*, prohibit murder, suicide, the eating of meat, the drinking of wine, self-mutilation, theft, adultery, gambling, drugs, tobacco, and the breaking of caste laws. He writes, 'None shall keep contact with those who hanker after women, and wealth, and practise sinful acts under the cloak of their hypocritical devotion and so-called wisdom.'

Another precept insists, 'None of my male devotees shall listen to discourses from the mouth of a woman nor shall enter into discussion with women, kings or their courtiers.'

Another says, 'None of my followers shall put on such a garment as is likely to expose any part of the body to view.'

He gives instructions about the hygienic and devotional activities of his followers, about how to combat afflictions due to an evil spirit, about behaviour during an eclipse, about how to greet the wise or reverent, about the respect due to the teacher. He puts restraints on the behaviour of wives; they 'shall serve their husbands, be they either blind or ailing or poor or impotent, in the manner in which they worship and serve God'. Some of these restraints remove them from temptation, while others prevent them from becoming a temptation to others; 'Devout wives shall not dress in a manner so as to expose their breasts, navel or thighs and thus attract the glance of males.' He makes particularly strict provision for the restrained behaviour of widows; he seems to see them as sexual tinder which might turn to flame under the merest spark: "They shall abstain from the touch of any male who may not be the nearest relative . . . These widow disciples shall take food only once a day and shall sleep on the floor and shall never witness animal postures in coition . . . The young widows shall never keep company in seclusion of young men, even if they are closely related to them, except under unforeseen circumstances . . .'

It may be imagined that the rules governing the ascetics, the monks, are most elaborately restrictive. Obviously they 'shall avoid all contacts or talks with females nor should they intentionally look at them', but they are never to talk about females, see pictures or statues of them – 'except those of Goddesses' – draw pictures of them themselves or touch their clothes. They are not to look at copulating animals. And 'they shall neither touch nor speak nor look at a man in the attire of a female'. They may even go against their Guru's orders if what he says threatens their celibacy. On the other hand, if it becomes a question of saving life, they are permitted to speak with and even touch a woman.

They are to conquer any taste they may have for good food. They are not to wear weapons or warlike clothes that might inspire fear. They may not sleep during the day, or at any time in a cot unless they are ill. They are to be patient with insults, are never to act as spies, may not hoard money, indulge in back-biting or act as eyewitnesses. Those who follow these precepts will attain liberation; those who do not will be excommunicated.

All this was written out and collected in 1826. From that time on it has been read daily, as is laid down in the book itself, by or to all the disciples of the sect. The severity of these injunc-tions did not prevent the spread of the sect, and from its strong-hold in Gujerat it has spread down the West Coast into Maharashtra and across the Indian Ocean to East Africa. Today, there is also a number of devotees among Indians in Britain.

Basically, Swami Sahajanand followed the philosophy of Ramanuja, that of visisht-advaita, which in very broad outline I have already described on page seven. An extra element in his thought, however, was the rather esoteric distinction he made between two aspects of Brahman, *akshara* and *purushottam*. The latter has been translated as 'highest of persons' and is con-sidered supreme over mankind. The former, translated as an abstract 'imperishable', is seen as the abode, the physical body, of purushottam, which thus becomes the highest level of god-hood. It is akshara (compared to which our cosmos is as an ant to an elephant) with which the devotee must make contact in order to serve at the feet of purushottam itself. In coming to be known as Swaminarayan, Swami Sahajanand accepted that he was him-self the incarnation of purushottam and is thus taken by his followers to have been a true avatar of God. This has given the sect a continuing intensity of devotion and supplied the spiritual power which has allowed generations of monks over nearly two centuries to live lives of such an extreme and restricted asceticism.

*

H. T. Davé is a man in late middle-age. He is above middle height, broad and well built. He gives a general impression of neatness and precision. His grey hair is clearly parted, his lips are firm, well defined. When he smiles they part to show small, even teeth. His eyes are small, though long, a little almond shaped. They are brown and clear and look out at one with a watchful friendliness. He has written several books about the Swaminarayana sect, notably *Life and Philosophy of Sri Swaminarayan*. 'This also,' he says, 'I owe to my Guru. I just sit down and I write. I studied commerce, I learned nothing of philosophy or anything like that. All comes from the Guru.'

He lives over a wild lane, a cornucopia of shops and tradesmen and smells and chatter and hammering and sawing and laughter, which flings at the visitor an endless profusion of wares and people. His small, neat apartment runs between two terraces on the second floor. We sit side by side on a black couch. On shelves around the room books stand, each covered in brown paper and carefully numbered. His wife covers her head when she sees me; later, we talk briefly about her son who has 're-nounced' and is now one of the sadhus of the sect. They show me his picture; his slightly anxious face peers out from under the stiff, almost absurd, turban that they wear as part of their habit.

Another, younger son pulls up a small table for us, then brings me water. A servant comes in later and puts down a sweet, subtly peppery, herb scented tea. Davé talks quickly, his words are precisely formed but tumble out one almost on top of the other. It is as if they were ejected, not only by a proselytizing fervour, but also by a pleasurable intellectual excitement; he is a man who enjoys his mastery of orthodoxy and takes delight in explanations.

'The philosophy of having a personal God is that if you want to improve and get rid of all the vices that you have, or even the baser instincts that the human mind possesses, it is better that you have a Brahmanized soul which is absolutely divine and manifests here on earth simply to relieve the people that he finds from maya. With us there is only one Guru because our fundamental belief is that the Lord is one – whether we call him by the name of Swaminarayan or Krishna or Brahman or Christ, God is one. He comes straight on the earth as an incarnation here and some emissaries also come with him, spiritual emissaries, divine emissaries; they go on manifesting here after he returns to his abode. The *shruti* says that the atman can be realized only by the grace of the Guru or by God. If God pours his grace on you, as Ramakrishna poured his grace on Vivekananda, or just as Swaminarayan poured his grace on our present Guruji – if God himself pours his grace we will be able to realize our souls.

'A spontaneous moment comes when this grace simply pours out. The disciple has to pray for it but he does not know when it will come. It comes spontaneously and when it comes the disciple realizes that it has come.

'We can't say that the Guru is merely a channel for divine grace which is passed through him without his control. For if we say that, it means ignorance in the Guru. But the Guru is absolutely divine, he cannot be said to have such ignorance that he doesn't know. He knows the moment when the grace is to be poured. You see, when you come in contact with our Guruji, he knows everything – he knows everything that is going to happen, he knows everything, not only of this world but of the other worlds also. But you see, he will behave with you as if he were absolutely a human being who doesn't know anything. But when the moment comes when he will reveal these things, then you will see.

'Now, first of all, when you accept a Guru, before you accept him, you have to know the attributes of the Guru – whether this is a Guru who will be able to deliver to me the things which I want. He must be perfectly Brahmanized, he must observe absolute celibacy, must have no worldly attributes, must have all divine attributes. So these things are the fundamental requirements for just finding out about a Guru. When once you accept a Guru, you have to dedicate yourself completely at his feet: that is the first condition. Second condition is that, even if you are away from him – it is not absolutely necessary that one is in close connection with him if you know the tenets he has prescribed for your living and you observe all these tenets perfectly – he will put you into certain circumstances in which you will find that your mind is in revolt against the tenets of the Guru; your body will revolt, your fixed notions will revolt; against this revolution of mind, body and ideas, you have to fix yourself tightly with the Guru, tight with the tenets of the Guru. If you succeed in that, then the Guru works; if you don't succeed, if you succumb to the ideas, the mind and the body, then the Guru doesn't work. And in our sect the tenets are extremely strict. But they are simple.

'Sometimes, Guru gives us tasks which we don't understand. Supposing you are near the Guru and the Guru tells you to go away from him on a certain mission. Now you feel that if you go away from the Guru in order to perform this mission you will lose the benefit of the Guru's darshan and his thoughts. You have that attachment. But the Guru desires that you should go there and if you don't obey the order the Guru is not pleased. Because he says, "When I give you an order there is always significance in that." It happened in the time of the second emissary of Lord Swaminarayan; a disciple came to him from a nearby village. Then the Guru told him, "I have to ask you to stay here fifteen days since I am going out of this temple. You stay here fifteen days and as soon as I return you can go to your village." This gentleman, unfortunately, didn't want to stay there and so without getting the permission of the Guru he went away from the temple. He didn't tell him anything, simply asked the people there to inform Swamiji that he was going. Now, when Swamiji heard that he had gone, he said, "I wanted him to stay there because there is some danger to his life. He does not realize it. But since he is mine, he belongs to me, he has taken shelter with me, I must protect him." After some miles of the man's journey, a serpent came and bit him. He was given the darshan. The Guru said, "Don't worry – trust Swaminarayan. You will not be affected by this poisonous serpent; but this was the reason why I wanted you to stay."

'If there are instructions which are morally unsound, Guru gives such instructions to test the tenacity of the disciple. In that case, the disciple should bow down and say, "Even if you have said this, I feel that it is going to affect my morality and so you will excuse me for not observing this." And then the Guru is pleased. There was a contemporary disciple of Swaminarayan; Swaminarayan was talking at a meeting where there were some ladies hearing his sermons. So Swaminarayan said to him, "Come and sit here with me, hear my discourse." Then the disciple thought that if he came to sit with the Lord, the Lord was talking with these ladies, he would also have sight of the ladies which was not according to the tenets prescribed for him as a sadhu – it was not his function, his duty, to have vision of ladies. So he said, "Even if you order me, I am not supposed, by your orders too, to come and sit before you." So Swaminarayan said, "I will cast you out!" He said, "All right, you may please do that, I will accept that, I will be very pleased to be outcast by you because I don't want to be outcast by being mixed with ladies and being immoral." So if you feel that the Guru's orders are morally unsound, then these orders are tests of morality.

'The technique of the Guru is such, that even if he realizes that he has been flooded with all divinity, that God has just poured himself in him, the greater state beyond knowing this is that he has no consciousness of this knowledge. Supposing I know that I have been flooded by the ultimate divinity and that I represent God, then there is that "I", and so "I" is different from God. That subtle ego of being an emissary of God here comes in the way of one's own redemption as well as the redemption of all the disciples who come to me. But the state here is so subtle that the Guru who has been graced by God does not even have that consciousness.

'Now, there are spiritual disciplines which are required of every disciple. One type of meditation has been prescribed by Swaminarayan. The first thing is that your mind cannot be focused on the divine form of God because your mind is too diffused; once you are meditating it spreads in all directions, all the things that you have seen or heard, all these things gather in the mind and you are deflected. So first of all, in your mind, you have to go with the Guru. When you have joined the Guru, you have stayed with him, you have seen him taking his bath, you have seen him performing puja, you have seen him eating his food, you have seen him resting, you have seen him having the darshan of God, waving lights before God – so you have to go with him during all these processes.

'So that is the first process and in that process, after the mind becomes entirely static, there are places in our bodies where we should meditate on the divine form of the Guru. The first mode of meditation which has been prescribed by Lord Swaminarayan is on the image of the Guru as it is seen before us by our eyes. When the meditation of the Guru in the eyes is complete, then you see the figure of the Guru on the inside of the eyelids. That is the first place. The second place is the forehead, the place of dream, the subtle state. The dream comes from there, that is its generating place; so sometimes you get surprising dreams, things which you have not seen, not even heard, not even contemplated – the reason is because the seat is here. So when you meditate upon the Guru here, then you control the subtle state. And the third is the heart in which, you see, all the desires are controlled. And the fourth is the *jiva*, the soul; as we go on we have to overcome these states: consciousness, the subtle, the deep sleep; all these states we have to control by these meditations.

'I joined this sect in 1939 when I came across the Guru who is the Guru of the present Guru. I had no affinity for this thing. I was secretary to Mr K. M. Munshi, who was the Home Minister here, and I was much more interested in administration; these sorts of religious or philosophical things were very far from me. In fact, I had no leanings towards it; I was never in search of it. But in 1939 this Guru was coming to Bombay and my elder brother told me that a very powerful saint was coming to Bombay and that he would like me to come and have his darshan. The first darshan which I had, I was terribly attracted. He also called me very close to him; he told me certain things which I was contemplating to do and he forbade me to do them. So I was surprised: how did this man whom I had never met, whom I had never told that I was going to do these things, tell me all this? So I thought there was some power in him. But I was terribly attracted towards him, I don't know why. Even I cannot find the reason for my attraction for him.

'And after some time my brother said to the Guruji, "Let me introduce him."

'He said, "I know him. I've known him since long." And again I was surprised – this was my first visit so how could he say, "I have known him since long?"

'Then I had the humility to ask, "This is the first time we

have met and you have told my brother that you have known me since long?"

'He said, "I have known you since your birth, during many births. I have always been with you. This time I'm going to give you a higher and higher place."

'Thereafter, I had a great attachment for him. I attended all the congregations, all the functions – there was not a single function I missed, and whenever Guruji used to come here I would sit with him for hours together, at nights to two or three o'clock, listening to his talks. Even to this day I am still surprised at how I am lifted and got so attached.

'In 1956 – I had my factory then – I was touring with Guruji and after two months we came to Ahmedabad. He asked me to go to a village near by for two days and then join him in Baroda. So after two days I went to Baroda and rejoined him. It was about four o'clock and he was just signing some letters. He told me that I would be going to Bombay that night. After giving me this order he called me once again. He said, "Your life is ending today. You have not come here for this mission of conducting a factory and earning money. God will give you a new lease of life provided you are prepared to serve his mission."

'I said, "All right." I had to carry out his orders implicitly. So I told him that my elder brother was with me as a partner. I came to Bombay the next morning. My wife had had a dream – my eldest son was here too – and in the dream she had seen my dead body carried out and she had been crying. So when I arrived in the early hours of the morning, around two o'clock, she told me she had had this dream.

'So I said it had been correct: "Guruji has also told me that this is my fate and that I should now retire from all these troublesome activities." The next morning, I went to tell my brother and since he is also attached to our Guruji he said, "All right." Since then I have retired; since 1956 I am totally concentrating myself to this institution and to Guruji.

'Now, there are certain restrictions on a man who follows the spiritual path, in his daily life also. Very early in the morning, we get up, we take our ablutions, and then perform puja in which we have to meditate upon the form of the Guru and get ourselves involved with all the activities of the Guru. So, as the Guru performs all his daily routines, we just help him to do all these things. We give him his bath, then we garland him, we put sandalwood paste on his forehead, then we give him his food – and that is all mental, that is all mental worship. And when you give him this mental worship you are with the Guru; so you forget yourself and you are always with the Guru as a matter of worship also . . .'

When I leave, he gives me his book on Sri Swaminarayan. I have the uncomfortable feeling as he signs it that it is his own, perhaps last, copy he is handing to me. This feeling is not, however, because the gift is made with any sense of strain. His face shows only friendliness; we part in a shower to and fro of compliments.

*

Dadar is in the suburbs of the city and, extravagantly, I take a taxi. The streets seethe. Crowds of bedraggled vendors squat at the edge of the pavement, vegetables spread on dirty newspapers beside them. Bullock carts, piled high with coal, rumble through the traffic; the nodding beasts are garlanded – someone loves them. A man bends between the shafts of a handcart to which is attached a great water barrel; he wears a ragged red turban, a greasy dhoti, grey hair falls over his forehead. In Mohamad Ali Road the shops are shut for Ramadan.

But farther on stand row upon row of stalls: furniture in unstable pyramids, then silk robes, slippers, shirts. People linger, watch each other, dart here and there, bend over bargaining, disdainfully fingering the embroidery, the printed cottons. A pile of gold coloured shoes gleams like a lighthouse in this endless, eddying sea. Then Byculla, where the buildings are submerged by the people in them, apartments divided into rooms, rooms sub-divided with a family in each sub-division, and around them the rooftop, the gallery, the corridor dwellers; outside, the doorway squatters, the pavement sleepers – that endless multi-purpose city pavement, pitch for beggar and itinerant salesmen, home for some, children's playground, sewer, rubbish dump, public lavatory . . .

The tower of the Sri Akshar Purushottam Bhavan rises opposite Dadar Station. Here the monks and sadhus of the sect live, work and study. Its stone is pale blue; against it the sadhus' ochre robes hang, sari long, brightly, like flags. I leave my sandals at the end of the bleak yard that runs alongside the monastery, where a surly, grey-haired watcher takes them into his charge. H. T. Davé greets me, his eyes hidden behind blue lenses and his dimpled smile thus made strangely sinister. He is as neat as before in spotless and religious white.

Inside, I am offered tea, hot, milky, sweet, overflowing into a stained saucer. Saffron robed, the monks crowd round the doorway looking in, or in the small reception-room and office, stand, half watching me, as ill at ease as I am myself.

The building is tall, with bare wooden stairs that wind to the attics. I look through a door at a great, bare assembly hall, where Sri Swaminarayan and the sect's present Guru, Sri Yogiji Maharaj, stand in brilliantly lit effigy, their portraits showing them benign yet watchful, their shrines dressed with bright garlands.

Through a door to the right, monks bend busily over kitchen work. One, wearing glasses Riviera dark, glances at me sharp faced; his head thrust forward, he looks for a moment like a gangster caught in an unlikely disguise. Elsewhere, there are the uncomfortable pallets, on which the monks sleep, stretched on the bare boards of a large room. Not that they are allowed much rest; they rise at four thirty in the morning and are supposed to pass the time in religious readings, prayers, discourses and the practice of yoga asanas. They eat at noon, meal times lasting half an hour. Whatever food they get they mix together, each in his bowl, adding water to make a lumpy, rather unpleasant gruel; in this way they are supposed to avoid any pleasure in eating.

Presumably their daily schedule keeps the sadhus too busy to allow impure thoughts to trouble them. Since many of them are young men who are aspirants in a puritan sect, this must be of great importance. The precepts of Sri Swaminarayan himself demonstrate the restrictions under which they live. They are not allowed to telephone in case a woman answers them, I was told, and to avoid temptation they may not go out unaccompanied. Should they touch a woman by accident in the street, they must take the first opportunity to wash themselves all over still wearing whatever clothes they had on at the time.

The head of the Akshar Bhavan – under the Guru, of course – is the mahant, Swami Keshavjivandasji. He is surprisingly young, in his middle thirties. He has a sombre, bony face, lips slightly pursed, the muscles under the skin rigid: an ascetic's face. Yet now and then his lips tremble faintly, his hand has a slight, intermittent quiver, and as we begin to talk he sweats nervously. All through our conversation the tremor flickers about his face like a ghost, like suppressed signals from some desperate invisible Doppelgänger. But the Swami looks into my eyes, looks deeply with no fear of scrutiny, he speaks softly and steadily and with great honesty. Now and then a shy, warm smile alters and humanizes his gaunt face. He seems a complex man, darkly within himself, sure of his vocation – yet, one senses, held to his vows by an effort rare among sadhus; renunciation in this poverty stricken and sexually repressed country often seems less of an effort than ordinary life. Many sadhus seem to develop easily, therefore, having no constant inner struggle to hold them back. In this man I sense that his vocation, whatever it has given him, has also demanded a steep price.

On a balcony a hundred yards away, a woman hangs out

washing. The monastery was placed here, in this overcrowded suburb, precisely to keep these holy aspirants within reach of temptation. Overcoming it then takes on a real meaning; in the serenity of the country they would be like children kept all their lives in a germ-free atmosphere, who then perhaps collapse and die at the first machinations of the influenza virus. The woman reaches up, clips a shirt in place. A young sadhu stands at the window, watches her, then moves away. Will he later do penance for this contamination? Swami Keshavjivandas leans forward to emphasize an opinion, tapping out the significant syllables on the table. This forcefulness seems strangely out of keeping with the even softness of his voice. His eyes look into mine as if with some unspoken, unspeakable question.

'We have come in contact with Swamiji simply through love. It was never in my life to take this path, but his affection and love only have drawn me to him. And before I came to him we had many questions, we used to ask many questions of him, but he never answered us. He would ward us off, he would say, "This person will answer you"; but we weren't satisfied. Now we realize that what we had asked him we have the actual experience today and in that way he has answered us. Because the other way the answer is only the solution for the mind not for the heart; but experience is different and that is why, since Guru has experienced, the disciple who comes in his contact should also reach a certain level.

'Unless and until he has reached that level, he will not understand. He should be patient, he should not come in a hurry to ask Guru to do everything in a moment, because this thing is all internal; this thing is not perceived by our outer eyes and we have to wait and if we are in a hurry and if we want everything to be done quickly and without perspiration then we are actually disappointed and we don't understand anything. The rain is showering but when it falls on hard stone it will go to the sea;

if the earth is soft then it penetrates. In the same way, he showers blessing always but if I am not ready for it then I cannot receive those blessings.

'So when can you receive blessing? When you are also about his level you can receive from him. Until then we have to take other sources to know the Guru because this source does not help us, because we are not ready and we are not understanding.

'If I come to a true Guru but if I am not ... Suppose a jeweller has some true jewels come to him; if he is not perfect in recognizing jewels he will not recognize them. In the same way, even if a true Guru comes to me I'll not recognize him and I may ward him off because I don't have the eyes, that knowledge, to know him. So I have to go to other sources. That other source is shastras, the scriptures.

'But even by knowing scriptures you cannot know the Guru. It is very high. If we have done some things in previous births, all that is collected and summed up and helps us to know him. And if we don't come to that, we have to depend on other persons who are experienced, we have to rely on their knowledge or their experience; they will tell us that this Guru is this way or that way. We see him in a different way, but if someone experienced tells us to see Guru in this way, we begin to see him that way; then we find that he is good. But without some experience ... If someone tells us that a tiger is like a cat it would mean nothing unless we had also seen a cat.

'And leaving aside all these things, Swami has shown us one way. That applies to all things. He has said, "Don't take a Guru, don't come to him; you should not be in a hurry to believe in him or to surrender to him, you should see his ancestors, his hierarchy, who was *his* Guru and how great they were; then you see the Guru himself. You should also see those who have come in contact with him and how they are being prepared and how they progress. Oh, you should see all these three things, and all living people can judge from that." That is not complete but that helps you and then afterwards ... And as we obey him we experience some things; then again he tells us further to obey ... orders us and we obey him again, and again we know him better.

'It is a very strange thing with many of us here. We are told by our Guru that if there is a jewel – I don't take myself to be a jewel, but just for an example – if there is a jewel and it is covered up with cow dung, when it is washed off it shines again. "In the same way," he says, "you have come here; due to your involvement with this world you had just lost yourself temporarily. But as soon as you come into contact with us you are drawn out from it." That is what our Guru has said and what we have experienced.

'I used to be at Jawalpur, at Christ Church Boys High School. We had to go to the church compulsorily. But because it was not my religion, in those times we used to think that since it was compulsory we must attend, but we never paid any heed to it. It did not help us in any way. But we were not taught our religion by anyone. Actually my father and mother, they were of this fold. But I did not feel like this at all.

'You see, there was Swamiji's Guru – I had the chance to see him, but three times I denied my father. He told me to come to him but I gave him lame excuses and ran away. Once he was only fifty yards away from me, the Swamiji's Guru, and my elder brother was pulling me back and I was pulling the other way and I won: I did not go to him. Then Swamiji himself used to come to our house; there were two staircases, so when he came one way I used to run by the other staircase. But once, you see, he approached from that second staircase. When I heard that he was coming I started running – but we met in front. He took hold of my hands and said, "Come, where are you running?" He took me, I stood before him; he took this ... my neck, but that hold also I broke and put his hand by his side. But he did not lose his temper and he was smiling; I was trying to harrass him, I was trying to rag him and trying to make him angry, but still he was smiling. How was it possible?

'From there I found interest in him. He was to stay for four days; this was on the very first day so I went to him for three days continuously. He would call me, he would bless me, he took so much care of me. I said, "My parents have never done like this to me," and that aroused something in me to know why was he behaving in this way. Was there any reason? Well, I found no reason: he was giving love freely, just like the free milk distribution, and from that time I found this partiality.

'To me, he looked changed: I began to love him. And during the vacation I went to him (he goes around to the villages to preach), I went to him for fifteen days. For all those fifteen days he himself . . . You see, there are so many other disciples who would obey him, but still, he personally made my bed and he would tell me, "Now go to sleep"; and in the morning he would wake me up. He treated me that way and I loved him very much and then when he said, "You want to leave the world? You want to come to this?" I said, "Yes."

'But after one hour I thought, "What have I done? I should not have said 'Yes' to him. It is wrong. I have not asked my parents."

'He said, "Your parents will give you leave." Now what should I do? Whatever I told him he gave me certain answers so that I could not argue with him.

'At this time I used to see Swamiji twice in a year. That was during the two vacations. But he would write letters to us and he would tell us that we were to behave this way; that we should not see pictures, we should not go in company of girls, we should fast and all that. That we did very gradually though physically we found it a strain. But still, keeping him in mind . . . Even though he is far away from here, if we will misbehave he will know it. We experience his presence wherever we are.

'The particular way we have chosen is very hard, because after surrendering sometimes it comes in our mind to throw this thing away and to go back to our original ways. Sometimes it does happen. But then at that time we don't take big steps. We approach our Guru, we tell it to him, we write to him. Then he again shows us the way. He gives us patience. He says, "I also asked that question; the questions that are coming to you came to me also but I continued with faith in my Guru and I am now here in this position. You see me as I am now." And so with that belief we come to our senses. But he does not himself claim to be divine; he says, "I was also like you but I have reached this stage and so you also can achieve this stage." Today I still find the temptations very hard, but due to Swamiji's grace I can introspect and then come to my level. Otherwise the temptation is great. For instance, persons come and they touch our feet and then something happens to us.

'You should have perfect faith in your Guru. If you even shake a little, even if you are highly disciplined, you break because of that. If there is even a slight doubt in your Guru that will bring down the great wall and that will be your downfall. It will not be growing easier for a disciple, but on the contrary he will be crushed, he will be thrown down on the earth.

'We know this partly by experience and partly by his saying so. Because we cannot have a complete idea of him, so many things are told by him. But he tells us only when he knows, "Now you will not doubt, you will have no doubt in you"; when he is quite sure that you will not take it for granted that he is speaking to please his ego, then he will tell you. Till then he will not tell you.

'Four years passed between my first and second initiation. I thought to myself, "I am educated. I know much more than many of my colleagues, why does Swamiji delay to give this to me? Many others are there who come from villages. They never knew anything, but still, they were given this directly." Earlier, I never got an answer to this question and I had not even asked

Guruji because, you see, I thought that this question should not be asked. But now I know that he has done a great thing to me. If he had given me this earlier, there would have been downfall. That ego would have come out of me and I would have thought myself this and that, and that would have destroyed me. But during those whole years, you see – I should not say it – I was treated in such a way that any other person would have run away.

'I give you one example: one day, Swamiji served us a lot of food. The previous day had been a fast, I had fasted. The next I should have been served with light food, but actually it was heavy food with sweets and all; immediately afterwards he told me to go to the station. Some person told Swamiji, "Don't send him to the station. We will do it." So Swamiji said, "No."

'Swamiji was still saying, "No, he should be sent." I had no shoes; they were broken, you see. Swamiji said, "You should go without shoes . . ." So I did that also. And he had told me to take a big vessel full of water, cold water. I had to serve a Swami who was to pass by through that station. And it was three miles away from this place. And Swamiji had told me, "Whatever remains, bring back; don't throw it out." I was with another person but that person, on the contrary . . . he danced around, he did not help me; he danced around and he teased me.

'I said, "What is Swamiji doing? I don't understand him. Why should I be treated like this?" But after all that, you see, when I came back, Swamiji patted me and all that anger . . . it diffused. Otherwise, great anger had been aroused in me and I would have done something. But then he came and he did this so nicely. And that told me that he knew everything.

'When the time came for my second diksha, it was planned. There was a big occasion at Madras; in the pinnacle of the temple, by the golden vessel – it took place there. Fifty went up to be initiated during that ceremony.

'As to the discipline here – Swamiji actually has ordered us to rise at four o'clock in the morning. That we don't do. [He laughs.] It is very hard. And once I read in Reader's Digest that practice makes a man perfect, but not getting up early. That has struck me. In some way it has drawn me back. [He laughs.] These things which come from an artist are caught up quickly, rather than the order given by Guru. We know that if we obey him we will achieve, but it is hard.

'After four we take our bath, cleaning our mouth and all that, and then we perform puja which is given by our Guru. There is some mantra which we have to chant, whereby God or Guru comes in our presence. Then we give him bath, mentally, and we serve him with food and all this; then all that is completed. And then we chant the mantra whereby he is to go away. Like that we hold our puja. Then some go for the studies. After puja, there is some time, about half an hour; during that we do scripture reading and interpretation. After that, at six o'clock, there is *arti*; that is, bearing of lights before God, in the mass. After that we are free, in the sense that everybody will do their personal things; that is, some go for their studies, some go to do their service, to cook or to clean and all that. And after that, at seven thirty, we take our breakfast and after that, at eight o'clock there is scripture reading again and everyone should attend this.

'The teaching is done by me. And I talk to them. Or even Mr Davé, he is there to teach us because he has developed great interest in us in this fold, and he has experienced so many things he can guide us nicely. There are others also; teaching is not only the monopoly of the saffron clothes. Swamiji says that whoever is fit for it can do this work. Even a small child could teach if he is fit. This teaching is only to saints and men; to ladies it is not asked us. But if they want to hear, it is done in such a way that we are not conscious of it.

'After that we go off again, some for cooking, some for study and all that. At noon we take lunch; there also we put this food before God and we chant some hymns before we eat and after that it is taken to be his *prasad* – graced by God – and then it is offered to all the disciples and not before that. We cannot even put it in our mouths. After that scripture reading is done for everybody. This daily reading is chosen by me, but the Sunday meeting is a special one and that is picked by Swamiji.

'After that the cleaning of vessels is done; this is not laid on one person because there is a rota and every fifteen days it is changed. After fifteen days another person comes and that way everyone has a chance; whether he likes it or not he has to do it.

'That goes up to two o'clock or two thirty. Then we take some rest because we have to get up early. Actually we should not take sleep in the afternoon, but we do it, and Swamiji allows it. Because if he is too strict, then we may break out.

'Then again at three thirty worship takes place, and then again we do our reading. Many times there are meetings; we go to centres to teach and some meetings are held here. And then again at seven there is arti. That arti is as it was at six o'clock in the morning. Actually that is not a fixed time; the morning one is fixed, but this is according to the sunset; when it is dark, then we should do it.

'After that hymns are again chanted and there will be scripture reading and at that time many come, other devotees besides our saints, because at that time they are free from their office and all that. And they also get time to hear us.

'Then again we take food although many don't take food in the evening. There are a few small saints, they take food, and others who are depressed and of that sort, they do. Actually we are supposed to eat only once, and that also in a wooden bowl. We have to mix everything in cold water and then we take it in that way. That is, we should not have taste of anything in particular. One taste, whether it is tasty or tasteless, is sufficient. That is what we actually have to do; but in that also, you see, we cheat ourselves. We do according to our capacity, we are all trying to please him, but still it is very difficult. But still, according to me, I can say that we are far better off because we are sincere, that is one thing. Whether we are able to or not, the sincerity is there and that is the great thing.

'And then at ten thirty, the cleaning of vessels; when all have finished, all get together. If Swamiji has written letters or something has to be read, something about the sect, or something is to be told us, it is done at night at about ten. From ten to eleven thirty there are again recitals to be done by everyone, all the devotees throughout this fold, whether they are saint or not. And that recital is to be said by everyone. Then we go to sleep. Some continue study until twelve or one, according to their need.

'Until we really know the fitness of a Guru, our surrender to him is partial. Even if we think that we have surrendered ourselves, actually we have not done it. We think that we have surrendered completely, but actually we have not. So you see both things go side by side: we think that Guru is perfect and we think that our surrender is also complete; but Guru is not perfect and your surrender also is not complete; so it works. But surrender goes on, there is no end to it. Lord Swaminarayan has said that once someone asked him, "Lord, show us one way by which you will be pleased with us, rather than our having to perform infinite things to please you." So Lord Swaminarayan said, "Complete surrender." So how great is this thing surrender? We actually don't know its value. You see, only when you know him completely, can you surrender completely. But you don't know yourself, so how can you surrender completely?

'And how to know ourselves – that is done by Swamiji, you see. Actually when we come to him we don't know anything, but Swamiji orders us to do something. And when we do that thing we get some light. Here is one incident. Once when I was with Swamiji he had told us to learn something by heart. We all went in one corner and started learning that passage by heart. Suddenly Swamiji began speaking. We all ran to him. Swamiji asked us, "Why have you come?"

'We told Swamiji, "Because you are speaking; if it was another person we would not have come, but because you are speaking we have come to hear you in order that when someone asks us questions we will know the answers."

'Swamiji said, "Go back and do what I have told you. That fountain of knowledge will come from within your heart if you obey me, but even if you come to me and hear me and not any-one else, nothing will happen. But when you obey me, only then it happens." You see, we have experienced that: one saint who is here, he does not attend any lectures or scripture readings or anything of that sort – he is always busy in his cooking depart-ment. He has taken that up completely. But still, when you hear him you ask, "How did this come to him, which we have learned after hearing, experiencing and all that; just by cooking he has learned all these things?"

'Because of the things that have happened, we have stuck to him. You may be given the answer perfectly, but still, to believe it is different. Swamiji has done that to us with his grace. But still, we don't give this explanation outside. The reason is, it is very hard to convince people. At the same time, if they are not convinced and they take up with this thing and then they leave it halfway, then they will interpret these things wrongly. They will say that there is nothing, it is all humbug. So it is better not to explain. A person like you, who comes here, it is very hard to give an explanation: there is writing and thinking – but that is not experiencing.'

Later, I eat with them; they crowd cheerfully round me as I mix the rather good vegetable curry and the rice, chew the raw vegetables, end with plantains. We eat in a bare room with a tiled floor. The 'saints', as they call themselves in English, sit in two rows, facing each other, cross-legged on rush mats. They stir their food together busily and water it as if genuinely afraid of being seduced in some way by its undiluted taste. To the right, through low, open windows, I can see a balcony and a whole world beyond, noisy, contumacious, sensual. In here, there is only low conversation and the soft gonging of metal vessels. On the wall hangs a framed photograph of the benevolent, garlanded figure of the Guru, pinned by the camera at some moment of appetite as he too bends over a simple bowl. But the young sadhus crowding round me laugh, watch me eagerly, then push each other away to give me room and privacy – more like a school than a monastery (and, indeed, this is in some sense a school, a centre for the sect's young aspirants, in which they learn Sanskrit, philosophy and a number of other subjects).

Silently, Swami Keshavjivandasji leads me to the door. I watch him intently as if he has secrets I can unravel. I think of him as a man who will be formidable if he survives. Around him, these young sadhus disport themselves like children; the older ones stand by, they smile, they let this or that happen. Only he is intense, burning within, obsessed by something – is it vocation, or the terror of failing it? Yet perhaps I dramatize and romanticize him; he speaks of other people's failings, failures, total defeats, as if they had no connection with him: he feels himself secure. And all the same, I look at him and wonder – every now and then, that trembling passes across his lips, swift as a humming bird's wing, a nothing that goes as quickly as it comes, leaving no more trace than the shadow of a cloud passing over a landscape.

At the door, at the head of the two or three steps that lead down into the narrow yard, he says his shy farewells. I retrieve my chappals, walk down the yard and out under the stone archway. I look back. The younger sadhu is still at the door, watching my departure. As I turn, he jerks around and scuttles out of sight

*

223

The then Guru of the Swaminarayanas was Swami Sri Jnan-jivandasji, usually called Sri Yogiji Maharaj; (he died, in his eighties, after suffering a heart attack early in 1971). He was born into a poor family in Saurashtra, spent his schooldays in chanting the 'Swaminarayana' mantra, and at the age of four-teen left home to join the sect's temple at Junagadh. He seems to have spent several years dutifully doing the most menial tasks and keeping his spiritual light hidden under a bushel. However, he was given his initiation and, emerging from what had occluded his brightness, joined Swami Sri Yagnapurushadasji, a doctrinal innovator whose new ideas seem to have caused some disturbance in the movement. Yogiji Maharaj became a stal-wart in the new faction which, a minority in the beginning, began increasingly to flourish. When Swami Yagnapurushadas died, Swami Jnanjivandas became the sect's new Guru.

He was fifth in succession from Swaminarayan himself. That founder claimed explicitly to be God – not out of vanity, say his followers, nor out of egotism or delusion, but simply because he was God. Addressing his five hundred *paramahansas* or saints, he talked of 'the inner recesses of my heart wherein I see immense light. In that light there is God seated, young and with a dark complexion, and that is I. You are all seated there before me, but this Gadhapur town, this verandah and so on are not visible to me. When you will get this knowledge of my form in all its infinity and profundity, you will be relieved of all worldly bondages . . .'

Since the Gurus of the sect pass in direct spiritual line of des-cent from Sri Swaminarayan, there may be a question whether this identity of leader and God has persisted through these half-dozen incarnations. However, H. T. Davé, speaking to me about the status and nature of the Guru, explained the distinc-tion. 'The Guru is the disciple of God,' he said. 'He is not God himself, but his disciple. He has become absolutely empty and has thus been filled with the divinity of God. He is not God *sui generis* – God is Swaminarayan. But he is the closest disciple of Swaminarayan, and that is why God works through him. That is the general notion that we possess; and we worship the Guru not only because we must worship the Guru, simply, but because we have to worship the Guru to reach God. He is the *via media* between us and God.'

When Swami Jnanjivandasji's path might have crossed mine in India, I was in hospital. It was therefore with some relief that I discovered he was coming to London to open a temple here for his followers and, perhaps incidentally, to celebrate his eightieth birthday. As a result, it was incongruously in Dollis Hill that I finally managed to meet him. All down the sapling lined suburban street with its lathe timbered, mock Tudor façades, suspicious housewives in flowered aprons were peering out of their front doors at this intrusion of an alien holiness into their uncomplicated lives. The Guru's haven was a house un-aesthetically at one with its neighbours. On its shrunken, sub-baronial porch, some devotee had formed out of blue sticky tape the words, 'Welcome, Yogiji Maharaj'.

In the hall, in battered schoals, lay the shoes of the devoted. Upstairs, their backs against the walls, sat ten or a dozen of the monks, among them several faces familiar to me from Dadar. Secluded, safe from the brusque temptations of London, they read, or spoke in low voice, or wrote busily on airmail forms.

In the centre of the room, near a window, stood an empty bed. From outside someone spoke, laughed in a low voice. Devotees, who had been sitting cross-legged on the floor and glancing curiously at me, scrambled to their feet. Smiling, round faced, his cheeks covered in a stubbly white beard, Yogiji Maharaj came in, helped by the arm of an attendant. He beamed all round, his wide mouth gaping with a genuine joy. At the bedside he leaned forward, then put his knees on the counter-pane. Rolling over on his back, he looked for a moment like some round, enormous baby about to gurgle out its pleasure at being in the world. Then, more sedately, he settled himself on the pillows, put his right foot on his left thigh, looked at me watchfully, waited for H. T. Davé to interpret my intentions, then my questions and his answers.

'It is by an inspiration given by God that I know that a certain disciple is fit to tread this path. Otherwise, it is difficult to sort out the particular disciple who is fit for it. Once somebody is accepted as a disciple, he has to observe certain rules, certain laws and certain holy injunctions given by the scriptures. If he has the tenacity to observe all these things, then he is further accepted; if he does not have that tenacity the Guru would not say anything, but automatically he would not remain in the fold. And tests are always necessary for the purification.

'The Guru is the symbolic form of God. God reveals himself through the true Guru, the Guru who has reached the Brahmanic state. So every activity that the Guru performs is a divine activity and the disciple has to observe it; he has to be under the influence of all the Guru's activities. And he must do whatever the Guru asks: if the Guru gives him the duties of cooking, of cleansing the temple, cleaning the house and so on – all the duties which the Guru imposes upon him – he must take as divine and must observe totally in order that he may progress. There is an instance in the Upanishads of a disciple who was told by his teacher, a man who had some four hundred disciples, "I have one cow here – you take it out to the country, and when you get four hundred cows from this one cow, then you can come back." He told that to the other four hundred disciples too, but they said, "We have come here to learn of the knowledge of God, we have come here to progress spiritually, not for this." But the one disciple did not question it – he said that the Guru's orders must be implicitly obeyed. So he went away; after ten years, when his one cow had multiplied so that there were four hundred, he returned – and the Guru's grace was showered on him and he was Brahmanized. So all the orders of the Guru are to be implicitly observed by the disciple who should take the Guru as a divine figure, the representative of God.

'Who can be a Guru? Not simply the man who has taken the saffron. A Guru is one who eradicates our ignorance, who lifts us. He is one who can interpret the scriptures in such a way that the disciple may know the significance of the spiritual path. He is one who carries within him the divine form of God and who cannot be moved by any outward influence. This is the real Guru. But Guru is not God – he is the symbolic or the representative form of God. Further, there is a spiritual hierarchy: the Guru does not inherit his place – his Guru was of equal spiritual status with him, and that Guru's Guru was of equal spiritual quality again. It is the spiritual qualities inherited from one's predecessors which make one the Guru; it is not sitting on the *gadi* and becoming the Guru like that. It is not like the appointment of a Pope or an Archbishop.

'Just as God is one, Guru is also one. There are other Gurus, but there are stages in their development. One can realize the Guru, not with the physical eye, but with the intuitional eye, the eye of knowledge. When the soul is purified by being detached from the influence of maya, with that consciousness one can know whether one is faced by a real or a spurious Guru.

'The performance of miracles has also a place in the spiritual life. The Guru performs them, not to show that he is the Guru, but when they are needed to attract the disciple. And then when the disciple is attached to the Guru, he gives him knowledge, purifies him and makes him fit for the worship of God. The miracles have no importance in the later stages of spiritual life. They are merely to attract the disciple, to make him feel that the Guru has some supernatural powers and that he may perform a miracle. But never to show that he is a great Guru – it is not for that that miracles are performed.

'There is, on the other hand, no sense in infusing the power of

227

God suddenly into a disciple. It is not going to have a lasting effect. But when the disciple becomes the truest instrument to sustain such power, then the Guru infuses that power. Then it will have a permanent effect on the disciple and will work through him for his benefit and the benefit of others. It is a power directed by the Guru who chooses the moment when the disciple is ready.

'When a disciple comes, he will have an urge within him to go on the spiritual path. But then he does not always have an intuitional feeling that he must observe all the rules of the sect, all the injunctions. This is not always the fact; there are instances in which the disciples are ready the moment they come to the institution, but there are others who are not ready. They have an urge, they come, and then they must observe all the rules of the institution. When the disciple observes all these rules sincerely, the Guru showers him with his blessing. He feels that here is a man who has sincerity, he may not have it from within, but he tries sincerely to observe all the rules. Then the Guru blesses him and his blessing then inspires him. So his behaviour may be only formal but the Guru's showering him with grace arouses his sincerity from within.

'Those who come to an institution or a fellowship and observe all the rules of that fellowship but feel a pressure as a result, they face a danger. And sometimes they have to leave the fellowship. But those who, although feeling the pressure, know that God is omnipotent and omnipresent and so observe all these rules in order to please him and propitiate him, they will please him and will in this way become very sincere and true disciples.

'The Christian conception, however, which sees the world as an essentially evil place, a place of trial, and its pleasures as wicked, that does not work with us. The scriptures prescribe that this world, which is evolved out of maya, has been evolved by the will of God in order that the souls here may ultimately be

redeemed. The world has therefore been created for a good purpose; it cannot be called bad. If one feels that the world is a place
wherein we have to attain our salvation, then the world doesn't
affect us like that – the creation is not bad. Human beings have
been created for a purpose and that purpose is to get salvation.

'The relationship between Guru and shishya is not a matter
of language. Both crave for that proximity which will make
them mentally one. And physically also, the disciple must never
infringe any of the orders of his Guru. When he is doing something he must just drop everything and go if his Guru tells him
to. So it is not a question of language but of feeling, of the inner
emotion.

'The definition of a Guru should always be this – that he is
one who knows the *Vedas*, the scriptures. But that does not mean
one who knows the books merely; the *Vedas* describe God, so
ultimately the Guru is one who knows God. And he should
be one who lives in God, that is, who is Brahamanized. So
those are the two qualifications of a Guru and that should be
sought for, for our ultimate salvation.'

Standing, ready to go, I watch as Yogiji Maharaj nods at me,
smiles at Davé. The sect's philosopher turns to me, smiling too. I
have been asked to join the sect; the price will be a certain
abstemiousness – neither adultery nor wine will be permitted
me. Whatever my views on the first, the second seems too heavy
a price to pay; I thank the Guru, but stammer out that I am not
yet ready for such spiritual progress. There is some laughter in
the room. Then, with a surprisingly heavy hand, Yogiji Maharaj
grabs my shoulder and gives me a short blessing. I feel embarrassed, hypocritical, yet curiously grateful.

A moment later, shod again, I am out in the summer street,
London exotic about me; in the distance the momentarily unexpected, the disorientating, rumble of the Underground.

THE ASHRAM: SWAMI MUKTANANDA

'Swami Muktananda Paramahansa – Adept Master of Siddha Yoga', the cover of the leaflet proclaims.* Above the title there is a drawing of the Swami: bearded and glowering, he stares without compromise into the eyes of the curious. The leaflet is published by the Sri Gurudev Ashram – his ashram.

Swami Muktananda Paramahansa, it tells us, was born on 16 May 1908, in a rich and pious family which lived in the vicinity of Mangalore, in Mysore State. From his boyhood he was imaginative, clever, jovial and mischievous. He was highly intelligent, but academic education did not appeal to him in the least; nor did any theories or dogmas interest him. He was one who could be convinced only by actual observation and direct experience.

The turning point came in his life through an incident which, at the age of fifteen, brought him face to face with the *avadhoot*, Swami Nityananda, who embraced him and gently stroked him on the cheeks. Within six months after this incident he left his home in quest of God.

The invisible hand of God guided him to the math of Siddharudha Swami in Hubli, south India. Here he took sannyasa and studied the elements of Vedanta and yoga. Soon after the mahasamadhi of Siddharudha Swami, he left Hubli and then began his lone wanderings in search of reality. For years, he roamed from place to place, visiting many a centre of pilgrimage, meeting various saints, sadhus and siddhas trying to know and realize the secret of the Ultimate Truth...

As ordained by divine will, his restless and rebellious spirit found inner peace and tranquillity on meeting Bhagawan Nityananda at

* A Paramahansa is an ascetic who has reached such a level of self-knowledge and self-control that no ordinary conventions bind him nor ordinary emotions disturb him. Although almost always a great Sanskrit scholar, he has transcended all doctrinal differences. A probationary period of at least twelve years must pass before he can achieve this status.

Ganeshpuri in 1947. It was a sort of reunion of the two after a lapse of about twenty-five years. Swamiji received the divine grace of his Guru in the form of shaktipat diksha; and after intense tapasya and sadhana of about nine years, he attained the ultimate goal.

By the end of 1956 Swamiji was told by Bhagawan Nityananda to settle down in Ganeshpuri. Bhagawan attained mahasamadhi in August 1961. The Guru and disciple were thus together for nearly five years and worked in unison towards fulfilment of the divine mission. Swamiji named his ashram as Sri Gurudev Ashram to perpetuate the sacred memory of his beloved Guru.

Many ashrams have a spiritual speciality, an approach or philosophy which the resident Guru considers most important or in which he is particularly adept. At Ganeshpuri, this is a process of instant initiation called shaktipat. *Shakti* means 'divine energy' and in Hinduism is conceived of as female. Thus it is the term applied to the wife of a god, to the female part of him – most particularly is this true in the Shakti-Shiva dualism. There are Shakta cults, also known as Tantrics after their holy literature, the Tantras, and in these cults the female principle is directly worshipped, sometimes in ways that an increasingly puritanical Hinduism has found it more and more difficult to acknowledge over the last two centuries or so.

Since shakti is the divine energy, and since the Guru is concerned with the transference of divine power, the use of that energy in such a transfer produces an immediate impact. That is shaktipat – the almost instantaneous transfer of divine energy, by touch or word or even look, from the Guru to the shishya. In yogic terms, what happens is the awakening of the *kundalini*, the coiled serpent sleeping at the base of the spine in that concept so difficult for the Westerner, the subtle body. Once awakened, either by the infusion of divine energy or by the special exercises of hatha yoga, it straightens its three and a half coils and, stiffened into a rod, rams its way upward through the six chakras, the downward facing lotuses, opening each as it passes.

Very few adepts manage in fact to persuade the kundalini up as far as the thousand petalled and final lotus in the head, but for it to reach even the first means that all sorts of occult powers and spiritual certainties and insights will be released.

This is a process which normally takes a lifetime; it is the claim of Swami Muktananda that through him it can be started, not only without the aspirant's spending weary years on yogic exercises – though these must be pursued, being both helpful and valuable in themselves – but also without his being aware of what is happening to him or even knowing what the process is. In other words, some newcomer may receive a charge of this energy within a day or two of his arrival at the ashram and so begin a spiritual journey which he may never have intended to make and the nature of which, at the beginning anyway, he will understand in only the sketchiest way.

What the leaflet tells us is,

The mission of Swamiji's life is to awaken divine consciousness in the aspirants by means of shaktipat diksha, and thereby further their spiritual development. Shaktipat is a subtle spiritual process by which the Guru transmits his divine power into the aspirant either by touch, word, look or thought. This is diksha or initiation. It marks the beginning of spiritual awareness in the disciple. This is also known as awakening of Kundalini shakti. It brings about the purification of nerves (*nadi shuddhi*) and this may make the initiated one perform automatic yogic exercises. This awakening of shakti also affords the aspirant wonderful spiritual experiences. Being blessed by the grace of the Guru, he also develops a sense of well-being. His attitude towards life undergoes a change. There is a spontaneous feeling of being at peace with himself and the world. All doubts resolve and he begins to grasp the significance of spiritual truths more clearly than ever. He feels the presence of divine grace around him, protecting and guiding him. Eventually he experiences divine existence as a positive reality, not a figment of abstract imagination.

This sadhana at the feet of an adept Guru is known as siddha yoga or gurukripa, that is, divine grace received from a perfect master. Swamiji is a great exponent of this siddha yoga.

Swamiji does not perform any miracles, nor does he encourage others to take interest in them. He gradually transforms an aspirant's desire to attain siddhis into a real spiritual urge. The greatest miracle that Swamiji performs is the invisible transformation of the ordinary life of frustration and confusion of an aspirant into a life of fulfilment.

Later, through a window, I am to hear the Swedish girl say, 'It felt like . . . all electricity – my arms were prickling and I moved without any volition . . . I had to move.' The French girl, nodding, 'And did you know your arms were moving?' A gesture, graceful, with the right hand. Then the English girl – who when she first came knew nothing of this or any Swami – 'Yes, at the beginning I was moving the whole time . . . and my voice was funny. It either came out thick – or not at all!' Like patients discussing a successful treatment, they will compare such notes in the sunshine, in the ashram garden, between bouts of hard and often pointless labour.

About shaktipat there is not as a matter of fact a complete unanimity of opinion among holy men. According to Swami Akhananda of Vrindaban, 'As for shaktipat, this transmission of energy happens when the grace of the Guru and the devotion of the shishya meet at the same point. Short of that there will be no such transmission; you can only say then that this is hypnotism. Sometimes such a transmission will be at the conscious behest of the Guru, at other times it may happen involuntarily. But the grace of the one and the devotion of the other must converge until they are at the same point and at the same level. If the shaktipat is given too soon, to shishyas who may not be ready to receive it, it shows that the Guru himself is not fit.'

According to Swami Amar Jyoti, 'Shaktipat is an initiation, sometimes directed by the Guru . . . As a Master he must be able to direct by concentration – he will catch your mind, a vibration kind of communication, like what you call telepathic communication elsewhere. There is vibration communication and he knows it. . . . But the Guru has to judge the instrument – with shaktipat, supposing you are not a responsive instrument, responsive or capable, then maybe it can sometimes do harm. That judgement lies with the Guru. Your nerves may or may not be able to stand it.'

Mahant Indresh Charandasji thinks, 'The transfer of power from Guru to disciple does exist, no doubt about it. No doubt about it. The moment the Guru says, "You are he," at that moment, just like an electric shock . . . The point is, you prepare the mind of the disciple and when you know the actual point has come you put the good thing into it! The seed is there. The seed is there and consequently the action takes place. But that a man is changed in a second – I don't believe it. A man cannot be changed in a second. He wants to be changed – so he has been changed! The Guru wants to change him – so he has been changed! The process is not completed in a second.'

Swami Padmanabhanand Saraswati in Benares has more faith in the Guru than some when it comes to transference of divine power to a disciple. 'As to shaktipat, it will never harm the shishya, not in the least. Because the power is given in such a way that it won't harm you. The Guru knows where it is to strike. No question of harm. The carpenter knows where the wood is to be touched, the smith knows where the iron is to be struck; so the Guru knows where the shishya is to be touched and at what point he is to be touched. And such a form of enlightenment will last because it is not the outward power – that can be lost – but it is a spiritual power. Once you have got it, you have got it permanently.'

It is this sort of certainty that, naturally enough, sustains Swami Muktananda's disciples at the ashram at Ganeshpuri. Setting off to visit this holy colony, therefore, I felt curiously vulnerable like some innocent in a fairy tale who, venturing out into an unstable and magical world, can never be sure that he will not return from it transformed into sad toad or glittering, unexpected prince.

*

The fans which hang in ranks from the high ceiling of Churchgate Station whirl in blurred unison so that one gets the impression of a gigantic Jules Verne airship about to launch itself with Victorian gravity into the sky. But, like these other struggling thousands, it is by train one leaves, clattering slowly through Bombay's suburbs, past coconut matting huts in cancerous colonies surrounded by sprawling moats of green-black water, past leprous concrete apartment blocks hung with stained saris which still flare now and then in the sun, past smart, modern factories with façades out of architectural magazines but already dirt streaked and flaking ... Later, on the flat land, there is a scattering of low, brown bushes, palm trees in loose order, long leaved mangoes, dusty jack-fruit, fluted *baobab*. We rumble over a causeway so narrow that, as I look down, it seems as if we are hovering over the water.

From the station, a taxi whirls me away, bouncing down straight roads ahead of its dust, past the brown, stubbled paddy fields. Hills rise near the road, soft and rounded, dappled with little dark green bushes like the tight curls on someone's head. The road forks; suddenly we have stopped beside a pair of iron gates like those to some grandiose Italian villa. Beyond, there is a narrow yard paved with small flagstones and shaded by two trees. A handful of middle-aged men and women turn to watch me climb from the taxi. This, a placard on the wall proclaims, is the Sri Gurudev Ashram.*

* Since I was there it has been much rebuilt. There are towers, now, a new audience hall, a new guest house. Swami Muktananda himself has, by visiting Britain and the United States, found wider recognition. I can only describe both as I saw them.

It stands at the top of a hill that slopes down into the small town of Ganeshpuri. A very small town, this, mostly one wide, dusty street lined with poky shops selling religious pictures and souvenirs, with cafés and small tea-shops, hotels and a 'bording' house. At the far end of the street rises the tomb of Swami Nityananda.

The ashram stands in some seventy acres of its own ground. The forecourt is backed by the main building where the offices and the audience hall are. Above and to the left, in a newer building, are the apartment of Swami Muktananda and the women's quarters. Behind this there are gardens, splendid with bougainvilia, and a caged white peacock named Moti. To the left of the first, walled garden is a cluster of buildings and court-yards – the halls where men and women eat, the kitchens, a new guest house still under construction and so on – while in the main garden, mostly scattered about a water tower to the right, stand the chambers and dormitories where male visitors or those permanently on the ashram sleep, their washrooms and lava-tories, stone benches for their occasional relaxation. A narrow double door in the back wall of this garden leads to a causeway which divides two patchwork stretches of small paddy fields. Beyond, on a low hill, there stand a cluster of well appointed bungalows and the marble lined meditation hall. This last is bare, very still; there is no motion in its air, sounds die within its walls. Its marble floor gleams faintly. A picture of Swami Nityananda dominates it, and others of him line the walls. The hill is quiet, bright with sunshine and bougainvilia. There are low, spear leaved guava trees. A yellow dog watches us, his ribs a deep corrugation under his skin. When I whistle, he runs away. The whole countryside is very still; on the slopes, two or three of the ashram's Westerners work at some improving task – improv-ing for them; it seems to have no value in itself. Outside the bungalows, long chairs stand on the terraces, prepared for the comfortable conversation of the faithful.

There is a great deal of social solidity about Swami Muktananda's flock: Bombay's rich professional and mercantile classes
are well represented. It is on their wealth, one must conclude,
that the wealth of the ashram is founded. Well groomed men,
Westernized all the week in their lightweight business suits, don
dhotis at the week-end and sink themselves again in their own
culture. The Indian, after all, in his very worldliness, is fulfilling
part of his religious obligation, passing through that householder
phase of his life which since Vedic times he has been enjoined to
do. Certainly none of the well-to-do followers of Swami Muktananda seem to feel any basic contradiction between the lives
they lead and the devotion they feel for their Guru.

*

A businessman in his late fifties, early sixties. He is unostenta-
tious, almost meek. His hair is grey, growing thin and brushed
back. He has the wide mobile mouth and toothy smile – a kind
of unconsciously ingratiating grimace – that many Indians have;
this has perhaps less to do with psychology than with a lack of
dental care in childhood. Despite a quiet dignity, a pervasive
and infectious seriousness, he is both friendly and forthcoming.
Looking at him, one would not guess that Gurus and their works
concerned him; polite, well dressed, he seems to carry no aura
of transcendental wisdom. Yet his attachment to Swami Muktananda is total and consuming, almost too much so to be
believable in so contained and retiring a man. But his sincerity
is utterly convincing.

'The concept of the relationship between Guru and shishya
is that of gravitation, in which the larger body attracts the
smaller one. With that gravitational pull, the Guru draws you
towards him. When we go a little further, we find that we don't
know the nature of this gravitation, how and why it works; we
know in what manner gravitation works, but why we do not.

'Fortunately, my wife also has an inclination to this aspect of life and we have no encumbrances in the form of children or anything. We are not very well off but we can manage our ends, so we can go on trying to pursue these activities. During the past fifteen or twenty years I must have visited about twenty sannyasis, stayed with them, heard their talks. And we went on studying ourselves in the various scriptural books and the Bible also, for I used to study at a college where they used to give scholarships only to those who had studied the scriptures. But after reading quite a lot, I found that there were things that the reading didn't tell me, particularly about meditation and how to control the activities of the mind. I tried to adopt the various postures advocated by our yogis – the asanas; but I never gained that meditation of the mind. It was only last year, about eight, nine months ago, that we thought of seeking some Master who could give us light. And we suddenly landed on Swami Muktananda and started going to his ashram. Of course I had been looking longer than that; when I went to see the sanyasis I sometimes put it to them that the shastras tells us that when you reach the proper stage you get the Guru. And one or two of them told me, "I am not your Guru: you'll find your Guru, but I'm not the one."

'So one day – it was a holiday, the Maharashtrian New Year's Day – we went to his ashram. There were three couples, we all went to see him. He was sitting there, giving a discourse. When the discourse was over, we sat there for about an hour. Then he said, "All six of you" – he didn't know us – "all six of you go now to the meditation hall and sit there for meditation." Without our asking, he told us this. So all the six of us went. But that day my mind was the same, I was thinking about all and sundry; I sat there for about ten minutes and came out. My wife sat there for about half an hour. Then we had lunch there and we went up for a rest; he has special rooms there where one can rest. And in the rest-room my wife said to me that she had been able to meditate during that time in the meditation hall. Then we came down and went for a cup of tea – there is a small hotel just near the ashram, a sort of place where you can have a cup of tea and a snack – but they told us that the milk for tea had not yet come although we could wait if we liked. But by then Babaji had come into the discourse-room, so we three gentlemen went in. The ladies said they would have a cup of tea and then come. We were sitting there and we had been sitting there for about ten minutes when somebody came and started asking, "Babaji, it is difficult for us to meditate, how do we get into it?"

'So Babaji turned round and said, "Look here, merely by making an effort you won't be able to go into meditation. By not making an effort, you'll never go into meditation. But besides, what you really need is a very high and intense desire. That intensity of the desire to get some guidance." He was confident that then one would go into meditation. He said, "In this high ashram, this hermitage, that power is always ready. It is in fact searching for individuals who will be able to go into meditation. And if the power finds that you are suitable, it will enter you." And then he said, "Look here, today six people have come from Bombay. I don't know them. But out of these six people, there is one fat lady, she got very good meditation today. She will just be coming."

'When he had finished the words, "She will just be coming", my wife entered the hall. He said, "Look here, she has come. Ask her, and you will know what it is."

'When he said this, my idea of my wife completely changed. Up to then, I had thought she was a person susceptible to outside influences and that her talk of meditation was just one of her usual ... moods, so to say. But when he himself said this, without our talking to him or anything, I was very much impressed.

'We sat there for another hour, and then again, at four o'clock, he said, "Go again for meditation." So we again sat. But for me the whole thing was the same; for ten or fifteen minutes I sat there and . . . My wife sat there for about an hour. When she came out, as is his usual practice, he was sitting in a chair outside.

'He said, "Mother, come." She went. Then he said, "During your meditation, you are reciting a very long mantra." During meditation, we were using a mantra given us by some other sanyasi. He said, "By using such a long mantra, it will be diffi-cult for you to go into meditation properly. You use the small mantra of *So-hum*" – he himself gave it to us. This gave me further conviction, because he even knew which mantra we were reciting.

'Thereafter, we have been visiting that place every week-end and have come across many incidents which have convinced us that here is a man who is really advanced and whom we should go to as closely as possible and get further help from. Although, once I was with a close disciple of Babaji and I suggested that we should go and meet him. That gentleman said, "Why do you want to do that? Babaji is everywhere. Just sit here, close your eyes and try to meditate. His grace is everywhere."

'After that man said that I sat down and to my great surprise on that day and from that day onward I have been able to sit for meditation for quite some time. Just I . . . forgot myself, which I had never been able to do before. And that is through his grace.

'Now I go almost every week-end when he is at Ganeshpuri. A lot of attraction develops and you feel like being with him, meeting him as much as you can. I don't ask him anything – I just sit absolutely silent. I only hear what he says. I don't ask him anything. Sometimes he talks, gives a discourse; normally we have a practice of reading certain parts of the scriptures together – we all sit together and read it aloud. Then he some-times talks and people listen to him. But Shankaracharya has written in a poem, "The lecture of the Guru is silent. The silent lecture of the Guru destroys all doubt in the disciple," and this, in some mystic manner, I have experienced. I can feel a communication.

She is very quiet, tall, friendly yet cool. Her husband is a naval officer, himself one of Swami Muktananda's devotees. When 'Babaji' comes to Bombay, he often stays in their apartment. Her face is thin and when she smiles it shows strong, unexpected lines. Her teeth are long, uneven, very white. Her high shoulders are hidden by the folds of her white sari. She wears sandals in pale, worked leather, bangles on her wrist, a miniature – of Swami Muktananda? – round her neck. Her black hair grows neat, grey wings. The dark eyes lie deep in her head and smile out at you as though to ambush you with an unexpected delight. She is happy, but in a contained way, as though she has just heard good news with which she will at any moment surprise you. The room where we talk is cool and calm, although outside the grey crows call anxiously to each other; around the walls and on occasional tables, pictures of Swami Muktananda watch us balefully, so that he seems like a silent and multiple witness to this interrogation of which he is the subject. Her silky sari stirs and twists in the draught from the fan overhead. She fidgets, covering her hand with her mouth as she talks, smoothing her long cheeks with her fingers. But her eyes continue to smile, her expression remains one of a strong, compassionate joy.

'I don't come from a religious background – not that formal type of religion. I come from a good family of educated people, but we were never religious in this sense that we used to go to the temple or worship in that traditional way. We were rather more Westernized people in our outlook because I come from the Punjab and that part of India has come more under Western influence. So I never practised religion in that sense; I was interested in reading serious books, right from my school days. As a matter of fact, all my brothers and sisters – our main interest has been books – reading books: literature, psychology, philosophy, and the study of human nature. So gradually I became interested more and more in serious reading. Then I started suffering from some ... you know ... mental troubles – fears, worries and nervousness, and I actually came into contact with one of the very good professors of psychology who was in Gujerat State ... In India, you know, especially in those days when I was a schoolgirl and I started suffering from these troubles, these mental troubles were not treated seriously. Like you go to a doctor when you have a cold or a fever; when you have fears or anxieties, your parents won't take you to a psychiatrist. My parents didn't know what a psychiatrist was! [She laughs.] So I was suffering; at the same time I didn't know what to do. My brother, who is a few years older than me, helped me a lot; he would bring books on psychology and tell me to read those, and I got more and more interested in psychology because I wanted to know what it was that was the cause of my troubles. And then he took me to one of his professors of psychology, and he was actually the head of the department of psychology of Punjab University. He used to treat patients also through these modern methods of psychology – psychoanalysis and all that; and he had been to America and studied there. He was a genius. He was very sympathetic to me and we became more like friends; later on, when I got married, he used to come and stay with me in Bombay when he came on some job ... Anyway, during those days when I used to have sittings with him, one day he said to me, "My dear girl, you will never be completely cured until you learn to meditate like a good Brahmin."

'At that time, I didn't understand the full significance of this. Then gradually, through psychology, I became interested in philosophy and religion. I started reading books; I even joined M.A. (Philosophy). First I joined M.A. (Psychology), but I couldn't continue because my mental troubles started increasing and then there was Partition and there were practical difficulties, our family was scattered, we had no home for some time . . . So I gave up studying psychology. He used to tell me that I should do some creative work: "You have so much extra energy, you must use it up in some way." So I first learned painting and I was very good at it also; but it didn't give me full satisfaction though I used to paint well and all the teachers used to praise them . . . Soon I started feeling frustrated in painting also. I said, "No, it's not giving me satisfaction," and I gave up painting also.

'Then I became a teacher. I thought loving children and teaching them may help me, and I became a very popular teacher with the children; I used to receive heaps of letters from my students. But even that didn't give me satisfaction, the complete satisfaction which I was seeking. So I gave up that also. You see, after some time I started thinking, "What is in painting, after all? What is in teaching?" It stopped giving me that happiness, that satisfaction, perhaps, that I was seeking consciously or unconsciously. I would start getting moods of depression and frustration without any reason. Then I would start doing something else, with the hope that that would set me right.

'Then I was a social worker for a year, and then gave up that also. Then I joined M.A. (Philosophy) – there were some other practical reasons also. Then this professor of mine said, "Why don't you get married? That may help you to become a little more settled and normal." I had no plan to get married during my school and college days; I always used to imagine myself as excelling in something and I looked down upon married life. "Everyone gets married – what is remarkable about marriage?" That was my attitude. And as it happened I was very good in my studies also – I used to come first in the class . . .

'But then I was suffering so much from mental depression, such intense depression that I used to cry like a child and it was more painful than any physical thing. I was in such a condition that I would do anything to get rid of mental suffering, so I agreed to get married. [She laughs.] And I got a very good husband – very intelligent, very calm, mature and ... But after some time, the same thing started all over again.

'Then, of course, it became more difficult. By then I had children and I couldn't ... like I gave up painting and I gave up teaching ... I couldn't give up my married life so easily [laughs], so then there was no way out left. One day, a friend of mine, while I was working as a social worker, a man who had been with Mahatma Gandhi for many years and had not married, a very mature person ... you know, he became a very good friend of mine and I opened my heart to him and he said, "Come, I'll take you to a person; he might help you."

'He took me to one Swamiji who was in charge of the Ramakrishna Mission in Delhi – an excellent person. I went to him and I told him everything. I also told him this: I said, "I want to join M.A. (Philosophy) because I've studied psychology to some extent and I want to get to the root of things." So he told me, "Instead of studying, why not live it and experience it? Studying won't help you much."

'Then I started practising ... I started trying to put these things into practice in my own life – like doing a little meditation, sitting for a few minutes ... And then I was told by some friends, and by Swamiji, that getting initiation from a Guru helps.

'They said that if husband and wife both take initiation it's better, so I went with my husband also and we both took initiation, and he gave us a mantra and we started repeating that mantra daily. I started sitting daily, in the morning and the evening, and repeating that mantra for some time.

'But still I found that it didn't help me much. I was still very restless, I would keep on looking at my watch [laughs] and I would get up after fifteen or twenty minutes. On the other hand, I was longing to have a real ... you know ... To get lost in spiritual experience, get lost in meditation and experience that blissful state which had been described in books. Now I had a clear-cut goal before me and I was longing to achieve that.

'Coming back to the practical side of life, we started building a house in Delhi. My husband had a very restricting job in those days so I was supervising the house. I used to go in the morning and come back in the evening. Most of these contractors are so dishonest and try to cheat you in every way; I being already over sensitive, highly strung, the worrying type, it became a great strain on my mind and I again started being troubled by those mental troubles: fears and nervousness, couldn't sleep at night, couldn't get those thoughts out of my mind ... And my physical health also broke down with the strain. Then one of my brothers who lived in Bombay came to Delhi on official duty, and he used to come and talk about this Swami Muktananda a great deal.

'It interested me, because he was in our family the most rational type of person, very practical minded; he never believed in these things, he was the last person to go to any religious person. Because he lived in the West for quite some time, his two boys were studying, one in England and one in America, and he was the director of a firm of engineers.

'But a time came when he started suffering from the same trouble from which I was suffering, but in a much more intense way; and he, of course, because he used to go to England and France and other countries, there also he took the best treatment and wasted a lot of money. But it didn't help him. He started taking tranquillizers in Delhi. Then all these intense worries, fears, insomnia, tranquillizers, brought about a serious heart attack. After that, his wife, who is M.A. in psychology and who understood him – she had been to the States ... When he was suffering, it was a great strain on her also. The stage was reached when she wanted some relief somewhere, so she thought of Ganeshpuri. Once or twice she had been there before; first she went there and spent one day there and felt peaceful on that day. She didn't tell him about her troubles, but Swamiji told her, when she was leaving in the evening, "Mother" – he calls every lady Mother – "Mother, come here every week-end, every Sunday."

'She said, "I can't come, Swamiji, because my husband won't let me; he's not interested in this sort of thing."

'So she went back home for a couple of days and she was relaxed and had more peace of mind; but by the end of the week she again started to feel that tension, again wanted to get away and spend the day at Ganeshpuri. She told my brother; she said she was going to this place for one day and she had explained everything to the servants and he would have no trouble. But to her surprise he said, "Don't go today, go Saturday. We'll go together tomorrow – I'll come also."

'She said, "No, no – that's not a place for you. You won't like it."

'"No, I feel like going, so what objection have you?"

'He pressed so hard that she agreed to it, and the next morning they both left together in the car and spent the whole day there. He didn't talk to Swamiji much, my brother, but when he came away he realized that that day after many, many months he had felt so relaxed that he had forgotten to take even a single pill. So naturally enough he wanted to go there again. And that's how he started going all the week-ends, going every week-end; then he started going on Friday evening and coming back Monday morning. Then they built a cottage there so that they'd have a place to live.

'Anyway, when he used to come to Delhi he used to talk about this, and we also found a marked change in him; his outlook was very positive and his health had improved and in every way we found a great change in him. We thought this man must be having some spiritual powers to change a person like him. So when he came on this occasion and saw me, he said, "You are on the verge of a mental and physical breakdown, so you'd better get away from this environment otherwise you'll end up in a mental home. The best place would be Ganeshpuri; why don't you come there for a fortnight? I have the cottage and you can stay there."

'Our house was not finished and my child was sick – he had chicken-pox – but everybody forced me to go away and have a change. So I came here for a fortnight and, during that fortnight, my whole life changed. All my mental troubles disappeared after I stayed at Ganeshpuri. That never came back.

'I experienced the happiest state of blissfulness; that was something which I never really expected to ... it was beyond expectations. I didn't talk to him much, I didn't tell him about my background; I just used to sit there in his presence, and during the first two or three days I felt I had made a mistake, you know, leaving Delhi and my sick child at home, and I thought it was wrong on my part to listen to my brother and do all this. But after two or three days some changes started taking place within me: for instance, while sitting there in the hall, in his presence, I used to feel so peaceful, so rested, that my mind would go deep into meditation for hours together; I'd sometimes sit there from six in the morning till twelve, and forget about my breakfast, forget about having tea or anything; I used to get so lost in meditation without any conscious effort – so much so I even forgot to write home. After the first two or three days, no thought about my children, about the house building, about my husband, entered my mind. I used to feel on top of the world. I was always well!

'In the mornings I used to get up at four o'clock, and at home I used to get up at six or seven. I'd get up at four in the morning and I'd feel like singing devotional songs; sometimes I used to feel so much joy in my heart, so much bliss, that I used to feel that I wouldn't be able to contain it; before that, during all my life, I have been ... well, sort of ... I don't know how to express it ... Even in my childhood I never experienced that happiness or joy because I was a serious type, thinking type, always full of fears and anxieties . . . So this was a unique experience for me, compared to that. When I was leaving, I didn't feel like going away. I cried and cried for hours – and then went on crying because I didn't want to leave that place. I was going back to that hell and I'd again suffer from the same fears and moroseness and . . . I wanted to stay there. But of course I couldn't, so he himself told me, "Don't worry, you'll come many times and I'll also come to Delhi."

'Then, when I went back, to my pleasant surprise that state of mind continued there! The same things were still there but it was as if they were not affecting me in the same way – the situation was exactly the same. Since then, a change has taken place and it has continued – that is more important. All this happened four and a half years ago.

'Everyone will describe Swamiji in a different way because it all depends on your own feelings; but I can explain to you how I feel. One thing is that he is different from all other saints that I ever met. Usually when people go to him they don't feel like talking. And previously when I used to go and visit such persons, I used to go with a list of questions I wanted to ask them [laughs], discuss my problems with them . . . But when I came to him, I never asked him anything. His silent influence works on you when you are in his presence – and if you are receptive to it. And that worked a thousand times more effectively than the lectures or the discussions one had with other saints. It's like giving an injection directly to a person or giving a blood transfusion – it works like that. The others are like slow acting medicines – pills and powders.

'Secondly, he has all their knowledge also – actually more than they have though his style is very simple . . . but it touches your heart. The words go deep into your heart. And he will express great truths in such a simple way and such a natural way.

'Then there is another difference in him from other saints. It is very difficult to understand his actions. Sometimes you will misunderstand him. In the beginning, that used to put off my husband. Most of the time he won't talk of scriptural things, he'll talk of just ordinary things if you go to him. He'll ask how your wife is, or your job – he'll talk about ordinary things, even politics, and he won't talk about spiritual topics. But you expect when you go to a saint that he'll be most of the time talking about spiritual subjects. And there are other actions of his that are rather difficult to understand; when one comes closer to him and develops a certain . . . love for him, or communion with him, then we start understanding all that's involved and why he does that.

'This is all very strange, you know, and I often wonder how it happened, because I was at that time very critical of everything, a doubting type: our whole family is that type. But ever since my first experience and my first contact with him, I've had deep faith in him, and such a high opinion of him that it has been going up and up rather than ever even for a moment doubting he was not what I thought. The more I come closer to him, the spirituality is revealed more and more to me and my faith in him becomes deeper and deeper . . .'

*

The darkness comes down, slowly at first, then like a lid shutting. Having arrived, I now seem a sort of parcel, something left lying around which it is no one's duty to clear. I stand in the dark forecourt, while around me the devoted pass to and fro. Finally I am taken to food, joining the lines of crouched eaters facing each other along the length of a grey terrace, their fingers busily scooping up gobbets of curry-corrupted rice.

When I am assigned a room mate, I fetch my small luggage; in picking it up, my chappal touches holy floor and I am quietly chastised. The place where I am to sleep stands near the water tower: a small hut, slant roofed, green shuttered. By the door there stands an earthenware jug of drinking water, and above the beds, hang furled mosquito nets, lifeless as exorcized ghosts.

David, upon whom I have been billeted, is American, has been here several months and expects to stay several more. He is tall, bony, with black hair cut very tight to the skull, shaved perhaps, thinning very slightly on the crown. He has grown a square, wiry beard. Sometimes he wears round, metal rimmed glasses; when he does not, you can see that he has pale brown eyes curiously flecked with dark specks. He seems very serious, even solemn, then suddenly is smiling; we begin to get on.

At nine o'clock, the lights must be put out. David clambers under his mosquito net, but I decide to brave the predators, putting my head under the blankets when I hear that venomous drone. I sleep badly; by two or three in the morning it is very cold. At around four o'clock drums are beaten, trumpets and conches cacophonically blown: thus the gods are brought to attention. Then the singing (actual or recorded) starts, within the main building but amplified for the world to get its benefit. Unexpectedly, the drone of those unified voices as they swing up and down the monotonous lines is beautiful, a chaste sound which rejects all decoration. Under his mosquito net I can see the dim, white clad figure of David, upright in morning meditation. At five o'clock, the pump begins, heaving into the waiting tanks the day's supply of water. From somewhere near by, dogs bark as if in response. A little before dawn, everyone in the ashram is expected to assemble and greet the new sun with chanted verses of the *Bhagavad Gita*.

After that, Swami Muktananda speaks to those who have come forward, or perhaps answers questions, or simply sits, a source of silent and indefinable power. Sometimes he sings in a husky but melodious voice; he is fond of music. At noon there is food, followed by a period of rest. Between three and four o'clock there is again a recitation, usually of the 'thousand names of God'. At four, the Guru appears for the second time to make himself available to his flock. At seven in the evening there is another arati, usually better attended than the pre-dawn worship. Supper follows, and then another holy recitation which is not obligatory on all. At nine in the evening, the last lights go out. After that, only the grumbling yellow dogs issue gruff challenges across the night or, on the road outside, an occasional tonga rolls, rough wheeled, down the hill to Ganeshpuri.

At six forty every morning, therefore, I assemble with the others in the L-shaped audience or darshan hall. (*Darshana* means 'beholding', important to Hindus since they believe that to see someone eminent or holy is to take into oneself some of his virtue.) The shaft of the L-shape is actually an extension of what is essentially a large square room; along it, behind a row of doors, are the ashram offices and the library, and through the door that leads from here into the forecourt the men enter. The women's entrance is farther along and brings one straight into the main part of the hall.

To the left of the women's entrance, and thus facing the shaft of the L, stands a large coloured picture of Swami Nityananda, his chin raised, his head a little to one side, his eyes almost aggressively wide, with a great bowl of naked belly below: he peers out at us like a precocious, irritable baby. Garlands and coloured lights hang about this portrait and, before it, the offerings of fruit or money made by the faithful lie in harvested heaps. Other garlands of jasmine and marigold hang by the gate outside, from the eaves above the door, from the ceiling. Garlanded too, in the far corner of the room, stands the white effigy of a god. To the right of this are the double doors that lead to Swami Muktananda's private quarters, and to the right of that again, his gadi, his seat or throne of rust-red plush with great padded arms. To the left of the gadi and facing it, the women sit; straight in front of it, the men. To the right, against the wall, a line of cushions marks the places set aside for more distinguished guests.

In the grey pre-dawn light the men and women slowly assemble, those who live on the ashram, visitors to it, people who live near by. Some wear blankets or heavy sweaters against the cold, a few carry cushions to sit on; in the course of an hour or so, sitting cross-legged on the hard floor becomes arduous even for an Indian. As they enter, they prostrate themselves before the empty gadi or before Swami Nityananda's portrait. A small boy falls flat on his face, scrambles up, grabs a copy of the Gita, makes a face at someone, then sits in front of the women. A young man in a woollen cap plays one soft note on a small harmonium while beside him a *tambura* player thrumbs a string, a muted, intermittent throbbing. People mutter to each other in low voices, or sit immobile, already sifting their psychic nourishment from the precious atmosphere. Outside, the last hour of the night dwindles silently.

The double doors swing open. Like an actor, Swami Mukta-nanda makes his entrance. He marches in, vigorous, of medium height, bearded. He wears ochre robes of fine material, an ochre shawl, a jersey. His ochre cap carries two pompoms which swing to and fro as he erupts in this dramatic way into the hall. Without a word or a glance for anyone, he walks straight to the door, stands there a moment looking out into the darkness, then steps out of sight. We wait in silence, almost with bated breath. We do not look round. Half a minute passes, then he returns. He marches to the low throne, sits down. A rush of devotees presses forward; they prostrate themselves, then settle into two rows facing each other and at right angles to the gadi. Those sitting there are privileged, sadhus, prominent devotees, old-established followers. They have their places, their precedence.

Reaching up, the Guru switches on a light illuminating the place where he sits, the lectern before it. He begins to lead the singing – his voice is loud though not unpleasantly so, and he puts in grace notes and breaks which the others do not permit themselves, or perhaps are not permitted. A beautiful girl with a clear, edged voice seconds him among the women.

Through the windows the quiet of the early morning seems to muffle our efforts. As we sing, more and more people steal in, doff their blankets, join the chanting. And suddenly it is light outside, the sun has risen after all, the last note dies away. Most people get to their feet, prostrate themselves again, then leave. The Guru sits, he gazes out at us. Later he sings to the electronic drone, while the women, remaining, listen raptly.

Next door there stands a chai shop and at this hour of the morning it becomes busy as the stiff and frozen devotees relax over tea. A young man comes over to me; he has travelled three days by train with his parents and two sisters all the way from the other side of India, from Bihar, to be with Swami Muktananda. Are there no Gurus in Bihar, I ask him.

'Yes, yes – but not like Baba.'

'What makes him different?'

He hesitates, perhaps not knowing the answer, perhaps only uncertain of the English for it. Then he smiles broadly.

'Baba is wonderful,' he says.

*

David is at ease with himself. He is not trying to become Indian, he is trying to become himself. He takes up no exaggerated attitudes of piety to what he is doing (one night I lent him a Simenon: later, when he came out of a long period of meditation, he gave me a big smile and said, 'Now I know who did it!'). He is not dedicated to becoming a sadhu, nor, like other Westerners I met, determined to unravel the secrets of the spiritual universe. He is relaxed, happy with the task he has set himself, one that is difficult enough without metaphysical embellishment. Perhaps this is because he approaches his new life from a position of strength – he was successful enough in his American existence not to feel apologetic. What could be done in that way, he did; in the end, he discovered it was not enough. Then he came to India.

'It's kind of hard to be brief about how I got here. It started when I was born. I'm not trying to be smart-ass or anything. But the most memorable, outstanding mind-whammy was my acid trip. You see, I was very deeply involved in manipulating my environment. I was working eighteen hours a day practising law, politics, part of the moderate Left trying to take over the party from within. Very good at it in our community. We did control the situation in our community. We had control of the city, getting the first Federal grants for the Negroes, we were doing all those things, getting jobs and recreation facilities, trying to improve the environment, fighting the big industries on pollution, doing all the things you do to try and make the whole living situation harmonious and worthwhile. I knew where I was going, I thought I had an objective. I thought I was a talented young man and I should use my talents to help other people, improve the society and the environment, I thought I could tell exactly what was right and what was wrong. And the whole of the problem was that the whole of society was run by a bunch of idiots; ignorance was rife, and greed. I really thought I knew exactly where it was at. And of course – I never did think about this aspect of it – but I obviously really enjoyed the exercise of power and playing that role; I always thought of myself as the little boy fighting against the big giants, too, which is very interesting. I always thought of myself as David facing Goliath.

'Well, everybody I'd known had taken acid for years, people I knew who were living around me, people I was running to. At college I went to a funny spade psychiatrist who was taking people on trips in '56, '57, '58, always talking to me about it. And I had read all the literature about it and I knew lots of people who had done it and I was very, very careful to read everything I could read about it and get a shrink to take me on a trip and do the whole thing in what I thought was a very objective way; because I was curious to know about myself.

'When I took acid it was like some large hand had reached over and ripped my exterior off. That's the only way to describe it. You don't think of having an interior and exterior, but it was as if there was no shell. I had total perception in every direction as far as I wanted to let it move. I started out in the beginning of the trip playing mind games. Everything was in extreme, vivid colours, extreme beautiful colours, and I could make any shape in as far a direction as I wanted to in every direction. I had no sense of up or down or sideways. And I could make any sound go with any of that shape. I could create symphonies, concerts, all variety of sounds and shapes and colours, all flowing in every direction as far as I wanted to make them go. I could see forever. I'd had some fun with my mind, smoked grass for twenty years since I was twelve, but I'd never even conceived of a mind having that kind of capacity. Never conceived of it. That was the first couple of hours. I've got to tell you about this trip because it really did it.

'Then I opened up my eyes and looked around and it became extremely obvious that everything I had ever believed in about reality was false. And there's something about acid, people say, "Well, it's a drug and how do you know that it isn't the drug and not you?" There's something about it that you know and there's no way you can convince someone that hasn't taken it, because you realize that you're seeing something, that something's been removed, an obstacle has been removed from your vision and you're seeing something and you simply know it's the truth. I don't feel the need of convincing anybody of it, I don't think; but I know it's the truth. You see everything as one great light show. You see everything as forms of light, everything you thought of as solid walls and hamburgers you can squeeze, things are soft and hard – it's just different forms of light and you see it quivering and moving and you see it rising and falling, you can see, literally see, mountains or flowers or trees wake up when the sun rises in the morning. You can smell and feel and hear them waking up. You can feel the vibrations from animals.

'Have you ever been around, like, a mouse or a little animal and ever notice how one-pointed they are on you? Like they'll be totally concentrated on everything you're doing, like you'd be if you were in a room with somebody that much bigger than you? Well, that's how you become about everything.

'And I looked out over San Francisco; I was in an apartment up high where I could see the port and the sea and the water and the people, and you could see everything that was happening, you could see the people scurrying around, you could feel them scurrying around and around and around: this big hum of people running around. You could see the pollution coming off them into the air. When a bird flew by you could just feel yourself flying by; you were the bird, you know. And you could see the absolute total futility of man doing things. It was just absolutely pointless. It became clear to me very fast that the only point was knowing what was happening, being aware; until one was aware of what was happening, all that scurrying around was a tremendous waste of effort and most of it was extremely negative and harmful. I mean people were doing so much more harm than good. Which is obvious even to someone who isn't very aware.

'I took a series of acid trips, spaced them out three to six months apart so I wouldn't burn myself because I could feel the mental exhaustion that it caused and I'd observed what it had done to people that had taken it too close together, and I never had any problems arise as a result.

'What happened then, I tried to get myself out of all the things I was in; I had a lot of financial commitments, I had just built an enormous house, you know, I had just socked myself in for a career, being the leader, great white hope, and I had to unravel myself out of a lot of financial things, political things. I had a big law practice with all kinds of dates for trials that we schedule a long time ahead. I stopped taking major cases, just slowly got out of it. I left two years ago. Left the office exactly two years ago now. Went and spent the summer in Europe and drove here, got here last November. I wasn't in a big hurry, I knew what I was going to do, but I wanted to kind of visit a lot of Sufis coming across because I was very interested in Sufism. I wasn't sure which road I was going to go on. Went and spent some time in Benares, here and there, and found out from a Sufi lady in Delhi that the highest yogi she knew going was Muktananda. So I came here.

'I came here looking for a Guru who was going to tell me how to get rid of greed and hatred and all that. I don't have any delusions about becoming realized, because that happens to one out of every million people who take up meditation. I put my goals probably more practically; I'd just like to get rid of greed and hatred and be able to feel that kind of love that I felt and I don't want to have to take drugs to do it. I don't want to destroy myself. I enjoy life. I knew absolutely nothing about shaktipat or kundalini; I'd read something about it but I didn't know much about it. So I came here and decided to do what they do here and see what happens.

'And what they do here is you do your chores every day and you go sit in front of Swami Muktananda for a certain period of time a day. And I did that. And after a while I started feeling some very strange sensations in my head and body. A very thick, honey, warm feeling, a feeling that I'd call ecstasy. And say that I'd never felt ecstasy before; I thought that sex was ecstasy, but this is another level of ecstasy, a level terribly more gripping, amazingly enough. You just feel . . . I have read other people's descriptions; someone who described his feelings in front of Raman Maharshi and it's exactly the way he described it. He said it feels like your mind is immersed in a thick sea of honey.

You know, it stops all mind chatter, it just stops; just "slurp", like jumping into a bath-tub full of vaseline. It just stops, but in the nicest way. And you have this warm, warm, warm, thick, thick feeling all through you, especially in your head, also in your body, in the trunk of your body. And it gets stronger and stronger and stronger.

'Then I went with him for a couple of weeks to Bombay and a couple of weeks in Baroda. And when I'm in front of him a lot of hours a day, then I'll even have it when I'm meditating when I'm not around him. And if you really get it strong, you can keep it and be a long way away from him. You know what this is supposed to do? Of course, the idea of meditation is to stop the mind chatter so you can see into yourself, see yourself past all the ego talk of past and future. In a very crude way – this is putting it in an extremely crude way – whilst your Guru helps what you're doing by giving you his grace, his one-pointedness is so powerful and so intense that, on a level that is not something that I know enough of to describe, he communicates that to you. But so many people that come here, people who didn't know that that was going to happen to them, people who just dropped in with other people, sat down and felt this sensation that I know it's not a product of my imagination; I know it's real, I know it's damned real because I have staggered and reeled around like I was high on dope or booze. It's not like booze and it's not like dope, it's like something else, but the closest thing in our experience would be like a drug. You know, you feel good, you feel warm, you feel thick, you feel loving: you feel good. It's obviously something in you, something's happening. You feel like some external thing has come into you. Now all I have to do is to be near him and I feel it. If I walk by where he is, I feel it. He gives off these vibrations and from everything I've read every saint gives off these vibrations.

'I can feel him coming. You know, like I'm allergic to cats and I can tell you when there's a cat in the house without even having to see it or even being in the house or even seeing any hair or anything. That's the way it is. You know he's there. You feel this intense feeling. You know it's a very real feeling, it's not vague, you know. It's not a little tingly thing you have to look for, it's Whapp! It's immediately the most present thing in your mind.'

*

The world is brown, a pale brown as far as I can see; to the hills thin beyond morning mist, everything seems dulled as if covered by a film of dust. The old green of the leaves, the earth, the tangled cactus hedges, the clumps of rocks, the wiry stubble of the rice, even the thinly chirping birds – all are brown, this pale brown: a dun, almost a golden yellow. Even the people: as I sit, two naked boys pass, leading a third in baggy shorts; their shining, black-brown skins are smudged into the same all-pervading colour. It is as if this dullness were in the light itself, in the atmosphere, infused into the very processes of vision.

The ashram is in the distance, the new block lifting above the pale grey, the near-white, of Swami Muktananda's apartment. A red flag flicks slowly to and fro in a collapsing breeze. I have walked away from the place into this monochrome landscape, overcome by claustrophobia. Everything is the Guru there, everything revolves round him, his is the only energy, love of him the only emotion, only his desires are legitimate. I look back, half-expecting to see him at an upstairs window, watching the world and me in it.

There comes a tinkling of bells, a sound too soft for gaiety, but peaceful, enhancing this stillness – the ashram cattle walk in a line along the nearby path, their shining backs brown or dappled, their soft eyes easy with the world. One, more curious, stops to examine me, its moist, lifted muzzle snuffling in my direction. The herd is led by a black Ugandan and is followed by a tall lad with long blond hair from the United States. They make a congruous, pastoral pair, both wrapped in loose white, each carrying a staff. I let them move on then slowly follow them back to the ashram. Behind me, a bird trills with a sudden energy, and from farther away comes the rhythmic sound of someone chopping branches. A child runs up to me, laughing, hand out: 'Paise. Paise, sahib.'

I miss lunch, preferring to lie down. I have a cold, perhaps influenza. The nights are frosty and I have woken up several times, shivering. I dose myself with aspirin, hoping to dull the almost constant headache. But at four in the afternoon I go back to the audience hall; this is the time when Swami Muktananda makes himself available again to those who want to hear him, speak to him, be near him, to those come for his darshan.

Again, as chanting ends, he bursts dramatically through those double doors. He wears dark glasses, his down turned mouth is set and firm, his thinning hair is covered by one of the ochre caps which he affects and which devotees present to him. He stands outside, looks up the road. A tonga rattles by, harness bells tinkling. When he steps energetically back in again, a small man runs up to him, his back half-bent, his voice high in complaint. He has been refused a seat on the line of cushions reserved for the privileged and wants that decision reversed. Swami Muktananda walks by him as if he were not there. The man subsides.

Letters from Europe or America are translated for him; this is the start of every afternoon's business. Then there is a rush forward of those who want to offer gifts, to prostrate themselves or ask questions. Because it is the week-end, there are fatter men in whiter dhotis than at other times, a greater crowd. As money and other gifts are offered, a tall, shaven-headed acolyte picks them up and lays them before the great picture of Swami Nityananda.

A man steps forward to make his farewells, a Westerner, a

scholar in Sanskrit and oriental studies, a stocky, broad shouldered man with spectacles, a bald head, a strong, greying beard.
He prostrates himself; sitting up, he looks heartbroken, like a
child miserable at leaving a party or a school where he has been
happy.

Swami Muktananda says, 'You'll take the shakti with you,
it'll get greater and greater. I'm very pleased with you, with your
fitness and your learning . . .'

'It's all yours! All due to you!'

The Guru says, 'It'll develop and you will be able to give the
shakti to others.'

'It's not developed enough for that. I don't feel it strongly
enough for that.'

His head is bowed, his voice small. Swami Muktananda nods
forcefully, his face thrusts forward.

'It'll develop. The force of the hatha yoga will make it
develop.'

He indicates the cushion beside him and the other man settles
there in the lotus position. Soon, his eyes are closed and he is
swaying.

A large young woman, very fat, perhaps pregnant, kneels
beside the Guru. She breathes heavily, she sways. Swami Muktananda looks at her. He is expressionless, which is to say that his
face is set in its usual fierce, arrogant lines. He puts both hands
beside his head and watches her, then looks restlessly away.
The woman leans slowly forward, her head touches the ground,
she is motionless for a while. Everything is very quiet. She leans
back, kneels again. Swami Muktananda bends forward towards
her, speaks with an unexpected softness, with an apparent great
affection. Is it a particular Guru, a swami whom he names, who
initiated her? Delighted, she agrees. They talk for a while, then
she withdraws.

An old man in a blue coat comes forward, does his obeisance,
then makes his complaint – his clothes, he says, are being burnt,

his sons are going out of their minds, he has come two hundred miles for help . . . Swami Muktananda tells him he is the victim of sorcery. He asks if a certain person, dark, thin, perhaps a physician, has visited the old man's house. 'Your troubles started from that moment.'

Then, for a long time, a young girl sits beside him. She has not long before been initiated by another Guru. Recently she has begun to achieve trance states and to experience strange sensations. She trembles, she is very tense. In samadhi, she says, she has been seeing lights. (Later, in the courtyard at the back, I will see her crouched beside his chair and weeping.)

A book has arrived. It is in English, on some aspect of religion. Professor Jain translates parts of it. Swami Muktananda's air is lofty, yet eager; his eyes gleam as if with pleasure at the comprehension of ideas. Perhaps he is often bored. Now he nods, he makes swift gestures with his hands.

A long silence follows. An old lady sits in the front rank of the women, her eyes closed, swaying slightly. Near me, an elderly man sits in rapt concentration, then, as someone stumbles against him in passing, looks up in sudden irritation. David, back very straight, head back, drinks in the source of his new energy. Swami Muktananda sits still, his elbow on the arm of the gadi, his hand high, finger and thumb together as, in a gesture already familiar to me, he turns his wrist slowly to and fro. I look around me. What do all these people see in him, what are they feeling in this silence, what is reaching them? David has told me, 'He's got like great teats all over him and we just suck and suck that heavy goodness out of him.' Some of the people are restless, moving their buttocks to ease the discomfort of the hard floor. But many are like David himself, immobile, absolutely still, a few with their eyes closed, but others watching their Guru with a kind of endless, yet expectant, curiosity, as though certain that some colossal and wonderfully enriching secret will at any moment be revealed to them.

When David gets up to go, I follow him. As an inmate of the ashram he has to work, in the mornings from eight thirty to ten thirty, in the afternoons from four thirty until six o'clock. The place has to be kept clean, land has to be cleared, rubbish has to be moved, the cattle must be tended, water carried. Among the Westerners, a mutinous feeling is beginning to develop. They claim they have not enough time to meditate, that they are kept at useless tasks too long, taken off useful ones too early. In the tea-shop, the French girl says, one morning, 'I could not work any more.' She leans back, white faced, her eyes are dull. 'I could not see any more – it was all black. We were picking up stones on the hillside and I could not, any more.' Her French accent is plaintive. For the Westerners, it is meditation they want, spiritual peace, contemplation. The Guru is a means to that end, a mentor and a focus. But he is not a god, an absolute in himself before whom one must abase oneself, as he is for the Indians. There is no virtue in such self-abnegation, they seem to feel, although to understand and even to transcend the self remains their aim. The conflict has its roots, perhaps, in the different view of what the self is: India sets nothing like the store on individuality that the West does.

My bones ache, I am beginning to shiver, the influenza is worse. David and one or two of the others suggest that it is Swami Muktananda's influence working on me. They can, they say, remember the aches they themselves felt when the shakti first began to work on them. I feel too miserable to argue, but go and lie down. Flat on the bed under my little window, I listen to the sounds of others, busy or gossiping about the ashram. I feel the hot throbbing of a high temperature begin its unpleasant rhythm below my temples.

In the evening, I go in with the others for the meal, rice and dal ladled out on stitched-together plantain leaves. Every night, the Guru sits to greet and take the obeisance of those who are, after all, guests in his house. Swami Muktananda, this evening, has set up a gadi in the half-finished porch of the new building. Lit from below by a lamp set on the floor, leaning slightly sideways, his dark, narrow eyes impassive, he looks like a feudal lord, perhaps a robber baron, accepting impassively the courtesies of his retainers. His energy is contained, yet very real; he looks a man of great power. Dramatic highlights turn his face into a mask of strength. I bow, the palms of my hands together, and he nods distantly. How much of the effect he makes is contrived, I wonder; then go on my way to where, cross-legged, I shall scoop up his succulent rice in my inexpert fingers.

Then back to pills again, pyjamas and two shirts, the single blanket folded double, a night of misery and cold, broken by bouts of shivering, rodents tumbling about the roof; at four, the strident clamour for the attention of the gods.

*

The major-domo, the principal lieutenant – Professor Jain. Once he taught English in a university but was always a seeker after spiritual certainty, determined to find the right method of belief, of life. 'For years I lived in my own way,' he writes, 'trying to strike out the path which would answer my needs and suit my disposition and personality. I wandered from one way to another, experimented with different modes of living at different times.' But he 'had intellectual contempt for bhakta types – I thought that they were basically weak creatures. "Why should they talk so glibly about God's or Guru's grace?" I would ask myself again and again.' Then he met Swami Muktananda; now he lives on the ashram, travels with his Guru, serves him in ways both high and low.

He is a small man, neat boned, sunken cheeked, his eyes long lidded, almond shaped. His voice is even, very quiet and controlled. His face is expressionless, his manner equable. His slight figure is to be seen everywhere, hurrying about his errands, his shaven head bowed in thought. Sometimes when he speaks to

people he touches them, holds them lightly by the wrist or fore-
arm. It is then as if another, more eager man is breaking
through; his smile, too, illuminates with an unexpected friendliness his usually sombre face. It is hard to tell how old he is –
perhaps in his thirties, perhaps twenty years older. He sits on a
stool outside the entrance of the audience hall, marigold garlands fluttering from the eaves above his head. When he
bends, a touch or two of grey glitters in the stubble on his long
skull.

'Perhaps we should begin with a very basic principle and say
that God is the Guru, and God is in everyone: that means the
Guru is inside. And it is only God who can bring you to your
Guru. But the problem for the seeker is that the God within is
not easily available, that in spite of wanting to, many people get
no access to the God within. What they get access to is past
impressions which are lying buried and which at times look like
inspiration. What is one going to do about it? And it is then that
one turns to a Guru, because it is only the Guru who can challenge your ego. And that's why the emphasis is laid on surrender; but when one starts to look at the concrete details of this
surrender, one finds that the relationship between Guru and disciple is a very complex and a very complete one. On the one
hand, it is as human as any human relationship, and on the other,
it is impersonal. He is a friend to you, he is a mother to you, he
is a father to you, he is a beloved, he is a master. With the Guru
you find that all these human relationships coalesce into one.
Therefore the Guru becomes the centre of all your emotions.

'And it is impersonal in the sense that, if you are talking with a
human friend, what is emerging from that is something very
limited which may have meaning only for the two of you and
which may have no meaning to anybody else. Whereas here, if
you are turning to the Guru as a friend, the ultimate outcome
will be significant for everybody else because through that you

265

will be discovering your supreme, divine personality. So it is human and yet not human, and it would apply to other people as much as it would to you.

'The Guru does not start preaching without knowing that he is realized – he is fully conscious of his own stature. Take the case of Ramakrishna – he knew he was an avatar of God. Or my own Guru, Swami Muktananda – he knows what heights he has attained. He is fully aware of the fact that he has achieved perfection and it is only after he has achieved perfection that he can set himself up as a Guru. It may be that there is always a chance of self-deception in some cases, but when his Guru is there, and assuming that he is fully realized, it is only on his authority that we come to accept his disciple as our Guru. His Guru declared that he had achieved perfection; then we find out from our own experience. That is, the Guru will not make a declaration as such; he will keep on suggesting it and we will keep on discovering it, but if it is necessary at times to give it an explicit form he will never fight shy of that. Because the Guru isn't humble; if he is hiding himself he is hiding himself not because he does not want to make it plain, but because he doesn't find it necessary to do so.

'I am not one of those who searched for a Guru for a long time. As a matter of fact I was sceptical about the whole institution, even the concept philosophically, because I had been educated in the concepts of Western philosophy. But as time went by, I discovered him as I discovered myself. I was introduced to him by a friend whom I dearly loved, but on me the impact was not sudden and startling. With me the relationship was gradual. In the beginning I was sceptical and it went on for some time. But I suspended my doubts; I neither accepted him nor rejected him but rather I spent more and more time with him while still keeping an open mind about him, while thinking that if he was a declared Guru he was not an ordinary human being. Until I came to my present stage when I was fully convinced that he is God in human form – and now I have not the least doubt about his divinity.

'That was one thing – constant observation and analysis; but even more important is the experience of his light inside you. The Guru is the one who lights the spark. And if that spark is lit then you are set on the path. So when I was set on the path I started having certain experiences myself, and I thought that if as a result of contact with him I am having all these experiences and I am changing in this particular manner, I'm moving in this particular direction, he cannot but be divine. Because nothing short of the divine could initiate this process and then, having initiated it, could extend and strengthen and could lead it surely to the heights.

'But I think it was the growth of love in me which solved this problem. In the course of time I started to feel more and more love for him. It is very much like human love and yet it is different. Because you are not just loving a body or a set of qualities or even a mind, but you know that you are not even aware of the full significance of what you are loving, but feel a part of emotion itself. And as this love grows stronger and stronger inside you all these doubts and questionings grow stale. Certainly my life changed in a practical way.

'As I grew towards him, I found that I lost all interest in earlier plans and earlier pursuits. I stopped going to the movies, I stopped having intellectual discussions and so on; and I started spending more and more time in meditation, the study of the scriptures and on sadhana. My life changed in every way; so much so that I gave up my job and I live with him now on his ashram. So I am totally committed now. One can never talk about the future, but as time goes by my conviction gets stronger.

'My family is religious and I come from a very strong religious background. Though I did go through a phase when I was not very interested in religion, during my childhood I was deeply attracted to religion and was carrying on religious practices. But then, for a number of years, I was induced to ignore that. That was the influence of Western ideas – I started living the life of a Western intellectual, as near as it was possible for me to do so. But once I started following these ideas, I found that they were incompatible with Western ideas.

'The basic difference is that the Western philosopher is seeing everything with his mind, and there's no doubt about it, the Western philosophical mind is very sharp, very acute. But the Indian philosopher does not only claim to go beyond the mind, he actually does go beyond the mind. And when you go beyond the mind you find that so many things which seemed so important to you are not important at all. For instance, for the Western philosopher, the world which he apprehends with his senses is of vital importance; but once you look beyond the mind, you no longer think it that important.

'All that I am interested in now is to become as perfect a disciple as I can. By that I mean, not to be any longer concerned with what I feel and what I think, but with what he feels, to discard my personal judgement and to be able to accept him completely in an emotional way – in other words, to completely overcome even the last vestige of resistance to him in me. And to obey him and account to him in small matters and in big matters, as a Westerner might obey his deity.

'Our acceptance of the Guru's divinity is a voluntary acceptance. Besides, the miracle is that we are getting so many foreigners to our ashram and we find that there's hardly any Western seeker who doesn't find it difficult to give himself to the Guru. Because he has been brought up to value his own mind, he has been taught to value what he feels, what he thinks; and he is afraid, as a matter of fact, of giving himself because he feels that he will then have nothing to hold on to. Whereas that isn't the case; if you look at it from the outside, that may appear to be the case, but if you are really able to give yourself and to accept

his will in every matter, to bring yourself completely in harmony
with his will, then you find your own true self in the process.
For instance, our Guru whom we call Baba – Baba submitted
entirely to his Guru, but that doesn't mean that he's a carbon-
paper copy of his Guru. He's very, very different from him in so
many ways. And giving yourself to him doesn't mean losing
your individuality; on the contrary, your individuality becomes
stronger. Just as Vivekananda was very different from Ramakrishna. So it may sound paradoxical, but the fact is that if you
make the completest possible surrender or subjection or sub-
mission to the Guru, then you are as a matter of fact establishing
your own true individuality. Previously I used to be in a state of
constant conflict because I couldn't accept myself fully, but
now I can do that and that has only come about as a result of
submitting to the Guru.

'Whether this is always true of those devotees who remain
householders in the city and do not set aside everything and live
on the ashram depends – you receive as much as you give.
Some of them of course are so devoted to him that even when
they are away from him they are continuously aware of his
presence. Some of these are the most devoted disciples possible
and very inspiring.

'Another thing to remember is that, as I told you, the Guru
knows exactly where you stand, and the corollary of that is that
he also knows exactly what is suited to your capacity. So the
more you submit yourself to him, the more unique will be the
things which he will recommend, that's to say, the more
uniquely adjusted to your temperament and needs would be the
practices recommended by him. And what practices depends
again on how much you want to be affected. It could be from
the minute and insignificant details like how to sit, right to how
to realize God. The practice of yoga, the practice of meditation,
japa; we lay a great deal of emphasis on communal chanting and,
what I have mentioned before, service to the Guru.

'But from these general terms you can't have a precise idea of how a practical disciple is being moulded by the Guru. Suppose that I am washing his bathroom, for instance; he sends me out to wash his bathroom today, but tomorrow he will give that to somebody else. Or during one period he may emphasize meditation, and then he may drop that and put the emphasis on something else. So all the time he is seeing what you need now, and he gives you that, and in that way he keeps on rounding you out. He keeps on eliminating all your embarrassments, he is all the time remoulding you, remoulding you in all your personal aspects. As a result of this, after a certain period of time, you find that you are an entirely different person, not only in the major things of life but also in the minor things. For instance, now I would not be careless even about minor things; if I were to go from this place, I would certainly switch off that fan, I would not leave any lamps unswitched off. I wouldn't leave any gas running, I would put a book back in its place after I'd used it: and it's all because of the training I've received from him. Before meeting him, I was very careless, you see, in these matters.

'Whenever the scriptures glorify the Guru-disciple relationship, the institution of the Guru, they say that we should remember that the Guru is self-realized. This is something which people in the West are likely to forget. The *Upanishads* declare again and again that one who is realized becomes God – there is no difference between them. It's not just a figure of speech. And that means that such a person can see not only a disciple's past but also his future – what is he going to be, say, fifteen years after. Maybe he has assigned a certain role to me which I am going to play out in twenty years, and during the next twenty years he will be preparing me continuously for that.

'All the actions and the moods of a saint of his stature are in the nature of what we call lila, which means sport; he is not the slave of his moods, he is not the slave of any sort of ideas or convictions, otherwise he couldn't be called liberated: liberation means liberation from personality. And there is certainly a deeper significance behind every little thing that he does. You may not understand it all the time. I remember a time when I used to try and understand it and if I didn't understand it I'd feel bewildered or something; sometimes my faith would receive a severe jolt also. But now I have come to discover that that was because of my intellectual approach towards him, which to my mind is not the right approach. What is the only genuine mode of understanding how a Guru functions is bhakti – devotion, faith, love.

'The definition of shishya is very wide. A person who comes here once every two years may claim to be a shishya of Baba's, and the same term may be applied to someone who stays with him twenty-four hours a day and is going to be with him for the rest of his life. So it's really wide; but a true shishya is one who has become one with his Guru or who is trying to become one with him. That is, who doesn't think what he doesn't want him to think, who doesn't even feel what he doesn't want him to feel. He doesn't will anything that he doesn't want him to will.

'Again, the almost physical awareness of him that some people have would vary from individual to individual. And you may feel it sometimes, not always. There are people who feel that all the time. There are people sitting in places as far away as New York and they continually feel his presence. It's all a question of how devoted you are to him, how much love you have for him. And you don't have to make an effort to feel the impact of the beloved. I mean, if you're in love, you will be all the time thinking about the beloved and, whether you are in the physical presence or not, he or she is always there in your mind. When you can feel his vibrations, distance isn't important. And you feel the vibrations in a physical way.

'There's no question that I'm now involved in a life-long

process. It can last for a number of lifetimes because there is so much in me which may not be in harmony with him. And if my goal is complete unison with him, then there's a lot that still has to be done. Quite a bit has been done in the past; it's a continuous process, you know. It's not like having done it once and for all. It has the suppleness and pliability of life. One can't say exactly where one is in this process, but one can be sure from a look at one's momentum that it must have begun earlier than this life.

*

In the morning I take a blanket in to the chanted recitation, sit on that, my hip joints burning, as verse after verse of the *Gita* unrolls. Afterwards, Professor Jain tells me to stand by – my formal interview with Swami Muktananda might take place this morning. I wait, then go out to the chai shop to try and wash the ache from my bones with tea. When I come back, Swami Muktananda is standing at the gate, the morning sun shining through his fine spun ochre robe, a canary coloured sweater on, the two bobbles swinging in his cap. As I greet him, the light flashes off his dark glasses, he makes one harsh sound – 'Ha!' – and waves me in. I look back from the door: his light blue Mercedes with the darkened windows and the air-conditioning has pulled up, a visible sign, perhaps, of the grace of God. He jokes with a little girl who swings away, giggling, offers a lift to a small boy until, overcome, the child hides his chubby face; finally gets in among the piled cushions on the back seat and is driven away.

Waiting for him to come back, I consider his changes of manner, his curious alterations of mood, even of appearance. In the morning, tender, singing softly, quiet; at lunch, old and hunched, his teeth out, greeting those going to the meal while seated humbly on a wooden kitchen chair; in the afternoon, smiling, approachable, almost gay, handing out sweets to children; with the importunate, regal in his disdain; with the hesitant and the shy, soft voiced and loving; then laughing as if flirtatious at a pretty girl or joking with the unafraid; in the evening, perhaps, once more imperial, spread on his low throne, leaning to one side, looking inscrutably down at his faithful. He is the only Guru I am to meet in India who employs these tricks of command, these psychological games to keep the rest of us constantly wrong-footed. No one knows which 'Babaji' he is about to see, not even what age he will be, since at times he looks a sad seventy, at others a vigorous and compelling forty. He dominates his own hall in ways which do not derive only from the fact that it is his, nor even from the unaided force of his personality. He uses, consciously or not, a technique, making a show of his vigour and energy, stamping in through those double doors, marching as if in a demonstration of superiority between the waiting rows of people with what appears to be a complete lack of concern for them or their wants, even their reality, then returning, making himself available in his own good time when they have waited, when they have been tamed once more by their own awareness of their need. One must not, however, forget that he is a Guru, a subtle teacher. If his many faces are designed to teach us a single lesson, it is up to us to unravel what it is.

Having brought the rich to his feet, he is rich himself (the ashram is run by a trust fund but the trustees are of course his devotees). He may not be attached to wealth but one gets the impression that he enjoys his life; he is too conscious in his arrogance, in his control, for that not to be true. Nevertheless, he has a true power, even if I have not felt it directly as the incapacitating shakti; he is a man who would be noticed anywhere. If the tricks are sometimes shallow, the effects go deep. If he uses a technique to project his personality, nevertheless the personality is there; there is no diminution in the effect he has as one gets closer to him. He inhabits his power to the limits, he is as big as his reputation. Whether that power is from God, or religious in any way, I cannot say; those about him think so, but they have been taught to think of all power as emanating from the divine. What I suspect is true is that, near him, you can only surrender to his force or leave. He is absolute monarch in his own domain and expects from all who stay in it their taxes of devotion. That leaves a larger question – does he take those taxes as his own, or are they the dues that go through him to God? Only he can answer that.

When I am finally settled on those prestigious red cushions at his side, the hall is not yet very full. I wait as he receives people, asks them questions, leans towards them to answer theirs, suddenly producing that unstrained smile which transforms his often cruel face. Finally he turns to me, flicking thumb and forefinger together in a gesture almost of impatience. He talks quickly, his harsh voice cutting through Jain's softer translation. More people gather – everyone, it seems, wants to see what sort of a fool I make of myself, what sort of fool 'Babaji' will make of me. But he settles to our talk, he becomes interested, he moves backward and forward in his seat. His dark eyes go from Jain to me, then back; he waits for my reactions, a new question or perhaps a smile. Just before noon, he gets abruptly to his feet.

Bathed in sweat, I lie down, refuse all food. 'Shaktipat', says David knowledgeably. I groan, feel my own heat flow over me like tides. But at four I am back again, next to that curiously barbarous dark red throne. My head inflates and contracts, it seems, and I am not sharp enough to ask the questions I would like or will think of later. An even larger crowd sits watchfully by as he tells me what I want to know, or what he thinks I should or need to know.

'I have met many saints, many self-realized persons during my journeys – people like Sri Aurobindo, Meher Baba, Anandamayee, Raman Maharshi and many others. But the Guru can be only one. You might have met many, just as a woman can meet many men – if we're talking about Indian women – but she'll marry only one. Once you have accepted one as your Guru, you don't have to go to any others. I met Swami Nitya-nanda before I began my travels. Then I met him again, while I was engaged on the spiritual search.

'The Guru must find out whether a particular person who has come to him is fit for self-realization. If you want to employ a manager for a big factory, you make sure he is fit for the job. In the same way, a Guru looks for certain qualities in a disciple. And he tests those qualities. He tests them in different ways. There is no course of examinations, or anything like that. [He laughs.] It would depend on the inner state of the disciple. What is really to be looked for is how far the particular disciple will be able to go on the path and how much natural stability he has. And then how much love he has for the Master. At times the Guru may even behave in a manner which is shocking. He may get angry with you but you may not be at fault – he has to test you. He will keep on testing you until he breaks the back of your pride. So one can take the Guru's moods and attitudes and so on as all a part of the process of teaching.

'The West has difficulties with the idea of the Guru as divine because of a certain stupidity on the part of a few people, because the Western people have been taught to look upon themselves as sinners. If they could look upon themselves as divine, it wouldn't be difficult to consider the Guru divine – once they considered themselves divine. Even the Bible teaches you that you are a sinner, and in prayer after prayer you keep on repeating that. And once you are convinced inside that you are a sinner, it becomes very difficult for you to look on the other person as God. Once a disciple follows the path which has been shown to him by the Guru, has realized himself, has had a true awakening to his own inner divinity, then he does not find it difficult to believe that the Guru is far greater than he. There are differing views on this, however, which one can distinguish in India also. There are people who consider the Guru a sort of sacred cow and consider that he himself is a god. But then there are others who give the Guru the highest position and regard him as God only because they realize the god quality within his (the Guru's) grace. Whatever view you take of another person will depend on the state of peace you are in. Shankaracharya realized God within and so he said, 'I am God.'

'When the Guru attains Guruhood, then the power that he gives is the power of God, his divine power. And then he makes it available to others. During the days of the British rule in India, the Collector would come and he had a certain amount of authority. Now, if you were to ask him whether his authority was his own or whether it was different from the authority of the Crown, what would he say? It's the same. Even though he uses this authority, yet he is drawing his power from the Crown. So one becomes a Guru only when one is able to draw upon the divine power.

'People say that to develop self-realization is a selfish process. But it's only when you have learned to love your own self that you can love others also. If you haven't learned to love yourself, then how can you love others? If at first you love yourself, then you can love your father, your child and everybody else: every other living creature. There is a centre of love inside you, just as there is anger. If you get in contact with that centre of love, even though that love is flowing from God, then you will be full of love. Even if you are a little intelligent, you know, you will get to know about it. Sometimes you may sit still, and then you may happen to cast your glance at somebody and for no reason you may be filled with anger. And then, after some time, that anger vanishes and you feel love for the other person. This means that feelings and tendencies are arising from inside you. That is why Indian philosophy has laid emphasis on three or four centres inside you. Love is one of these centres, and a yogi, once he has been able to realize this centre, will always be full of love and joy, whether he is in pleasure or in pain. Once you have made contact with this centre of love, well, then you are laughing even when you ought to cry; but if you are not in contact with that centre, you may be living in the greatest comfort and still you will be crying.

'When one talks of these centres, of the chakras and the kundalini, the language is not symbolic. For instance, whatever you are doing during the waking state tires you finally. You might have made millions of rupees or you might have done anything else – you might have won a kingdom. Even that would tire you. Now, when you go to sleep and afterwards you feel completely refreshed, that means during this time you have gone into your centre of rest. Now that – is it imaginary or is it true? [A pause follows this and then he says, "I want an answer to my question." Thinking something irrelevant about the ambivalent nature of dreams, I murmur that perhaps sleep may in some ways be both real and imaginary. He makes a gesture of impatience.] It can't be imaginary, because if it were imaginary you would not feel refreshed in the morning. If it were imaginary, then people wouldn't have to spend so much on sleeping pills just to get to sleep. Huge factories have been set up in America where millions of people are working just to make those pills. You should read some books on the subject!

'There was a girl here who was only eighteen, and she began dancing and smiling, and one could see that innocence was shining in her face. Now that couldn't have been imaginary. But these things are deeper than the subtle body, even. Their roots go deeper. This has to be realized and these things are worthy of being realized.

'I have no need of the devotion of the disciples. But then, if it is devotion which is the chief attainment of a particular disciple ... Now, whether he gives me devotion or not does not affect me at all; but that inner devotion is the chief gain of the disciple.

'As for shaktipat, sometimes the divine power is directed by the Guru, sometimes it works through him so that he becomes a channel for it. Both are true. Shakti does sometimes work independently of any personal powers of the Guru, and any conscious thought of passing the shakti on to the disciple is a secondary factor. There are certain Gurus who instruct their disciples to sit on a particular day at a particular time and that at that time the shaktipat will take place. I don't work in such a conscious manner nor do I think about a particular devotee, either. I don't even care when they are going to receive it. A certain professor came here from South Africa and he was a great scholar; he held high degrees and he had studied Vedanta and philosophy and he was a very good student of both. He was here for three months. I never talked to him. Then, during the last week before he left he received so much shakti from me that he started weeping and laughing, and other signs also appeared.* I don't think about it and for this reason: I know the whim of the shakti very well; Shakti herself is omniscient and she has knowledge, and so it is shakti which looks after the disciples. I don't exercise the shakti power by any conscious wish. It is only that teacher whose shakti is not omniscient who will consciously think of helping the disciple. I don't have to think about it. There's a girl here who came eight years ago and who is meditating very well . . . meditating intensely; and I've never spoken to her at all. It was only today that I went up to see her because she had been having intense experiences. One aspect of the kundalini is omniscience, so this shakti understands the disciple through and through. So I don't have to think about the disciple. It is the force which knows.'

And Swami Muktananda has written:

Since countless ages, shaktipat has been used as a secretly concealed means of initiation by the great sages. Concisely, to transmit

* This is the man I had seen making his humble farewell.

one's own glory and lustre of divine Enlightenment into the disciple, and give him an instantaneous direct experience of Brahman, the eternal spirit, is the secret meaning of shaktipat . . .

In every human being there dwells the divine energy, the Kundalini shakti. This energy has two aspects: one manifests samsara, the ephemeral worldly existence, while the other leads to the highest truth. When the Guru transmits his soul power to the disciple, the latter aspect of the Kundalini shakti is automatically activated and set into full operation . . .

When the attributeless, formless, changeless reality which underlies the entire universe as a whole and which is the pure ultimate consciousness is stirred up, then this divine energy begins to operate in it. In fact, she is the power of becoming, released out of the eternal being, expressing herself through all names, all forms and all changes that we call the world. Indeed, she is the most magnificent power – Sri kundalini shakti – of the supreme reality. To set into operation this Kundalini in an individual being is known as shaktipat, call it a favour, blessing, diksha, gurukripa or by any other term, and one who gives shaktipat diksha is a Guru.

'In the West now, some people are beginning to discover new experiences while under drugs. It's not the drug which is causing the experience. What the drug does is that it turns your mind inwards, and when the mind turns inwards then it has certain unusual experiences. So in India also, you'll find a lot of sadhus who are taking drugs like *charas* and so on. But it would not be true to say that any route, even drugs, that leads you inward is a good route. The drugs induce a state of intoxication and under that you have certain experiences which are not always good. But in Vedanta, there is a state in which no drug can affect you and no physical causes can affect you. Something similar is induced by doctors through chloroform; under the effects of chloroform they can perform an operation and the patient doesn't feel any pain. So in this state something similar happens. But being under chloroform cannot be described as the state of samadhi. You should have your experiences through the practice of yoga, not through drugs. That is why you should turn your mind inwards through yogic practices. Besides, after some time you become habituated to drugs and they stop being a stimulus. They become just like an item of ordinary food.

'I have a large number of devotees in the West. Last year one of them wrote to me and told me that he'd invited his mother to a meal at an hotel – after three years! He felt very happy about this. But in India we don't want to keep our parents away from us. It's not that we are wrongly attached to them, but because we love them. Let me tell you about a little conversation I heard in Delhi last year – and don't mind it. Now, there were two ladies from the West. They said that the latest trend in the West was to have special houses – special residential areas, you know – for the older people, and different areas for the younger people. [There is some laughter at this, from those in the darshan hall.] They asked me what my views were on this. I said I wanted to pronounce no opinion on the subject, but then I told them that, besides being a sadhu, I was also a farmer and moved among farmers. Sometimes one finds oxen and bulls which have become ill and I ask the farmers why they look after such old and helpless cattle, and the farmer might say that that particular bull had been bought by his father and looked after by his father and he wanted it to die in his care. So, in our country, we won't even let our father's bull die away from us, but in your country you put away your own parents. [Laughter again at this.]

'Most of these rooms here were built for me by my Guru. Now I'm putting up new buildings and a lot of people have suggested that these rooms should be demolished. But I don't feel like demolishing any of them. We value the things we get from our parents. It's because of our love for our own parents, brothers and sisters, and our nearest and dearest, that we're able to extend so much love to you. If we were living here in your manner then we wouldn't have given you such love.

'You know, the people of this new age think they're very

clever, but the consequences of their cleverness are not going to be good. For instance, there is the value that is set on certain achievements. There was a time when people used to take pride in having visited India, particularly the people who discovered India first. They must have taken a great deal of pride in it. But these days, it can't be a matter of great pride to come here because everybody can come here now. Similarly, you cannot keep on taking pride in the achievement of having gone to the moon. This sense of achievement will not be lasting. It will become very ordinary, and that is an experience which seems to be inherent in this kind of attempt. So can you really describe it as a success? Because it is bound to be followed by a sense of failure. Now, the astronauts have gone to the moon. They're going to go higher than the moon eventually. There are worlds in the universe which are farther away than the moon. In our scriptures these worlds are described and it is also said that there are inhabitants on the moon, that the moon is inhabited . . . Success in the material field is a relative thing and the sense of pride in such success does not last long. Supposing that today you have made a hydrogen bomb and you think that you have a special achievement to your credit, but tomorrow somebody makes something much bigger . . . and, you know, that sense of achievement is gone!'

In the night, I shiver, terrible shuddering spasms that threaten to throw me out of bed. At six I rise and finish my small packing, sweating, despite the pre-dawn cold, in my own feverish summer. Outside, everything is still; blanketed figures stand in the forecourt, talking in low voices. David walks with me to the chai shop, where I drink glasses of hot, over-sweet milk.

At the small, thatch roofed bus stop opposite the ashram I wait for the Bombay bus. A little way up the road, two men and a boy crouch round a small fire of grass and twigs and straw; it dies to a glow every now and again before, replenished, it rises up once more. People go into the small temple, pray briefly, then walk on up the road. Already behind me the sky has a stretched, transparent look, the first beginnings of the dawn. More devotees gather at the doors of the audience hall. Professor Jain passes, shakes me warmly by the hand. Bruno and the blond American come by, call out, 'Come back some time!' A South African lady wishes me luck – it seems suddenly as though I have friends. Normally, there is an unconscious arrogance about the ashram. People are friendly but preoccupied. They make no concessions to your unfamiliarity, your lack of knowledge of their routine. The stranger must do the accommodating – 'Babaji's' devotees have room for only one concern in their ashram lives. The outsider, perhaps quite properly, finds no way to their real attention; to do that, he must become an insider like the rest. And then, paradoxically, he will need no one's attention or concern: the world will have narrowed to the operation of *gurukripa*, the Guru's grace.

Round the dipping corner from Ganeshpuri comes the clattering bus. 'Bombay!' shouts the conductor and 'Bombay!' I shout. I slump in a seat, my reactions blurred by fever. Through the far window, across a long landscape stopped by jagged hills, the uncomplicated dawn continues. Red, ochre, gold – Swami's colours – and then the untethered sun burning its way inch by inch above the horizon.

Back in Bombay, I discover it is not shaktipat at all that has caused my troubles: it is hepatitis. My next stop is hospital.

5
The Godmen's Meaning

As I travelled about India, visiting Gurus, interviewing disciples and would-be disciples, I found myself more and more drawn into their world. It is so alien in its intensity from anything that we have, and I felt myself to be so unqualified to stand critically aloof, that for a long time even to want to do so seemed an impertinence. What to an extent liberated me from these pressures was my increasing impatience with the narrowness, the repression, the authoritarianism and consequent intellectual stagnation of Indian society as a whole. Of course such a judgement is a generalization to which anyone who knows India or Indians can indicate exceptions. But, as Nirad Chaudhuri says in his *Autobiography of an Unknown Indian*, 'In a country like India, so vast and so populous, the individuals who form the exceptions may well run into millions. But in spite of their numbers taken independently they are negligible when pitted against the hundreds of millions who constitute the norm.'

Certainly the Guru-shishya relationship has its roots in Indian society at least as deeply as it does in the Hindu religion; that is – to explain what may seem a very artificial distinction – in the kind of society it actually is rather than in what it says in its explicit philosophy. We ought therefore to glance at some of the social factors which may have helped to build the veneration in which these Masters are held.

It seems an almost universal illusion that other societies are having a better sexual time than we are ourselves. I call this an illusion because, although it may or may not be true, we are prepared to believe it on the thinnest of evidence, the most unreliable of rumours. Our belief in the potency, desirability, knowledge, and complex performance of lovers seems to increase with their distance from us. Only this can explain the prevalent North European notion that Spaniards and Italians make the most satisfactory sexual partners the Continent offers a footloose girl. In the same way, the *Kama Sutra* and the temple carvings of Khajuraho seem to have persuaded many Europeans that India is a land where for centuries the wilder extravagances of sexual indulgence have been a commonplace. If they make the journey, perhaps sustained by this supposition, they may be bewildered to find themselves in a society which, by European standards, stands somewhere in the eighteen sixties. India is a puritan country. Its women are still largely subjugated, by father first, later by husband. Its daughters remain virgins and so do most of its sons, unless they can pluck up the money for a prostitute or the courage for a 'tribal' woman (the 'tribals', outside the main structure of society, heirs to a vestigial older culture, do not have the same taboos that hedge in the generality of Indians).

Indian puritanism arises, I suspect, out of the very glorification of sexuality that has misled the West. Sexual ecstasy became a symbol for the ecstasy of man's union with God. This coupling of the earthly and the divine must, I would imagine, make any ordinary copulation a psychologically uncomfortable experience. Its end result can only be to devalue the physical. At that point, the Hindu comes face to face with strange ideas about the value and the power of semen, *bindu*, a word with strong metaphysical associations. It is avoiding the loss of semen as much as the pleasures of sex which lies behind the insistence on celibacy in holy men. There are, in fact, exercises by which advanced yogis may draw up spilled semen, which suggests that it is not the pleasure of orgasm so much as the draining of 'strength' which is mainly to be avoided.

But repression in Indian society goes further than the purely sexual. The emotions themselves are suppressed. To show one's feelings in public is considered almost obscene. This is made easier because so many relationships are a matter of duty, and of a duty that no one questions. In my hotel in Bombay there was a cleaner; during the war, he was a batman to an R.A.F. officer who wanted to take him back to Britain in 1945. The man's older brother – the head of the family since their father had died – refused to let him go. Later, he was offered work as a steward on a ship and again his brother insisted that he stay on the small family farm. Later again, he wanted to go to the ashram of a Guru to whom he had become devoted; his brother instead made him get married. After his life had been thoroughly blighted by these repeated calls to duty, his brother left to marry a rich woman who owned land in Burma. When I asked this gentle cleaner why he thought his brother had so consistently stopped him from doing what he wanted, he said at once, 'Because he loves me'. No other reason presented itself to him – not jealousy, vindictiveness, the pride of authority: his brother was his brother, *ergo* he loved him.

In the West, we are free to work for the approval of those we love or respect and whom we would like to love and respect us. Not so the Indian, who fits into his family situation and his social stratum as inevitably as a part of a machine. There is never any question of his laying himself down, to be accepted or rejected totally, taking that gamble with himself which romantic love has taught us to do, sometimes many times with different people. For the average and particularly the middle-class Indian, there are often only two directions he can go to prove that he can love, that he can be loved. One is towards homosexuality, the other towards the Guru. (These are not, of course, mutually exclusive.)

I myself doubt if many of the young men who walk intertwined through the Bombay dusk are in any overt sense homosexuals; they are the pathetic victims of that social stricture which prevents displays of tenderness between the sexes. The human animal, it may be, needs to test his desirability and to display affection and these boys are taking the only opportunity their world allows them to do so. Because these displays are socially acceptable, there is no need for those taking part in them to make any close examination of their motives.

India, indeed, is in a condition of what one might call pre-Freudian innocence: there is a lack of knowledge about the work of Freud and subsequent psychoanalysts which permits even Indian intellectuals certain kinds of self-deception many Westerners are now able to avoid. Self-awareness has its drawbacks; it seems to me that we have lost spontaneity and warmth as we have learned to be suspicious of the id and its unacceptable desires. Nevertheless, for many in the West, it is probably true that certain kinds of previously unconscious behaviour can now be seen for what they are. Not so in India, a country where, for all that has been said and written about the depths of the psyche, the appearance of things still counts for a great deal. There is very little recognition of the turbulent motives which might underlie acceptable behaviour.

This blindness paradoxically gives the Indian the freedom of his emotions – at least in those areas in which they have not been inhibited by conditioning. It is for this reason that he can only very rarely have sexual relations with girls of his own class, but can form passionate friendships and express them with caresses; and it is for this reason that he can succumb to the Guru's personality with the love-like *coup de foudre* of which this book has given so many examples. Such emotion seems to him entirely without overtones and in no way to be suspected, particularly as its turmoil has so often been charted in his scriptures and is thus supported by what is perhaps most important of all to him: tradition.

That there are parallels between the relationships of lovers and those of Guru and disciple is evidenced by the language in which the latter is described. There is always the proviso made, however, that the emotion the disciple feels for the Guru is different from, or at least quite transcends, that which the lover feels for the beloved. Such a disclaimer seems enough to make most Indians believe that what they feel is in fact a quite different emotion, the more so as they believe the object of it to be divine.

That the roots of such feelings may lie in frustration need not lessen their intensity or their genuineness. The ease with which the disciple accepts his totally subservient role, on the other hand, may not be entirely the result of the deep feeling he has for his Guru. The fact is that the Guru-shishya relationship is in some ways almost an ideal version of that between the Indian father and his son. I suspect that there are few countries other than India where one could find an advertisement in the matrimonial columns of the newspapers beginning, 'Youth of forty seeks wife . . .' From almost his earliest days, and certainly from the age of four or five, the young Indian is expected to conform absolutely to his father's wishes and commands. So comprehensively is this discipline imposed and accepted, that for the rest of his life the average Indian is almost incapable of doing anything of which his father disapproves.

In this situation, the Guru can appear as a rescuer. For, with him, the whole conditioned mechanism of happy slavery can come into operation without conflict. He is the father who has been chosen; in this way, the disciple remains free in his bondage, bound in his freedom. Taught to be non-attached, he can cut himself off from his family without guilt.

In the actual, rather than the ideal, plane, it certainly seems clear that the reasons disciples give for their surrender to the Guru have more to do with theology than with experience, that what they say about their Guru and what is apparent to the detached observer are not always in agreement. The pressures of the disciple's need thrust him into the role that Hindu tradition has prepared for him and he sees his Guru in the way that role prescribes. The relationship itself, which at first glance appears to be dominated by the powerful and developed personality of the Guru, finally exists because of the disciple's will that it should. It is he who agrees to see the Guru as divine, he who surrenders.

It is only when the shishya has thus committed himself that the Master can begin his work. In this sense, then, the value of a Guru as Guru lies in his acting as a focus for the spiritual drive of the disciple, rather than in himself as a realized man or even as a good or a wise one. The driving force in the relationship is not the godhead of the Guru but the need of the disciple.

No man, therefore, puts as it were a brass plate on the door to advertise his spiritual qualities. A person who has devoted himself to his sadhana with the intensity which has allowed him to reach the bliss, the timeless certainty he seeks, may on the way have collected devotees who find, perhaps more and more as time goes on, that he is a channel through which they can draw the power to follow him along the difficult path he has picked out. His fame may spread or he may inherit the fame of his Master. But in any case it is usually they who cluster, not he who invites, though there are exceptions to this pattern.

This mechanism is partly disguised by the totality of the disciple's abasement, by the power of the Guru. Most of all, it goes largely unnoticed because the pattern of the Guru-disciple relationship is so fixed in Indian expectation that its configuration – detached Guru, doting shishya – seems settled in a permanence which puts it beyond anything as ephemeral as analysis. For example, there is no question that some Gurus are very powerful people; but what is the nature of their power? For the disciples, there can be no doubt – the power is divine. Where else does power come from? No explanation, psychological or physiological, exists to challenge this theology. And, after all, has that power not been developed by years of effort and only in a religious context? Does that not prove that what the Guru has received as a result is of divine origin? This certainty makes the process of surrendering to him, so difficult and sometimes unpalatable to the Westerner, a very straightforward task for the Indian devotee.

The sadhus are the religious Bohemians of India; hundreds of thousands of them march across its poverty-stricken plains, their bowls stretch over the thresholds of a million peasant huts, demanding a pinch of rice, a drop or two of dal. Many may be frauds, settling for a comparatively easy life in a country where three hundred million peasants are under-employed or have no work or land of any kind: after all, the coin of asceticism has been devalued in the last fifty years by the millions who have been forced to live in rags and in starvation. But they reinforce an awareness of the transcendent wherever they go; by the fact of their existence, they make India a country stitched and patterned by religion. For this reason, the psychological contortions most Westerners have to go through before they can even begin their spiritual development, particularly in a religious context, are rarely suffered by any Indian, however Westernized. One window in his ancestral mansion has always looked out on the transcendental.

Because the process is so familiar, Indian disciples find it easier to make their commitment total. One result of this, however, is that their view of the Guru is coloured by the very totality with which they have given themselves to him. Their investment is so extreme that it becomes more and more impossible with every succeeding year even to consider an alternative. The more they give themselves, one might almost say, the less they see what they have given themselves to. The relationship with the Guru finally becomes a closed circle, around which the currents of demand, satisfaction and consequent dependence endlessly swirl.

The corollary of this state of affairs is that one is constantly being asked to believe in the value of the relationship because of the intensity with which it has been entered into and is being maintained. To accept that is to become party to what may well be a condition of delusion, both self-imposed and commonly held. There is a story I have been told of a disciple who, after many years of meditation and the practice of hatha yoga, felt convinced that he could fly. And with arms extended he leaped off a cliff, to fall and die like any other mortal. It is obvious to a rational outsider that the intensity of a man's subjective feelings are no guarantee that they relate, even distortedly, to any objective reality. In his highly subjective states of auto- (or God- or Guru-) intoxication, the joyful way in which the disciple throws himself over the cliff of surrender does not of itself mean that he will fly, nor even that flight is possible: too often it seemed to me that he was not flying, but falling.

I do not criticize the institution as such, nor deny that other and higher states exist; nor do I deny that I met Gurus who had relationships at such levels with their disciples. Far from it; all I am saying is that many of those most heavily involved seem never to have put the dangers, the real possibility of delusion, squarely to themselves. In one way, this hardly matters; the essence of the Guru-shishya relationship lies in the subjective states it causes, and those who have written on this subject say again and again that a flawed Guru can take his disciples partway along the road. Yet if we are to accept that a certain condition exists only because all those taking part in it tell us it exists, we are left with no standpoint from which to regard it at all.

This reflects, for me, the sort of intellectual mustiness which pervades a good deal of Guru-shishya relationships. Too much of it has gone unquestioned for too long; not only that, there is no technique for forcing the disciple to re-examine his preconceptions, not only about the world and himself as a man, but about the Guru, the ashram and himself as a disciple: about the whole Guru-disciple connection, in fact. That is already given, and it dominates his life so thoroughly that he cannot look at it.

Of great importance in preventing any real examination of the institution of the Guru by those most closely involved with it is the reverence, the devotion, in which he is held. His godhead is taken literally and, as God is hidden by the effulgence of his own perfection, so the Guru is hidden by the borrowed blaze of this accepted divinity. Surrender to the Guru has been made the prime condition; in this way the Guru-shishya relationship seems to me to have become in many cases, many places, moribund, almost degenerate. I know that there have always been Gurus concerned with the transcendental, that they were working at the same time as the early Vedic Gurus, yet it seems to me that some of the essential virtue drained from the tradition with the invention of writing. From then on, the Guru was no longer the only repository of divine knowledge; manuscripts appeared which could partly take his place. The main purpose for which the institution had been developed had been overtaken by one kind of technological change. There remained the bones of a formalized relationship to be inhabited by, as it were, a soul which if left to itself might have preferred a quite different skeleton. The rigidity of formal teacher-pupil relationships imposed restrictions and damaging inflexibilities on the Master-disciple relationship with its very different and far less easily defined objectives. The increasing inhibition of ordinary feelings and their expression between people, with at the same time the development of the bhakti cults and their emphasis on an extreme emotionalism in the religious context, left the Guru as the focus for the displaced love of a frustrated people. In some such way, the present exaggerated emphasis on surrender may have come into existence.

A result has been that the whole society is permeated by, and perhaps suffers from, relationships based on that between Guru and disciple, so emotionally powerful and uniquely true. Authority, whether in its academic, industrial or political aspect, demands and unfortunately receives a deference which would seem outrageous in the West. Paradoxically, the Guru can himself act as a safety-valve in this too tightly organized society. He and his disciples, and sadhus generally, form an alternative order to the normal hierarchies of India. Outside caste and class, they can operate as the Catholic Church did in the Middle Ages, giving an intelligent boy of peasant or shopkeeper background an opportunity to display talent, or at least to live partly off his abilities and not only within his inherited social limits.

I have been critical of the Guru and his relationships with his disciples, and I have tried to draw some connections between the inhibition of Indian society as a whole and the intensity of feeling the Guru arouses. But I have no intention of being smart-alecky about it and ignoring what the institution means to those who help to form and perpetuate it. At its highest, it offers solutions and experiences which we in the West have either never had or, long ago and perhaps foolishly, discarded. It has answered the needs of millions for thousands of years. It has drawn to itself men of great practical and intellectual distinction from within India and from outside. It has survived conquerors and profound cultural changes and continues to offer its elusive rewards to those who come to it wholeheartedly, accepting its philosophy and its discipline. Most of those I met who had done so seemed to me men and women who had benefited as a result; they were quiet, certain, happy, dedicated – their lives were rich, their inner world expanding. They did not merely tell me so, they seemed to be people of whom it was true. If their original decision had its roots in neurosis – and given the continuing religious priorities of Indian culture, I do not believe this was by any means so – they had long ago learned to cope with their problems. I go by appearances here, by the impression they gave me, but I met too many calmed in this way not to feel I am right. If I am to be truthful then I must include this feeling, this impression.

It is a continuing error of the West to think that what has been explained has been understood. Another is to think an explanation devalues what has been explained; if we find an atheist who was early rejected by his father, we leap for the parallel and imagine it renders negligible his belief. Truth and, even more so, value seem to me to reside elsewhere; explanation helps towards their discovery but cannot substitute for it. There is more to the Guru-shishya relationship than frustrated sexuality or the psychological wounds inflicted by over-authoritarian fathers.

*

Perhaps the disadvantages of Indian rigidity are matched by those of Western flexibility. Ironic, to suffer from what you most pride yourself on. But it may be that some essential paradox underlies all human development; certainly it lurks within and dangerously underneath any view of man which, by implication, isolates him from the natural universe around him. We cannot control what we do not see and we cannot see what we are part of. We have tried to avoid the subsequent distortion by taking ourselves out of the landscape; but after two centuries of rational objectivity, we find we were there all the time, classifying, ordering, analysing and dissecting, the ubiquitous observer, a madman who all this time had thought himself invisible.

Our belief in human rationality, supported by Rousseau-based ideas of an essential human goodness, has led us to put a higher and higher value on human individuality. Instead we find we are the heirs of the pre-human hominids, great shouldered bone wielders, shaggy coated weapon gatherers, vegetarian murderers. Our great heroes and their patriotic causes turn out to be the consequence of thousands of years of selective breeding, their medals and stirring speeches the echo of the snarls, the war dances and painted masks of ancient ancestors protective about hearth and cattle and the village fence.

Today, we are baffled not so much by our problems as by the solutions we have chosen. We opted for liberty, enshrining our new political freedoms in this or that version of democracy, only to be threatened in almost all departments of life by the tyranny of majority. We demanded and, to an extent, achieved new economic freedoms, only to breed a generation dissatisfied with what those freedoms brought. We tried for freedom from sickness and ended with over-population. We tried for technological freedom and ended with the befouling motorcar. We act as if we still believed in the perfectability of man; but that bright and splendid balloon was brought to earth in 1914 and buried under twenty million corpses. We talk as if Freud, Nietzsche, Heidegger, Einstein and all those who followed or surpassed them have not for ever altered what we think of man and the place where he lives. Our culture shakes, like a house loose on its foundations. Sub-cultures appear, conformist, exclusive, intolerant; either loutishly confusing universal love with general copulation or desperately hanging on to the tweed jackets and club memberships, the inhibitions and irrelevant loyalties of a discredited past.

Here and there, hope finds something to cling to. Some of the young move beyond drugs to the asking again of long-forgotten questions. Neither the aridities of scientific materialism nor those of linguistic analysis will put them off. They are rediscovering ancient needs and, it may be, ancient ways of satisfying them.

But the majority of people are bewildered. The talk is of alienation. Queues form for psychiatric treatment, for mental hospital places. No household is without its sleeping pills, few without tranquillizers. People are lost, frightened of their freedom, cut off from others in this islanded self they inhabit. Once they belonged to classes, to neighbourhoods, to guilds or villages, to wide and boisterous families. Now they have been isolated, trapped with wife or husband in some indifferent suburb. They are the casualties of battles against the old social systems whom the victors never mention. Since we insist on change, we can see no value in experience; the old lose their historic asset and

294

are left to lie in their own piss at the expense of the State. But, ignored, they will not go away. They remain, a sign and a warning to the most exuberant teenager – himself soon to be a harassed forty year old. Where can he turn then, as his discomfort changes into terror?

His need – our need – is answered by the psychoanalyst. Our self capsizes; he will salvage the hulk, right and reanimate it. We go to him, to the analyst, urbane, attentive, patient, for that understanding which will have to do us in place of some astounding, all embracing love. Realizing this, many people have asked me if the Guru is really anything more than his Asiatic equivalent.

This comparison so often made or implied between the psychoanalyst and the Guru seems to me to say more about the overvalued position of the analyst than anything useful about the Guru. There are, certainly, points of similarity: each functions by taking part in a relationship with someone whose mental state he has been asked to change. But one stumbles on a fundamental difference right at the beginning – the analyst is a doctor; the Guru is a teacher.

This difference is not lessened by the fact that their views of the self, rooted in contrasting and sometimes opposing philosophies, have very little in common. For the Guru, that section of the mind which identifies and makes us aware of the self is part of what must be transcended; the analyst, quite to the contrary, usually sees it as his task to reinforce or even reconstruct the ego sense. One after all deals with the spiritual aspirant, the other with the psychologically maimed.

Since the analyst-patient relationship is essentially therapeutic, the subject of it is by definition the patient; the analyst never figures in it as himself. He remains neutral, a wall off which the patient may, awkwardly at first and then with more and more expertise, bounce his unbalanced psyche, until he finally understands its idiosyncrasies of flight and ricochet, when he retrieves it. Everything that occurs has as its objective the development of that understanding. But to foster such intense self scrutiny is not the Guru's function at all; he would consider a great deal of it no more than pandering to that lowest conscious self which operates so self-destructively in the illusory world. The Guru is a model and the disciple must try and emulate him. The Guru is the realized man and the disciple must strive to be like him. The Guru is the Swami, the man who has risen to the highest levels, and it must be the disciple's only intention to rise to a level as high or higher. The extreme version of this, as we have seen repeated again and again, is that the disciple 'merges' with the Guru. The general oneness of the universe finds particular expression in the oneness of Master and disciple.

Why does the patient come to the analyst? Because his obsessions, delusions, hysteria, compulsions, tics or perversions have made it more or less impossible for him to live in the ordinary world in an ordinary way. What does the analyst try to do? He wants to discover and redress the causes of this distressing behaviour, he wants to rebuild his patient's capacity to love, he wants to give him ambition, energy, hope, he wants him to marry and have a family and keep up his insurance payments. Whatever doubts the analyst may have about the nature of the society we inhabit, there is no question that he would consider someone who learned while under his care to live in this admirable way as cured, and cured by him. (To talk of 'cure' is now unfashionable, which underlines psychotherapists' new uncertainty about themselves; but it will do as a shorthand term.)

Not so the Guru: for him, it is precisely that 'real' world which has trapped the self, has separated it from the eternal Absolute of which it is an illusory part. The disciple who comes to the Guru must, either in physical fact or in metaphysical theory, give up that world. Only then will he be ready to begin his progress towards illumination and the truth. The 'real' world of the analyst, therefore, becomes the 'unreal' world of the Guru. Where the first wants his patients to fit into it more and more successfully, the second wants his disciples to have less and less to do with it. Where the analyst wants his patients finally to leave him, the Guru wants his disciples finally to come to him, to merge with him. Where the patient stops being a patient in order to become himself, an accountant or a plumber, functioning and at peace, the disciple's ultimate aim is to become a Guru or to reach the same level of mystical insight.

It is true that the Guru's disciple, once accepted, often discovers a new confidence and so may function better in society. But that is not, unlike the patient, his primary aim in going to the Guru. What he wants is to leave the world, to break the birth-death-birth cycle, to merge with the Guru and thus with the Absolute – not to operate in the world at all, in fact, to cease to exist as an entity. He is entering into a religious contract, so to speak, and those are his religious aims. The only way in which any real parallel can be drawn between the Guru and the psycho-analyst is by saying that both the birth-death-birth cycle and the disciple's intentions are to be taken as symbolic, and that maya, for example, is not the illusion of physical reality, but is instead the illusion which is social institutions.

I myself cannot see how maya can be defined so narrowly. Certainly it is unlikely that Shankara, arch conserver of the caste system that he was, intended maya to be a concept synonymous with social institutions. No alteration to his basic concepts has been permitted in the twelve centuries since he propounded them. In fact, I find the continuing and literal acceptance of Shankara's philosophy a depressing example of the inhibiting effect of authority on profound speculation. Nevertheless it continues, proving once again how much the Indian suffers from social and philosophical rigidities.

It is plain that, in practical terms, to transcend these rigidities should be the first step in his liberation. Yet it is at this precise point that a paradox built into the structure itself intervenes: in a society which allows for the path of liberation, 'the liberated man' is only one more of the acceptable roles that can be chosen. The liberty of social action which the individual then has is ultimately unreal, because it is permitted him on the very condition that he is a holy man. In the social sense his liberation is a fraud, precisely because he must leave the ordinary world and be seen to have left it before he feels able, or is allowed, to exercise his freedoms. This is not to say that he is a fraud as a holy man, nor that he has not managed to sever his attachments to people and to passions; it does seem to mean that he has not transcended society.

There are, of course, many men who are on the path to liberation but still operate in the world. By the nature of things, I met no one who was self-realized but living an ordinary life, someone whose light was fierce but hidden by some necessary bushel. They are rumoured to exist, and I may have passed a dozen such people on city pavements or the dirt roads of country towns, but they remained saints in disguise, spiritual princes travelling incognito. Some of the people I did meet were Guru's disciples and at the same time merchants, say, or stockbrokers; yet they often seemed to derive their sense of self from the very attempt to overcome it, or at least to find confidence and sometimes the ability to act from their acceptance by the Guru. The concern of the Guru was the measure of their worth. They always 'knew' what the Guru wanted and in this way a weak ego structure (undermined by a parental authority often unquestioned through four decades) was probably being shored up rather than broken down. This too I saw as a consequence of the known and expected role the Guru plays in society; in becoming disciples, these men were playing parts that had been written into the Indian script many centuries ago and could therefore be accepted without difficulty. Like the sadhu in his ochre robe or loincloth, they were discovering their freedom within the social structure, not outside it. Liberation from the worldly point of view was taking place only in appearance; from the spiritual point of view, however, the story was frequently different in that through meditation the disciple was achieving some measure of illumination – that is, he was subjectively experiencing those states which he had always known to expect and which he understood as mystical.

In India it seems as if he can only reach this point by staying within tradition and accepting the sanction of established forms. I am forced to wonder what in that case is the real nature of his transformation. This leads me back to something I have mentioned before, something which deeply disappointed me since the literature had not prepared me for it, namely that the attitudes of both Gurus and disciples seemed too conditioned by the long tradition that lay behind them. Disciples travelled a route very well mapped, giving one the suspicion that they were following too fervently, too meticulously, the deep footmarks of the generations that had gone that way before them.

All this is a far cry from the psychoanalyst and the work he does. And the gap is not narrowed by the general Indian ignorance of psychiatric theory and technique. To say that this disbars them from any psychological insight would be nonsense; it would be like saying that no one in the West knew anything of the human psyche until the middle of the nineteenth century, and we have enough evidence from authoritative witnesses like Sophocles, Shakespeare, Boccacio or Dickens to refute such naïvety. Yet it does seem to me to make many of the sadhus' and Gurus' insights partial, and to leave some of those who profess to have them looking curiously superficial in their judgements. I recognize how arrogant such an assertion sounds; but I met too many men deep in the processes of Hindu religious life who seemed to have such an imperfect awareness of their own motivation or sexual nature to conclude anything else.

That a successful sadhana leads to confidence, to calm, is not to be denied. But it is not, I think, the calm that follows a successful analysis; its basis is more control than understanding, more the avoidance of stress than the acceptance and surmounting of its causes. To some extent, too, it is the calm of men who have been given a simple goal and the means to achieve it, and have worked or are working successfully towards it, supported by the care and attention of someone they venerate. Thus protected, it is not surprising that they achieve contentment. Nor do I intend to imply that such contentment is unreal; far from it. But it is not achieved by means which are in any way comparable to those used by the analyst; it is most important never to forget that we are discussing a religious phenomenon. Therefore the successes, the experiences which deep meditation brings, mark progress in a context seen as infinitely more important than the one which the ordinary world provides. Yet it is a context essentially simple, dominated by the word of the Guru and calibrated by the depth, intensity and duration of the mystical experience.

It is this all-pervasive domination of the Guru, the necessary surrender of the disciple and the nature of the resulting relationship, which makes Westerners turn to the analyst-patient connection for a comparison. Conversely, it is transference, that curious one-way love affair of the patient with his analyst, which most makes that connection resemble the one between disciple and Guru. 'Transference' in psychoanalysis, of course, means exactly what it says: the transfer of an emotion from an earlier object to the person – that restrained, amorphous person – of the analyst. As I have said, the involvement of the disciple with the Guru seems to me much more the bursting out of intense emotion in people who have learned love as a duty. When it happens there is no question of the emotion having been transferred. It is the emotion itself, hitherto denied an object. Once established, it is often felt life-long, and it has the Guru for its only object. Nor is there, in what passes between Guru and disciple, that rediscovery of the past which is not only what analysis is about, but itself leads to an intensification of transference as the original emotions are explored and reawakened. The relationship looks forwards and its goal is the spiritual emancipation of the disciple, his arrival at the point at which the Guru already has his being.

Not cure but illumination, then, the actual experience of oneness, is the end to which all sadhana is directed. The essential process of sadhana is control, and, through control, sublimation. The means of control are psychological as in meditation; physical as in the yogic asanas; and social as in the attempt to achieve non-attachment. If these are successful, they leave the disciple in a condition of psychic emptiness which, in this as in other religions, can then be filled by revelation and a new spiritual certainty. The funnel through which these are poured is the intensity of the disciple's devotion to his Guru; it is his constant concentration on that single, divine figure which opens the channel along which the Guru can pass his own convictions and, it may be, his own psychic energy.

One must not forget, too, that while analyst and patient form a unit which usually operates only while actually in being with both members physically present and the therapy in full swing, the disciple does most of his work alone, is engaged on changing himself and only turns to the Guru when in difficulties. Such difficulties do from time to time occur. If without any preparation, you try to concentrate upon a single point, physical or intellectual, it will not be long before irrelevancies crowd in on you like chattering children. Sadhana is a technique for stilling and controlling this horde which constantly bustles about among our thoughts, a reminder of and bond with maya. In this process, the Guru can be crucial by constantly refocusing the disciple's attention. Again and again he will offer the right question – not, 'How do I attain liberation?', but 'Who is it that seeks to do so?' Thus prodded, the disciple is brought back to his primary task of self-examination.

But this is not, as in analysis, an examination which searches for the hidden roots of sickness; rather it looks with increasing penetration and steadiness at what is going on now, hunting out distraction, quelling irrelevance. It is concentration, stillness, one-pointedness that is being sought, and a method that is being perfected; not the healing of such wounds as the psyche may bear.

What is the point of reaching such an intensity of concentration? It is to unite with the object of it, to feel that you have become a part of this external fact and it has become a part of you. In this way, your sense of its objectivity and your subjectivity begin to swim together until you realize both are illusory. In the light of that, one can begin to understand much more clearly the disciple's sense of 'merging with' the Guru, since it is the Guru whom he so often takes as the fixed point in his meditation.

Lurking out of sight, however, there is I suspect another dimension. The technique the disciple learns is, of course, in many of its aspects an ascetic one, involving a great deal of discomfort directly through tapas and the asanas, indirectly through the short hours of sleep it insists on, the long periods of immobility, the kinds of menial work demanded of disciples, the plain and often inadequate food. One might therefore consider whether the masochistic element in all this does not put the disciple into another bondage which he is not at all fitted to recognize. This is one of the consequences, it seems to me, of the inadequate knowledge of Western psychoanalytical theories which I have already mentioned. Fenichel says in *The Psychoanalytical Theory of Neurosis* that, 'the very act of mortifying (the flesh) becomes a distorted expression of the blocked sexuality'. In the Guru-disciple relationship not only is this the case, but the self-mortification is done at the behest of the Guru in the light of the intense feeling between them and, in part, in order to gain his approval. In this way a true sado-masochistic connection may be set up without the awareness of either of the participants who, without knowing what to look for, can hardly be expected to defend themselves against it. So with all the energy of such subterranean sexuality, their relationship is cemented into indestructability. Of course, from the point of view of the gratification both partners need in a continuing relationship, subconscious involvements of this sort may be essential; yet they ought to be understood and allowed for. Certainly, whatever sado-masochism there may be in the relationship between analyst and patient, it is rarely reinforced by any ascetic practices. An equally great danger, naturally, is the establishment of an unconsciously homosexual or even heterosexual relationship between Guru and disciple, and this too is not always avoided. Given the displacement of emotion I have mentioned, this is not, of course, surprising.

I have been trying to suggest that the parallel too often drawn between Guru and psychoanalyst is nothing like as comfortably close as some Western authorities have tried to prove; efforts to use Indian ideas in a Western psychoanalytical context always seem to me to come out looking short on penetration but long on pious hope. I have a suspicion that the word 'liberation' has caused much of the trouble: for us it means to be free of, yet in, society; in Hinduism, it means to be free of society, of the body, of differentiation, of birth and death. It is not a mundane but a metaphysical concept, and to ignore this is to distort it.

This is not to say that the insights offered within the Indian frame of reference are not at least as profound as those Western psychotherapy offers. But they are different, they start from different premises, they have different objectives; they are made and their results administered by men very different from psychoanalysts. It may be that we have become the victims of what not long ago freed us: the concept of the self-determined individual. Since anthropologists and ethologists, neurologists and psychologists have been showing us the limitations of this idea, we have become more aware of the distortions it forced upon us. By insisting that the difference between things and persons is an illusion, by saying 'all is one', Hinduism offers us liberation from the necessity to maintain a self by force, by the constant exercise of will. Paradoxically, the real self, unobserved, unconsidered and so unconstrained, blossoms when not artificially cultivated. Engaged in a quite different order of reality, unconcerned about a self which they regard with suspicion, yet socially absolutely safe because of the role they have taken up, sadhus seem to suffer from no self-alienation. Their personality inhabits them right to the skin, as it were; there is no gap, no emptiness which must be closed or filled with effort. There is no need to be anything, but the freedom simply to be.

The theoretical basis for such ease is the notion of totality; total man, neither arbitrarily divided within himself, nor divided from a total world. Since everything has being equally, *is* to the same totality, having its origin and continuance in the Being of Brahman, there is no need to maintain a false self for others: others and you are not separate, they cannot threaten you. It is true that such a view of the self takes hardly any account of the instincts or the unconscious drives; these, as we have seen, are to be controlled and stilled in order to let the 'true self' emerge. They too, therefore, so far as they are considered at all, are thought to be a part of the world illusion, attaching us to maya by a thousand tough Lilliputian wires. Once these are broken, action takes place only in the finally unreal 'real world' of objects and differentiation; success in that plane, therefore, will never be able to elate a true and developing adept, failure will never drive him to despair.

There are obviously details in Indian or Western practice which might usefully be examined by the other: for instance,

the Indian insistence on physical preparation for a mental discipline, based on a refusal to make an absolute distinction
between mind and body, could with advantage be looked at by
Western psychiatrists; while Indian Gurus, rendered by a sudden miracle less complacent, might glance at Western ideas
about the results of repression. But it is not at this level that the
synthesis between East and West can most usefully be made.
Indian attitudes to personality, Indian disciplines for self-examination, will only help us if we take them up long before we
reach the point where we have to rush to the analyst to help
clear up our conflicts. They must be practised when we are still
healthily a part of society. The narrowness of our sense of ourselves, our rigidity, our emphasis on the opposition and not the
unity of phenomena, our self-destructive sense that we are the
'masters' of our environment because essentially separate from
it, our devaluation of dream, reflection, inwardness, our over-
valuation of external alertness, action, image, our passions for
lists and definitions which makes us think that what is neither
listed nor defined does not exist – it is in these areas, the very
ground in which neurosis roots, that we may need to import
some part of Indian thinking. Such a modification may limit a
little of our present freedom of choice – itself more apparent
than real, more spoken than realized, and so a cause of great
disturbance in many of us – but in return we may get a sense of
identity as wide as the universe.

*

In India, where the visible and the invisible merge into each
other, where the seen is illusory and so no more significant than
the otherwise perceived, a range of behaviour is permitted which
stretches well over the borders of what we would call madness.
As a result, the schizoid and the paranoic have an area within
society in which they can operate and usefully connect with
their fellow citizens. This is not to say that they occupy the

passive position of the holy fool, tolerated for his supposed innocence, but rather that the ideas society as a whole has about the
cosmos can accommodate a vast number of personal demons,
assumptions of omnipotence, invisibility, astral travel, methods
of communication with the gods, obsessions, eccentricities, distortions of perception, hysteria.

We give our mad no opportunity to compromise with their
delusions; instead, we put them behind walls as if to drive
them farther into their personal universe. But the Indian remains and finds his delusions accepted, part of a common
mythology. 'I am Napoleon' condemns us to four walls, barred
windows and shock therapy; for an Indian, 'I am Ramakrishna'
would be a serious claim, to be examined carefully and accepted
or rejected on its merits and in its own terms.

In contrast to the Indian, our concept of 'reality' seems very
narrow, narrower than that held by the majority of the people in
the world, and Western man himself at least until the seventeenth
century. By devising finer and finer instruments to aid the senses
we have been able to go on exploring this reality with impressive
results, thus continuously reinforcing what we already believed:
that nature was external to us, separated and essentially inert.
As a result, we could exploit it and, by extension, each other.

It seems, however, to have remained constantly – and curiously – the case that our actual experience has not entirely confirmed this idea of 'reality' by which we were organizing our
intellectual, commercial and political lives. That there was such
a disparity and that it caused a certain strain may be deduced
from the category 'the supernatural' which we were forced to
create. Had this been descriptive only of the incomprehensible
doings of God – who having created the logic of nature might
have been expected to rise above it from time to time – one
would have been able to understand both its meaning and the
refusal of most scientists to investigate it. Instead it became – it
remains – a rag-bag into which we have swept any scrap of

experience, theory or information which could not be fitted into, and so challenge, our straightened and impoverished definition of the real. Once shunted into this intellectual limbo it can be disregarded, since one definition covers everything from divine ecstasy to acupuncture, from telepathy to graphology. Because many of these 'skills' or 'sciences' are clearly bogus, they have always damned the others by association. Even those most disposed to think such things interesting or potentially important chose a term, 'extra-sensory perception', which contains a paradox so self-defeating it leaves us no alternative to magic as an explanation of the phenomena it describes. As a result, that minority of serious men who, in every generation, have felt that here was a *terra incognita* which was not necessarily cloud-cuckoo-land, have always been regarded as sound on the whole but forgivably cranky in this; after all, did not the great Newton himself devote more years to alchemy than to mathematics?

The Indian, however, knew that the distinction between within and without was false, that the more one tried to manipulate the world, the farther one got from the truth. He himself was the world, was everyone; and everyone was part of him. There was a single indivisible unity; to destroy one part of it was to destroy a part of himself. If he tortured, exploited, despoiled, he was going against the fundamentals of Indian belief. He did so, often – although many of India's invaders and later overlords came from farther west – but never to the point where Indian thought itself became corrupted.

My belief is that the toughness of these fundamental ideas came not merely from the long centuries during which they had been held; it came from the experience of the many thousands in every generation who turned to the Guru and under him learned to go into the state of samadhi. In this condition, their knowledge of what the philosophers taught became direct. Ideas of universal unity did not remain words in a text-book, however persuasive. They became a part of every successful disciple's own experience. The essential vision of Hinduism could become, as it were, the actual vision of every Hindu. What the religion preached, he could live.

Thus in one way or another the relationship between Guru and disciple became a channel through which the essential belief of Hinduism in the unity of all phenomena was passed. To the extent that this relationship continues to exist in India, 'westernization' – in, it must be admitted, both its good and its bad aspects – will be resisted. There is no way in which the Guru-shishya tradition, with its emphasis on samadhi and on the merging of Master and disciple, can ever come to an accommodation with a philosophy which takes the material world to be real, separate and malleable. It is as if the Guru stood for a grammar that is all subject, while the West opposed it with one that is all predicate.

In considering why this should be so, it seems as if the West has turned out more predictably than India. Three thousand years ago, to judge from the philosophies, there was no lack of materialists clustered about the Indus. The philosophical school of Charvaka (in the *Mahabharata* an atheistic demon of that name is reduced to ashes by the power of Brahminical eyes) taught that there were only the four elements of earth, water, fire and air, that nature itself is the only creative force and only what we can perceive exists, that heaven is found in the enjoyment of delicious food, beautiful women, fine clothes and so on, while hell is what one suffers through one's enemies and their weapons, or through disease; death was the only liberation and the wise did not concern themselves with it. Austerities were left to those foolish enough to be duped by chants, ash smearing and other rituals, which existed only to offer a living to people too stupid or feeble to earn it any other way. Charvakas argued that men could not expect to avoid pain or discomfort; these were a part of life. But, like the Epicurians, they said that such unpleasantness should be kept to the minimum and happiness striven for – a happiness they defined in very concrete terms as the owning of cattle, successful trading, political administration, and so on. It is no wonder that these doctrines were known as Lokayata: *loka* means 'this world', but the word also means 'that which is found among people'.

The Ajiyikas, a sect which flourished around 700 B.C.,* believed that there was no ultimate cause for anything. Creatures behaved as they did because it was their nature to do so. The sect had an atomic theory, possibly the oldest in the world, which said that everything was made from atoms of water, earth, air, fire and a fifth, vital element. Nothing you did would alter what happened; they therefore rejected the theory of *karma*, preferring that of an uncontrollable destiny which they called *niyati* (it has also been translated as 'necessity'). Their doctrines are seen as forerunners of Lokayata.

The Vaiseshika philosophy, founded by a sage called Kanada within a century or so of the beginning of the Christian era, was also atomist. It taught that reality was understood through experiencing it; the soul was an inherent part of consciousness and was not therefore independent of the organism to which it was bound; everything was governed by karma, in that every occurrence had to have a cause. The dynamic qualities of matter itself did away with the need for a Creator. The Nyaya was a similar philosophy, founded possibly a century or so earlier. It believed in external reality too, and thought that man's highest aim was a total knowledge of it (*nisreyasa*).

* They were a rather repulsive bunch of ascetics, the members of which were initiated by being buried up to the neck while others of the sect plucked out their hair. Their self-imposed ordeals often crippled or mutilated them, and included holding red hot metal, breaking bones, squatting for weeks at a time and living in large earthen vessels. At the same time they had curious sexual habits, principally for occult purposes, and were sometimes found in the company of prostitutes. I do not understand what connection, if any, there is between their doctrine and their behaviour.

It is astonishing that, on such a basis, the *Vedas* retained their hold and no flourishing sciences were built. It is hard to see why this should be so, unless there was some factor in the national psychology which dragged the attention of the Indian intellectual to the within rather than the without. Today, however, there are many fine Indian physicists and the Tata Institute of Fundamental Research in Bombay is among the most prestigious scientific centres in the world.

More important may be the great hold that Buddhism had for so long on India, with its doctrine that life was suffering and that the stability of the material was an illusion, that there were only events and no basic elements (a doctrine, this last, which it has taken Western man the best part of three millennia to arrive at). When the Hindu revival came, it was Shankara's ideas that largely structured subsequent belief. Taught that there was no essential difference between man and nature and that to think there was one was the result of ignorance, Indian intellectuals can have had little inducement to discover how nature worked or what it was made of. They assumed they knew its essence; its illusory outer covering did not draw their interest.

Three factors, it seems to me, then stabilized thought in India, so that even today its general pattern, where it has not been modified by fundamentally different ideas from outside, remains what it was a thousand years ago. The first is, again, the innate conservatism of Indian society, cemented by parental authority; the young cannot strike out on their own and so are prevented from discovering new directions, new paths. The second factor is the waves of foreign invaders and rulers, who have for long periods made Hindus aliens in their own country. Their external pressure seems to have forced Hinduism into the complex, variegated, yet essentially rigid and unchanging pattern it still presents today. And the third is the Guru, whose disciples, by their surrender to him, their total devotion and acceptance, gave themselves little room for innovation and who, by institution-alizing authority in a religious context, gave authority through-out the society an extra edge, a greater significance.

The West, on the other hand, liberated individual intelli-gence in a scientific revolution which set fact before hypothesis, both in importance and in time. Observation and measurement decided the shape of theory. Since close observation followed by logical deduction seemed a method before which all secrets would fall and since curiosity insisted that it was the duty of secrets thus to let themselves be unravelled – the preoccupa-tions of the Greeks would not be questioned like their methods – Western man was free to race on and on down the almost unbelievable paths that suddenly stretched before him. Only the Church, to our continuing derision, thought that no good would come of it: Galileo's whispered, 'E pur si muove!' blares down the centuries like a bugle call. It is only today that we are beginning to look round at what we have made of the earth and of the lives of our hemmed in, multiplying race. Everywhere there is a feeling that things have gone wrong; we are like people in an unfamiliar landscape, plagued by the conviction that our compass is misleading us. We stumble on in the direction we chose long ago because we cannot quite face that our mistake has such a history, that we have wasted so much time.

It may be, though, that a change is coming in the West. A new generation is making the effort to face a quite different horizon. It is like watching the second wave of an attack; twenty years ago, there was a partly abortive effort at a breakout. This was after the existentialists, and particularly Sartre, had offered us their vision of personal authenticity and so at least squarely faced the philosophical problems of the post-Christian world. But still they accepted the basic configuration of the Western world; all they preached was that we should not simply be sheep, but should consciously choose our sheephood. Authenticity, their watchword, proved very hard to achieve, however. The majority took to a pseudo-existentialism, a holiday from morality. That choice by its nature is always moral escaped them, and their enthusiasm dribbled away in the noisy cellars of a thousand imitation St Germains.

Now we are witnessing a new assault on those same walls, led in part by older thinkers, in part by a new generation struggling to assert different values, demanding the old, elusive freedoms in a new way. What has changed the nature of youth's contribution to this revolution is, quite simply, drugs, and LSD 25 in particular. There is no need for me to discuss the use of this or other drugs in detail – there is a large and increasing literature on the subject, including notably the writings of Timothy Leary, Sidney Cohen's *Drugs of Hallucination*, William Braden's *The Private Sea: LSD and the Search for God*, works by Alan Watts and several others.

What acid has given us – given particularly the young who are the main experimenters – is the experience on which to base a new kind of perception. At the beginning of Dr Cohen's book there is a long letter written by a student immediately after his first experience of LSD 25; a few sentences explain how the drug can raise unexpected issues in the mind of someone who takes it: 'I met myself and found that I'm really not me after all. Or perhaps I should say that I have found out what it is like to exist. For that's all there was left at that instant, at that instant when feeling, thinking, being, all were caught up into one ebbing unity; a unity which was me, but not me, too. A me not me which stood there nakedly and pointed back at itself in a sorrowful joy, and asked "Why?". That's all, just "Why?". But then the "why" didn't matter and it just *was*! . . . I do know that from now on I'm going to feel a little different about the kind of language we use to describe psychotics and their "little worlds". . . . I'm going to look a little closer at what the mystics are trying to tell us; at what the philosophers have to say about this.'

What is important to realize is that the drug experience has not been for these people an end, but a beginning. It has opened up areas of themselves, it has posed questions. And not only for them; a whole generation has become aware of these questions because they have been posed by their contemporaries. Whether they themselves take acid or not, they have taken part in forming a climate of opinion in which, for the first time for centuries, a large number of Westerners is asking questions which can only be answered in the language of mysticism. The very nature of the LSD experience for some people – the sense of universal unity it brings them, of the pointlessness of so much of what we do, of the self as being without boundary – ensures this.

In other words, many of those who have passed through this experience ('passed through' is important here; to be valuable the experience should lead to questions which transcend and leave behind the drug-taking phase), and many others who know as a result that such an experience is possible, find themselves looking for a world view into which it will fit. They have been handed a key to that inner landscape from which Western man has been so long excluded; now they need a map, a pathway ... and a guide. For it seems to be a shortcoming of the drug experience that of itself it is no more than that: an experience, something felt at the level of the senses, posing questions at the deeper levels, but by its nature being unable to answer them. Sensation is enough, of course, for many, but for a substantial minority it is not.

I have the feeling that the majority of people have not yet understood that with the hallucinogenic drugs, a completely new factor has come into and begun to alter the way we in the West perceive reality. New to the modern West, at least; other cultures and our own in earlier times have a longer history of such awareness. From examining these cultures, one can see that there are dangers. The open gateway to another, kinder world invites the hard pressed to pass through it – again and again. What seems to me significant is that it is in these countries, particularly in Asia, that the Master has assumed such importance. I am not sure, naturally, that there is a connection, but it seems likely that once the existence of alternative kinds of perception has been discovered, someone takes on the role of explaining them or finding alternative routes to them, of giving them a human framework.

It is, in any case, to Zen, to Buddhism in general, to Sufism, to the Hindu Gurus, that many of those who have passed through this strange rearrangement of the self have turned. Many have gone to India or Japan; Indian and Japanese teachers have travelled to the West. Often misunderstanding, over-intensity, the cultural gap, have made the results apparently ludicrous. The basic concepts themselves, upon which these alien religions are founded, can hardly be described in Western languages, let alone understood. But a large number of Westerners continue, doggedly convinced that it is only from here that they will be given a context into which their discoveries about the world will fit. The underground press of America and Britain is filled with the symbolism of Asia, articles spread its doctrines and disciplines, the terms of which have become common currency among a large proportion of a whole generation. Those who believed that the young are irreligious are going to have to think again. They are religious. What they are not is Christian.

It seems at first sight strange that in this condition of spiritual bewilderment those in search of ways out of their dilemma should not have turned to what lay nearest to hand, the Christian religion. Christians may insist that those who turn elsewhere are people undisciplined in mind or spirit, searching for new sensations and mistaking them for new beliefs; and to an extent they may be right. What they are not seeing, however, is that for many people the need for new beliefs is created by their new sensations, that it is precisely because of the nature of these sensations that they are turning from Christianity.

What seems clear is that there is a new and increasing interest in the religions of the East, particularly Zen Buddhism, Sufism and that part of Hinduism which is concerned with illumination and which has the Guru as its guardian. What these have in common is that all three offer the aspirant, who puts himself in the hands of his teachers and has the will and the humility to learn, a direct experience which he finds both overwhelming and totally satisfying. What is more, he discovers how to fit this experience into a framework of philosophy or theology built to accommodate it. He thus has a bridge between what he feels and what he knows or believes, and so relieves the isolation which is the price of his inward journey.

Mysticism, a subject once among the most esoteric, has become in however hazy a fashion a part of contemporary knowledge, and even, among the young, of expectation. With the same fervour their parents and grandparents pursued high incomes and the comforts they bought, possession of which would, on the one hand, mark them out from their parents and, on the other, bring them closer to their admired superiors and masters. The demand for more and better things took on the flags, fervour, speeches, parades and martyrs of a crusade. Great systems were built on the need for economic justice. In that war, battles remain; but many people have taken their spoils and set up in oblivious comfort far behind the lines. It is their children who have repudiated both the war and its victories and turned inwards for their comfort.

This is, naturally, too tidy a picture; the fight against obvious injustices in society goes on. But at the same time, there is a movement which does not simply want to change the structure of society or distribute the conveniences and comforts society has to offer in a new way; instead, it turns its back on the whole philosophy upon which our societies have been built, sometimes upon the very concept, 'society', itself. Its concern is not with external structure but with internal reality, not with the reasoned but with the felt. Its concern is not general truth but individual validity, not acting but being.

All faith is fuelled not by dogma nor any over-precise definition of God, but finally, I imagine, by the direct experience of some alternative or additional plane of existence, approached through a special illumination. That such a plane does or does not objectively exist in any of the terms religion lays down is not the point; even if, as I think, it answers a purely human need, what is important is that the perception is so interpreted, and unless such perception continuously revives the aridities of theology, the faith itself must clot and slow and weaken.

It is the cultivation of this perception which Christianity offers to so few, and to those so reluctantly. It is as if those who manage to break through to it do so alone, by chance, or by a particular faculty of the imagination which allows them to concentrate on the fact of Christ or the transcendence of God with an intensity which makes these real in a way dogma might not have predicted.

One may ask whether a religion, not reinforced generation after generation by a direct mystical experience in at least a sizeable minority of its adherents, can survive for long.* For even the most devout are balked on the threshold of experience by the problem of Christianity's dualism. While the *Chandogya Upanishad* says, 'Now the light which shines above this heaven, above all, above everything, in the highest worlds beyond which there are no higher, verily, that is the same as this light which is here within the person', Christianity, one foot supported by Old Testament theism and the other by the philosophy of

---

* In Islam, while the prophet or law giver (*nabi*), whose line ended with Mohammed, is called the 'inspired by God', the realized holy man (*wali*) is known as 'regenerator of religion'. Thus the once for all revelation can be constantly refreshed.

ancient Greece, has from its beginnings stressed the essential 'otherness' of God. The God of the Jews, however much he may change and develop in the course of the millennia recorded in the Old Testament, remains the tribal Father, the demanding and occasionally irritated figure to whom all the other characters are answerable, whether they know it or not. It may be a forgiving God to whom David addresses his Psalms, and who comes to magnificent flower in the Palestine of Jesus. But man and God remain separate, their separateness emphasized by the uniqueness of Christ's divinity.

Unofficially, of course, the story is somewhat different, since the orthodoxies of Christianity have always been at intervals tested and even plagued by mystics claiming a direct experience of divinity. But that they were often put down by the orthodox is certain. Aquinas has his own definition of mystic ecstasy of which the highest level is direct contemplation of the divine essence. A long step remains between this and union with it. In the thirteenth century Beguines and Almaricians took up the doctrine of mystic oneness and were crushed for their 'pantheism', which Catholic scholars have always equated with atheism on the very ground that it denies the distinction between God and his created universe.

The Brethren of the Free Spirit, a little later, declared that man was essentially divine and therefore could by contemplation and detachment from the world of the senses unite himself with God. Since the man who had realized his divinity had the spirit of God within him, he was free to act as that spirit moved him. As a result, the Brethren seem to have gone in for a joyful but too easily censurable carnality; whether it was this which most affronted the Church or their belief that man, potentially divine, had no need for dogma and sacrament, it is hard to say. What is true is that for centuries thereafter inquisitors were busy burning mystics for their adherence to these or similar ideas.

Even Meister Eckhart, famous now and perhaps even thought

by some an adornment of the Church, who taught that there is a ground of the soul which is of a level with the divine, with which and through which we may realize God, was accused of heresy. When he died, he was preparing his defence against charges which were to be laid against him in Avignon. They had been brought with all the authority of Pope John XXII behind them; among the points in his teachings they condemned was his argument of a common divinity between man and God.

Mystics within Christendom, therefore, often found themselves in a great deal of theoretical difficulty. As Professor W. T. Stace puts it in his *Mysticism and Philosophy*, 'Although the Christian mystics themselves can generally be quoted ... on the side of dualism, it remains a question whether this would have been their view if they were not overborne and subjected to threats by the theologians and ecclesiastical authorities of the Church.' He goes on to describe how Christian mystics reconciled official dualism with their experience; sometimes their only means was a considerable ambiguity of expression. They had to do so since they knew where their allegiance lay; yet often the facts of the experience spoke despite themselves. 'The monist and the dualist describe the undifferentiated unity in practically identical language, but the monist believes that he himself is included in it; whilst the dualist, for cultural and theological reasons, regards himself as still outside it.'

It seems to me, therefore, that if this experience of 'the undifferentiated unity' is central to what I have called illumination, central to the experience to gain which the disciple seeks his Guru, then it is an experience to which Christianity is structurally opposed. The result has been that mystic ecstasy has been available, or has come, only to a small, a tiny and almost irrelevant minority among Christians, and that nothing in the organization of most Churches or denominations has tended towards their encouragement.

Instead, there have always been on the fringes of Christian

society sects and secret societies dedicated to giving their adherents precisely that experience which the Church itself normally gave them no opportunity to achieve. Of these, the most
important was probably witchcraft, which has always afforded its
devotees high excitement, ecstasy and trance. But various orders
and societies came into being, each offering a mixture of mysticism and magic in its prospectus. Many of these may have had
connections with the Middle East, the Arab world and so with
Sufism, of which they would have been a weak echo. The
Alumbrados of Spain, according to Arkon Daraul in his book
Secret Societies, had a 'method of carrying out their spiritual
concentration which links them strongly to the Sufi mystics. As
with the Sufis, (they) practised concentration upon the will of
their master or teacher in a supernatural or "illuminated"
union of minds. The Alumbrados were put down in 1623 by an
edict of the Grand Inquisition.' They in turn had links with the
Rosicrucians who were to be found in many of the cities of
Western Europe from the seventeenth century on; in London a
lodge was founded by a number of eminent scholars. There were
the Carbonari of Italy, whose origins may go back to pre-
Christian times and whose 'initiates' (to quote Daraul again)
'believed that they could, by contemplation and throwing themselves into a trance, gain information about secret matters'.
And many of these go back, of course, to the Gnostic groups
which flourished well into the Christian era until forced into
dissolution or the utmost secrecy by the heresy-sniffing atten-
tions of the Church. The Gnostics, as their name implies,
believed they had knowledge; a special knowledge, knowledge
itself, as it were – the ultimate fact of the universe. They
believed that this world was the creation of a corrupt and evil
god; full awareness of ourselves and our situation would finally
release us and allow us to rise to that level where the real God
existed. Most important among their institutions was discipleship, through which and under the guidance of a Master they

would make this attempt to identify themselves with the ultimate power, the world's final energy. Each aspirant would have a path towards illumination plotted for him by the Master and so would arrive by a unique process at his final mystic achievement.

What the existence of these societies and groups seems to point to is an overspill of the dissatisfied from the central experience of Christianity. Not even the Reformation which made available a large number of sects, some of them in many ways extreme, made the secret societies less attractive; nor, then or earlier, had persecution been able to curb them. It is as if they answered a deep and abiding need in Western man, a need with which the Church could not cope. It is true that often it was a desire for power over nature or other men that led people in this direction, a feeling that their own abilities could perhaps do with the boost of magic. It is true that there was always, especially about witchcraft, an aura of sexuality which would have been attractive to some people otherwise frustrated in a world suspiciously obsessed with stamping out lust and the sins of the flesh. But what this constant underground of spiritual guerrillas offered was not only a body of theory which could accommodate the mystic's experience of wholeness, but also techniques and guidance which would enable him more easily, and perhaps more often, to reach such illumination. They were freedom fighters, keeping alive an alternative vision during a long period of intellectual tyranny. It occurs to me that the persistence of this spiritual ambition suggests a deep psychological need for it. Perhaps, just as a society needs music, it needs mysticism. Not all men can play the violin or sing basso profundo; not everyone even has an ear for a true note. But a whole society, a whole culture without music is unthinkable, and those who make that music do so for us all. In the same way, a society might need the pathway to the inward self kept open, even if not everyone can travel it, or even understand its importance.

It seems to me that it is this constant, if often nearly fretted through, thread in Western spirituality which is now plainly in sight and being grasped and followed by a greater and greater proportion of the younger generations. And it is a thread which leads, not back to Golgotha and Bethlehem but past them, to a point farther away and earlier in time. For those who even now would prefer to turn to what their own culture teaches, who would find Christianity more comfortable if only they could find a way into it, the old theology offers no comfort; and neither, I imagine, does the new.

By secularizing the language about the concept of God, the new Protestant theologians from Barth to Alitzer may well rescue an intellectually viable structure of a sort around which they will be able to swing with all the old monkey-like agility of schoolmen. But religion is not for the theologians; it exists – revelation apart – to answer a human need. For that reason, if there is to be a new departure, its beginnings will have to be popular, chaotic, unschematic and emotional, not elitist, tidy, programmed and intellectual. In September 1970, the Archbishop of Canterbury told the Festival of Preaching at York that young people were turning to Eastern religions and by-passing the Christian Church because it concentrated so much on practical activity. 'Contemplation has become very widespread in the modern world and there is a world-wide longing for it, but the Christian Church has perhaps failed to be contemplative enough.' Yet how can a religion concerned with sin and thus with man in action take any stand on contemplative ground? Man's relationship to man – and to woman – is usually in the secular world, and while the idea of love is taught best in the act of loving, the idea of sin demands policemen. So the Church moved out, into power, politics, diplomacy. Constantine's state religion remains, though hydra-headed now, the voice of an official morality, of an official divinity.

More than that, Christianity, committed to its transcendent

God, was always vulnerable to an alternative theory of physical existence, to the consequences of a full exploration of man's physical environment. It is this involvement with the physical, a perhaps unavoidable consequence of its essential dualism, which on the one hand makes it so vulnerable to the logical picture of the world presented by scientific materialism, while enabling it on the other to offer so little to the non-Christian mystic in search of a world-view into which his experiences fit. If it can only be the direct awareness of divinity which constantly re-creates religion's principal moment of conception, such awareness can never have been available to more than a minority. That minority within Christianity may once have been sizeable, but it has now perhaps diminished to the point at which the whole religion is robbed of vitality. It was available to a minority because the European mystic had nowhere else to turn. He felt his illumination to be a religious experience – what other terms of reference had he? – and so he turned to his religion. But Christianity, reluctant to cater to people whose perceptions threatened its dogma and whose enthusiasm chastened its clergy, always provided an uncomfortable matrix for the mystic experience. The Eastern religions on the other hand, structured to provide that experience, can rediscover vigour in the large numbers who have found through those structures the way to illumination.

How could a theologian like Bultmann more effectively shut that door than by conceding to an unconcerned materialist world that the Biblical Jesus was largely a matter of myth and as such not worth our attention? He has accepted a definition of reality where all that can happen is known, and that which is unknown cannot happen – the dreariest kind of old-fashioned scientism. But I have seen Jesus' Palestine, or something very like it: it exists in many parts of India. Groups of itinerant holy men, travelling preachers, ascetics, mystics, prophets and miracle-workers people its landscape. Many are charlatans, or deluded, or insane, catering to the superstitions of those whose beliefs go no deeper, but their existence means that most Indians live cheek by jowl with the miraculous, as those who heard Jesus also did.

It is we who, with impoverished perceptions, gibber as though in terror of what they clearly saw and lucidly recorded. Their mental capacities were no less than ours, in geological time they are our contemporaries; why have we such contempt for their perception? The age of miracles is over, we say with some self-satisfaction; but is it over because for seven thousand years humanity deluded itself and in many parts of the world continues to do so, or because for three centuries we have rejected the harsh self-disciplines necessary to hone our inner awareness to the sharpness which the miraculous demands?

Illumination looks for a faith through which it may be explained; and faith needs a focus less than abstract, however much one may realize that beyond the assimilable myth there is an Absolute which can only be considered in abstract terms. The Hindu can reconcile his tens of thousands of *devatas* and avatars, his gods great and small, with the Absolute which is Brahman, he can achieve unity with the vast totality of things through his connection with and devotion to the particularity of his Guru.

'The real purpose of myth', Bultmann writes, 'is to speak of the transcendent power which controls the world and man, but that purpose is impeded and obscured by the terms in which it is expressed.' It seems to me that it is only impeded and obscured because we allow one set of terms – the scientific materialistic, the rational – to blot out all others, on that pernicious 'either-or' pattern which has so diminished Western man's universe. And myth, in any case, retains its power – otherwise the statement 'God is dead' would wipe out the need for all theology.

The point is that Christianity is a Western religion, steeped in Western man's dualism, convinced of the reality of a world 'out

there', differentiated, subject to causality, eternally to be external to us. It accepts the reality and the uniqueness of the
individual. It allows no scope for the idea of merging. It will
have no truck with paradox, however sublime. Tillich's God –
'the infinite inexhaustible ground of history . . . the ground and
aim of our social life' – still leaves the individual looking outside
himself, and into a singularly arid prospect. That is no God
who will explain illumination. And in that lies Christianity's
dilemma; it can no longer sustain what it has believed about
God for nearly twenty centuries. The God 'out there' becomes
so implausible, even his servants abandon him. Yet it offers us
no way but exhortation to experience the God within, no way of
reaching him, no theory or technique which would bring him to
reality. It intellectualizes, refining and refining concepts which
from the beginning were irrelevant. Illumination needs an
inner centre; for the religious, Christianity may never be the
route they take to find it now. Hinduism and its related religions,
Tao, Zen and Sufi, have spent thousands of years on that road.
It has been made smooth; and from its far, brilliant end the
singing voices of long-arrived pilgrims seem to float back to us,
and the guides stand ready.

*

If the Christian God, the transcendent 'other', is not, as I have
suggested, the deity reached by self-realization, he is at least the
one our culture makes available. Conversely, although it might
make philosophical sense of certain very intense subjective states
to equate Brahman with Being, that Hindu absolute is separated
from us by a vast cultural gap. Many will always be unable to
leap it; a majority, even of those who think it is not beyond them,
end up tragically or grotesquely far short of where they hoped to
land. Yet the questions, the needs, which prompted their
attempt are real and will not be forgotten. One or two individuals
strolling on the moon have for ever altered the dimensions of

our physical environment; in the same way, the minority asking these questions is, I suspect, altering Western man's psychological environment.

What their questions are concerned with is the nature of subjective experience, the value of objective knowledge, and the connection, between the two, which turns out to be closer and more nearly indestructible than we have assumed in three hundred years. It is by ignoring this subjective element that we have been able to believe in an external world not only knowable – which is probably the case – but actually as we 'know' it to be. And this, in face of the many different ways there are of 'knowing' it, seems unlikely, can be no more than an assertion. Western man, like the rest of sense-imprisoned humanity, only knows the world in a way peculiar to himself. Like the rest, he proves his knowledge by tests he himself sets up. The Indian sadhu who knows the world in other ways, knows it no less than does the Western physicist, or economist, or sociologist. He too has his tests, and they too confirm him in his certainties.

If the sadhu's, the Guru's, convictions have value for us, if they stem from and point to something essentially true about the human being and his nature, then it seems to me that the West can only achieve that truth in its own terms. It cannot borrow cultural references from six thousand miles away and somehow graft them onto its own language and ideas. There is rarely a lasting value in hybrids of that sort. If Western man is preoccupied with the 'reality' of the physical world, he will first have to be convinced that the states which the shishya achieves through his Guru are 'real' in that sense. He will have to be convinced that trance states reached after prolonged meditation are not delusions on the part of those who say they can attain them. Only then will his training allow him to approach them without suspicion and only in that way will his defences be, as it were, turned against him, so that his very belief in objectivity will lead him to accept the reality of such subjective experiences.

Once this has been established, he may go on to consider if such states are valuable; at least he will have to modify that construct, 'the external world', by the means of which he has been able for centuries to ignore his own sometimes untidy subjectivity. And once he has been forced to include this in his picture of the world, he will find that it has automatically become very different – as regards time, matter, causality, energy – from previous perceptions.

It seems to me that one proof might lie in the cultural field. Embedded in a number of widely different cultures and sub-cultures are descriptions of the trance state. If they tally with one another where any cultural interchange is highly unlikely, one may imagine that they refer to an identifiable and identical condition. For example, in his essay *Experiences of the Mystic Light*, Mircea Eliade considers a farflung phenomenon in the world of mysticism: the observation of light – slow effulgence or lightning flash – in highly charged states reported among the priests, sages and shamans. The light in these mystic visions was not always experienced as light by itself, but shone on, through or around other objects. Immediately – to continue with this one aspect of trance – one thinks how vivid colour and a strange brightness suffuse so much of the reported LSD world. If we pursue this phenomenon further, we discover that, in sensory deprivation experiments, visual hallucinations are most commonly experienced. Dr Cohen prints a table which shows to what an extent the results of those experiments overlap the experiences of those who have taken LSD.

The weakness of the construction, 'Light is seen in trance – I have seen light – therefore I have been in trance', will be clear to any student of logic. Light, too, is a very obvious metaphor for godhead and therefore one would expect it to appear in the religious symbology of many cultures. Once it has appeared, it may become the raw material out of which delusions are built. Nevertheless, such correlations in the reported details of trance states, wherever and however induced, if properly pursued and listed, might provide a basis for their wider acceptance and for further enquiry.

Physical proofs, provided by doctors, physiologists and psychologists, that changes occur in brain rhythm and blood oxygen during deep meditation may go further in a sceptical culture to persuade the reluctant that something 'real' is going on. For example, a paper by Dr R. K. Wallace, entitled *Physiological Effects of Transcendental Meditation*, was published in March 1970 in *Science*, the journal of the American Association for the Advancement of Science. Fifteen students, with no noticeable mental or physical disabilities, who had practised meditation for anything between six months and three years, were tested for an hour or so under laboratory conditions; each of them spent some thirty minutes in meditation. 'Oxygen consumption, heart rate, skin resistance, and electroencephalograph measurements were recorded before, during and after ... meditation. There were significant changes between the control period and the meditation period in all measurements. During meditation, oxygen consumption and heart rate decreased, skin resistance increased, and the electroencephalogram showed specific changes in certain frequencies. These results seem to distinguish the state produced by transcendental meditation from commonly encountered states of consciousness and suggest it may have a practical application.'

What this and all the various experiments that have been made on the physical control of yogis seem to prove is that there are many ways, based on our own empirical methods, in which one can approach these highly subjective conditions. Nor should the residual awe we still have in the face of religious phenomena hold us back; Hinduism more than most faiths gives foothold to the atheist. Buddhism, which is derived from it, was never a religion concerned with deity, but with the self, the universe, and the relationship between them.

Not only, therefore, may we be able to verify this strange experience in our own manner, but it may also be possible to approach it without altering our present post-Christian, humanist standpoint. I see no need to blunt the chopping edge of Western man's mind, honed on so many complex problems over the last two or three hundred years, because of the false supposition that mysticism in its fragility will be unable to survive its blows. On the contrary, the mumbo-jumbo, the moaning and the incense, the finger cymbals, the poeticizing, the androgynous propagandists in their robes, the prevailing odour of *ganja*, although they may all help to induce a psychological state in which trance can be more easily achieved, have served as a barrier precisely against those minds which might most penetratingly have examined this phenomenon.

But why should we want to examine and perhaps use these resources of the mind? Why now, when we discarded them so many centuries ago?

The present crisis in Western consciousness seems to me to stem from the very success which that consciousness has brought us. We have, after all, largely become what nineteenth-century visionaries hoped we would; embracing their certainties, we built the future they had foreseen. Literacy, democracy, technology can stand like honours on our fading banners. But what did we lose? What did we fail to gain? What price were we forced to pay, what cramping of the soul and impoverishment of the imagination have we suffered? Put the question a different way: we sent men to the moon – did we ever seriously consider not sending them? Was a free decision taken, a choice made? Or were we run away with by technology, doing what we could do because we could do it, not doing what we should do because we thought it should be done? And what of the weapons we have created? What of the dying birds, the unbreathable air?

One result of such questioning has been to set up new doubts, especially among the younger scientists. They are beginning to

challenge that most deeply embedded Western institution –
scientific curiosity itself. They have stopped, it seems, believing
in the right to discovery as a moral absolute. Values, they are
beginning to feel, have a part to play; and even as this is realized,
it becomes plain that they always did, that Western man's curiosity always implied a moral right to knowledge which only the
Church ever questioned – and the Church could be ignored,
having its own interests to defend.

As western man has become aware that there is a flaw in his
world-view, he has tried to correct it, but always by the methods
he has grown used to applying, themselves the consequence of
his distorted viewpoint. He searches for mechanistic explanations, sets up the social sciences, extends his technological
dominion. He adjusts the difference between expectation and
actuality by self-delusion, shifting his definition of civilization
whenever the old one gets too hard-pressed. His criteria are self-
justifying, accepting implicitly the attitudes and aims they might
be questioning. They remain so by the exclusion of some part of
the truth. He cannot include Belsen in his picture of himself; on
the other hand, the moon landing is treated as an apotheosis of
homo faber. He achieves this self-deception by a semantic trick
which makes an identifiable body of men responsible for the
events he would rather ignore, man himself responsible for
those he wants to glory in. Thus the Nazis built Belsen, but
man landed on the moon.

At the same time we prefer to rely on our objective achievements – mass-produced comfort, mass-responsive institutions –
to prove what we are. As a result we are forced to give ideology
and technological achievement a quasi-spiritual significance.
Anyone who doubts this ought to look again at the literature of
scientific discovery or the rhetoric of space travel.

This view of man only as tool maker – that is, as proving his
humanity by the tools he makes and, by extension, the control
those tools give him; thus becoming, he assumes, more 'human'

as his tools become more complex and his control more complete – has raised a purely mechanical efficiency into an exalted ideal. In its name, powerful hierarchies grow up, baffling bureaucracies, autocracies of unexpected power.

That we should have developed in this way in the West seems to me the inevitable result of the separation we make between man and the rest of the natural order. The hierarchy God-man-nature, with free will a major factor in the programme, always made the world man's oyster. Perhaps that was God's trap; if it was, then we leaped proudly into it some twenty-five centuries ago, under the bright blue Athenian sky. In time, scientific method itself developed into a pseudo-theology implying an absolute; ideas in the form of theories and postulates seem to prove the researcher a constantly tentative sceptic, but are in fact part of a refining process implying absolute knowledge. Once scientific objectivity had been established as the right frame of mind in which to regard natural phenomena, the way was clear for considering man too as an object. Psychology and psychoanalysis, when they finally developed, were forced to construct pseudo-physical cause and effect models to explain the workings of the psyche.

For longer than we realize, we have relied upon the humanity of our institutions to save us. Under pressure of increasing population, of higher and higher material expectations, of consequent frustration and increasingly bitter industrial and social strife, these have begun to sag a little. And they themselves, of course, have had the same bias in their founding; man as object is their main concern: hierarchy, cause and effect, precise definition, prescribed limits. They depend upon the illusion that we know who we are, why we act as we do, what the extent of our responsibilities ought to be. They are concerned with action, not with conviction, they shore up the external, devalue the internal.

But now a change – which may be only transitory and which I

may be optimistically exaggerating – is taking place in Western consciousness. I have mentioned that there is, among younger scientists, a growing doubt about the absolute value of scientific research as such. And I have also mentioned at some length the changes in attitude of many of the young, particularly as a result of taking LSD 25. (I must here emphasize that I do not advocate its wide, unsupervised use; I have no desire to help carry further Timothy Leary's dimming torch. But it is being used and certain intellectual attitudes have developed as a result, not only among those who actually take it, but in the whole generation to which this group belongs.) Their prevailing mood is a fairly sickly mixture of pseudo-Asiatic exoticism and a self-conscious sweetness, a knowing and sophisticated innocence. But at its heart there is a conviction that Western modes of thought and behaviour have been inadequate and are now threadbare, a conviction which is, I think, quite tough and durable, supported as it is both by the evidence in front of us and by other, more 'legitimate', groups and thinkers.

The political young, now often the revolutionary and the violent – who may be taken as overlapping in some ways the more contemplative school – have in many cases given up the attempt to make the existing system work. It no longer seems to them to answer human needs. They have an intuition that kinds of joy are being stifled, kinds of immediate communication of one man with another, kinds of personal achievement and satisfaction. They are rebelling against the existence of money, therefore, not the existence of poverty; against politics, not against a particular party; against the drabness of most men's work, not against low wages. They are not offering an alternative programme, but turning against programmes as such. They stand, in short, for the subjective needs of man, for a society in which he can get to know what these needs are by discovering himself, where the hierarchies disappear because they are not needed by men who have become fully themselves.

331

Whether this is as practical a programme as it is sympathetic is doubtful. We are, after all, descended from the ape-like hominids and the likelihood is that they, and thus we, had a deep implanted need for hierarchy and structure. Biology makes us overlords, aggressors, murderers, and will try to trip us when we attempt to change; the violent young enjoy their violence too much for it not to outweigh much of what they preach. But it remains significant that their dissatisfactions should be so widely shared, that the belief in individual self-realization, however phrased, should be so widespread. I doubt if in modern times there has ever been such a mistrust of objectivity, of materialism, such a drive towards dream, trance, subjective knowledge.

Not that those who most mistrust scientific objectivity are necessarily the ones who rush eagerly towards the mystic's solution. They are, on the contrary, engaged in the effort to construct a new basis for science, one which recognizes the presence of the human observer and his relationship to what is observed.

The ideas of Michael Polanyi, for instance, a scientist turned philosopher, best known for his book *Personal Knowledge*, distinguish clearly between knowledge and knowing. He does not say that knowledge does not exist, but rather that what is passed objectively from mind to mind is not yet knowledge. 'Nothing that is said, written or printed, can mean anything of itself: for it is only a *person* who utters something – or who listens to it or reads it – who can mean something *by* it,' he writes in his *The Study of Man*. And in his essay on C. P. Snow's attempted analysis of the gap between science and the old humanistic culture, also entitled *The Two Cultures*, Professor Polanyi writes, 'Scientific rationalism served man well as long as it was moving towards its false ideals from a great distance. But this could not last. Eventually the truth-bearing power of its absurd ideals was bound to be spent and its stark absurdity to assert itself. This is what has happened in the twentieth century. Scientific obscurantism has pervaded our culture and now distorts even science itself by imposing on it false ideals of exactitude.'

He gives as an example the evolutionist's problem with consciousness, which he must acknowledge as useful since it has not hindered survival, but which his mechanistic attitudes prevent him from accepting as a cause which can set a living body in motion. Professor Polanyi ends the essay by asserting that: 'A humanistic revisionism can be secured only by revising the claims of science itself. The first task must be to emancipate biological science, including psychology, from the scourge of physicalism; the absurdity now imposed on the sciences of life must be eliminated. The task is difficult, for it calls in question an ideal of impersonal objectivity on which alone we feel it safe to rely. Yet this absurd ideal must be discarded. And if once we succeed in this task, we shall find that science no longer threatens man's responsible existence and that we can restart the great work of the Enlightenment without danger of the traps that have so disastrously ensnared its progress in the present century.'

The psychoanalyst R. D. Laing makes a similar point in his book *The Divided Self*: 'It seems extraordinary that whereas the physical and biological sciences of it-processes have generally won the day against tendencies to personalize the world of things or to read human intentions into the animal world, an authentic science of persons has hardly got started by reason of the inveterate tendency to depersonalize or reify persons.'

He goes on to say that his book is about 'people who experience themselves as automata, as robots, as bits of machinery, or even as animals. Such persons are rightly regarded as crazy. Yet why do we not regard a theory that seeks to transmute persons into automata or animals as equally crazy? The experience of oneself and others as persons is primary and self-validating. It exists prior to the scientific or philosophical difficulties about how such experience is possible or how it is to be explained.'

Dr Laing refuses to accept that objectivity, as it might be

understood by a physicist, has any validity here. Such an attitude he feels, depersonalizes the patient, rendering him, as the word implies, an object for study rather than a particular man or woman. He is concerned with the unity of human experience, which does not permit him to make the deep division between 'sane' and 'mad' upon which so much psychiatric definition depends. This means that he takes the state of being of the schizophrenic as seriously as he does that of someone who functions in a recognizably sane manner; he does not devalue the patient, even by implication, through considering him impaired and therefore lesser.

Taking this further, Dr Laing recognizes that, not only must the insane be taken seriously as themselves, but they may also be explorers in areas we have neglected. In *The Politics of Experience* he writes: 'The madman is ... confused. He muddles ego with self, inner with outer, natural and supernatural. Nevertheless, he often can be for us, even through his profound wretchedness and disintegration, the hierophant of the sacred. An exile from the scene of being as we know it, he is an alien, a stranger, signalling to us from the void in which he is foundering, a void which may be peopled by presences that we do not even dream of.'

Not the mad, but the so-called primitive, should be our teachers in the opinion of Claude Lévi-Strauss. He believes in scientific method as the only one that leads to true knowledge, but makes no judgements that derive from this conviction ascribing a superior position to our culture, an inferior one to others which have developed in a different way. Thus he does not recoil from objectivity but rather broadens it to include the observer and his society, in this way refuting by implication the thesis that 'out there' can be examined without references to 'in here'. In *A World on the Wane* he points out: 'Implicitly we claim for our own society, for its customs, and for its norms, a position of privilege, since an observer from a different social group would pass different verdicts upon those same examples .... If we are to get back to a position of objectivity we should abstain from all judgements of this sort. We have to admit that human societies can choose among a gamut of possibilities. These choices cannot be compared with each other: one is as good as another.' His theory of structuralism, by pointing out underlying similarities in the very logic of societies, implies a human unity. The exclusive position of Western man at the top of some mythical tree of development begins to look extremely insecure.

Western man's assertion of pre-eminence, then, has come under anthropological attack, psychoanalysts readjust the inadequacies of his view of man as object, philosophers dispute the true objectivity of his knowledge. But physics itself, since the acceptance of quantum mechanics and relativity, has been forced to turn its back on the strict rules of the Newtonian universe. Quantum theory states that all forms of energy are released in discrete units, called quanta; a quantum of light is called photon. The theory most usefully deals with phenomena which are so small that classical, nineteenth-century physics cannot describe them. Its rules do not apply to them; but since all matter is built out of such infinitesimal particles, this subtly falsifies Newtonian physics. It works only because its scale permits the investigator a coarseness of definition, rather in the way that £10 or fifty pence may be much the same to a rich man.

In quantum theory, randomness becomes respectable, partly because the scientist cannot avoid reckoning with it. Particles cannot be kept under continuous observation; for instance, when two electrons scatter there is no telling which particle in the final stage of this event was which in the initial stage. Out of quantum theory there arose, formulated some forty years ago, the Uncertainty Principle of Heisenberg. This for the first time recognized that the observer, by his actions, modifies the object he is observing, a fact which can be ignored in a practical sense when we deal with matter in its ordinary dimensions or conditions, but which becomes more and more important the nearer we approach the limits of observation.

To determine, for example, the position of a sub-atomic particle, it has to be examined in light of an extremely short wavelength. However, the shorter the wavelength, the greater the energy of each photon. For a scientist to observe the particle at all, at least one photon must interact with it. In doing so, the particle gains energy from it, and thus momentum. As a result, the more precisely you can determine the particle's position, the less certain you will be about its increasing momentum. There is no way out of this dilemma – in order to examine anything at all, an exchange of energy and momentum takes place which alters that object's original properties. One result is that predictions about the future of a particle's path cannot be made with any certainty. To this extent, the laws of cause and effect have to be ignored; the scientist himself is reduced to dealing in probabilities.

It would be easy to make too much of this long-accepted development in physics. Yet it is curious how little it has altered our views of science, how much it could alter our view of the world. As a former student under Einstein, Professor Ernest Hutten, puts it in his book, *The Ideas of Physics*: 'Human knowledge must, of necessity, bear the human imprint. This does not mean, of course, that the laws of physics, for instance, now become tinged with the experimenter's personality or that scientific knowledge is a matter of arbitrary, 'subjective' decision. On the contrary, what we want to do is to abandon, if not to abolish, the supernatural, superhuman view of what a law of nature is and of the power of science.'

So that we are confronted with the absurdity that when we turn to the very citadel of positivism, to science, to physics itself, we discover the echoing halls and weed grown courtyards of an abandoned ruin; for half a century the garrison has been sporting in wide and distant meadows, led to a new freedom by Einstein, Planck and Heisenberg. Meanwhile the rest of us, cowed by those sombre walls, the solidity of those battlements, the long tradition of oppressive rule they represent, have continued serflike in our ideological duty. We have attempted to be more and more 'scientific'. We have ignored the distortions this has led to, we have denied our humanity, we have defined fact, evidence and logic as narrowly as madmen. And all the time the prince bishops of our sad religion, themselves apostate long ago, have been breaking the very rules we thought they stood for.

It takes a long time for new ideas to overcome the inertia of a whole society; like some giant liner, prodded by its fussy, attendant tugs, it comes about slowly, almost imperceptibly at first, then more and more quickly. It may be that Western society has been swinging to a new course while hardly anyone aboard noticed, that only now are the passengers beginning to turn and point as they discover the altered configuration of the shoreward landmarks. The course may not, indeed, be new at all; in the calculations of history, the West's attempt to chart the world as it is, without realizing that men can do no more than point out how it seems to be, may well be seen as a passing intellectual aberration, brave in its own way, but always doomed. Its aridities will then be regarded with the horror with which we now think of the extremes of Puritanism. Its standards will become incomprehensible, its narrowness laughable, its disciplines material for footnotes in some examination of discarded ideas.

What will replace it? First, surely, a new science, incorporating and extending the old, based in part on the humble acceptance of human senses, human scale. We are present in the world, and to the extent that that is accepted, our total being becomes important and must be allowed for. No truthful statement can be made by excising or censoring a part of what we know of ourselves and, by extension, of others. Accepting our role, we may be able to make science not man's enemy, as it now so often seems, not a machine which carries us in unsought directions by its inexorable processes, but something more natural, a particular way of understanding the world which neither occludes all others nor dominates us.

One of the alternative ways in which we may then come to understand ourselves is through some version of that interior journey offered by the mystic disciplines of the East. It may even be, as our populations grow, as the pressure on each man's self increases, that we will have to learn to make that journey in order to survive.

If these areas of mental experience are to be usefully explored, we cannot ignore the enormous body of knowledge locked up in the literature and traditions of Asia. For Teilhard de Chardin, evolution was the struggle towards consciousness. Once achieved, consciously controlled evolution would begin to express itself in cultural convergence with, in the far distance, that slightly suspect Omega Point of ultimate development. There is no question that, physically and technologically, we have reached the stage when cultural convergence is so simple as to appear inevitable. It may even be that its occurrence is an essential preliminary to our survival. The barriers against it are psychological. If, however, the new frontier on which man's struggle for understanding is to be fought lies within each one of us, such barriers must come down so that we can turn to those who have been warriors on similar battlefields for millennia.

One thing we shall discover is that, in every society which has developed techniques for inducing meditation and trance, there has grown up an institution on the Master-disciple pattern to propagate those techniques. From Persia to Japan the teachers wait, century by century, to induct yet another generation into these mysteries. Invested as they are with all the majesty of religion, we think them very alien, but stripped of their divinity they may be better understood.

The function that the Master, the Guru, performs is complex and perhaps essential. He is, first, the focus of the disciple's attention and emotion. In normal life, these are dispersed, elicited by many events and people; the Guru cures this condition of dispersal, draws the disciple's energies together in a way which may be a necessary preliminary to redirecting that energy inwards. Second, the Guru, a human being demonstrably similar to the disciple, sets the experience within a human scale. The myth of his divinity may add intensity to the disciple's devotion; the fact of his humanity allows the disciple to operate without being crushed by a constant sense of eternity, omniscience, omnipotence, without a feeling that he is contending with the Absolute without allies. Third, it is clear that the Guru can help the disciple directly, either by explaining difficulties, helping to solve problems met with while practising the technique, general encouragement, or by scolding, setting the disciple baffling problems, even by violence. Fourth, he is the repository of whatever doctrine, religious or scientific, is currently in use to explain the disciple's experiences. This may be very important because insanity, or at best disorientation, might otherwise be the outcome for the disciple. Fifth, he is the example, the proof that the way leads somewhere and somewhere worthwhile. His own sanity, detachment, serenity, strength, integration and loving kindness show that the hard journey the disciple has to make will prove worth it in the end. And possibly, sixth, he may be a source of a developed mental power which, transferred to the disciple, can transform the latter's inner life.

If I am right and Western man's next adventure will be the struggle to discover himself, then he will need such a figure by his side. But the Master will not be imported from cultures in which he already has a place, precisely because his roots lie in those cultures. I have tried to show how in many ways the relationship between Guru and shishya is determined by the facts of Indian society; anything similar that develops in the West must be equally a part of Western culture. But if, in detail, the figure which emerges here has little in common with the ochre robed godman of India, peacefully tyrannical in his ashram; if new explanations have to be found for his powers, and the devotion that is given him is couched in different terms; if the very qualities we look for in him alter with our altered demands – in essence he will still be the Guru, the guide and mentor of the inward path.

Glossary

acharya. A savant, exponent of religious lore.

advaita. Non-dualistic, the name given to Shankara's monistic philosophy.

agni. Holy fire, from the Lord of Fire whose name it was.

akshara. The Indestructible, one of the attributes of Brahman and sometimes a synonym for God.

ananda. Spiritual bliss, one of the constant qualities achieved by the realized.

arati. Sung prayers, accompanied by the waving of lights before the effigy of God or Guru (sometimes spelled arti).

asanas. The prescribed postures for meditation, an important element in the teaching and practice of hatha yoga.

ashram. A retreat, hence the secluded abode of a holy man; the home of a Guru and the centre of his activities. Also the name given to the four stages of Hindu life.

atman. The soul, or inner Self; thus, transcending difference, the single universal Soul.

avatar. An incarnation of God, occurring when the state of the world seems to call for it.

betel. A leaf which is wrapped around particles of areca nut and chewed.

Bhagavad Gita. Literally 'God's Song', the section of the *Mahabharata* in which Krishna sets out for Arjuna the tenets of a correct and pious life; perhaps the most famous piece of India's holy literature and the one most widely consulted.

Bhagavan. The Exalted, the Lord, the personal God, as compared with the undifferentiated Being which is Brahman.

bhakti. Intense devotion to God. Hence bhakta, one who feels such fervour.

bidis. Indian cigarettes, both very strong and very cheap.

Brahman. The Universal, the Absolute, all-containing Being.

brahmin. The caste of the teachers of religious knowledge.

brahmacharya. The first stage of orthodox life, thus a Vedic student or religious neophyte, dedicated to an ascetic life; hence, any celibate.

chai. Tea.

chakras. The centres or 'lotuses' in the spinal column of the subtle body which must be opened by the exercises of hatha yoga in order to bring enlightenment and realization.

charas. Narcotic extracted from resin of the hemp plant.

charpoy. A light, wooden-framed string bed.

chela. Disciple of a Guru.

cit. The consciousness to be achieved in self-realization.

dakshina. Voluntary fee given to priest or Guru for the performance of a ritual, or for religious instruction.

darshan. Sight of a holy, or otherwise great, person; such visual contact is believed to add virtue to the beholder.

deva. A deity; the feminine is *devi* and there are thousands of these and related celestial beings.

dharma. Ethics, the prescribed code of conduct.

dhoti. Piece of fine cloth wrapped round the waist, tugged between the legs and tied; traditional and hence the dress of the orthodox.

dhyana. Meditation in its intense form; the Sanskrit root of the Japanese word 'zen'.

diksha. Initiation of a disciple by his Guru, usually by giving him a mantra, sometimes only by touch or look.

Diwali. A five-day multiple festival held in late autumn.

gadi. Position or office, hence seat symbolic of these; the Guru's throne.

ganja. Dried leaves of the hemp plant, smoked as a narcotic.

ghanapathi. Proficient in the *Vedas*.

ghat. A steep place; hence the steps leading to a river or bathing place.

gopis. The girl cowherds with whom Krishna played at Vrindaban, incarnations of devas.

grihasta. The second, householder stage of a Hindu's life.

guru. The bringer of light; hence any teacher.

gurukripa. The grace of the Guru.

Hanuman. Chief of the monkey allies of Rama in the *Ramayana*, of divine birth and exalted for his devoted service; known as the Monkey God.

hatha yoga. Complex physical exercises giving spiritual enlightenment and occult powers, as well as physical health, to the practitioner.

Holi. A spring festival, now largely sacred to Krishna, celebrated by throwing coloured powders and dyed water.

homa. Traditional fire sacrifice.

Ishwara. God; the Creator.

japa. Repetition, silent or audible, of a name of God or a mantra.

jiva. Individual soul, sometimes combined with atman in the form *jivatman.*

jnana. Knowledge in the absolute sense which derives from the realization of sacred truth; hence jnana yoga, the path which leads to such knowledge.

kanya. Unmarried woman, a virgin; hence used of those women dedicated to a spiritual life; a nun.

karma. The actions one performs, and the destiny created by the actions one performed in earlier incarnations; hence karma yoga, the way of duty, in which one performs right actions for no reward but spiritual development.

Krishna. An avatar of Vishnu; but for most bhaktas, God himself, absolute in his own spiritual domain and not merely an incarnation.

kshattriya. One of the warrior caste from whom the kings and princes sprang.

Kundalini. The serpent coiled at the foot of the spine in the subtle body, or invisibly in our gross, normal body, which, when awakened by the exercises of hatha yoga and by meditation, bursts through the chakras from the lowest to the highest and last in the brain, thus opening up the spiritual self to God-realization.

lakh. One hundred thousand; a hundred lakhs make one crore.

lila. Sport or game of God, a concept enabling the faithful to accept the otherwise inexplicable.

lingam. The phallic symbol of Shiva, almost certainly pre-Vedic in origin.

Mahabharatha. Sanskrit epic poem of some 200,000 lines, venerated as a work of religious teaching.

mahant. Head of a monastery.

mahatma. Literally 'great soul', used of a man of developed spirituality.

mahala. Sect.

mantra. Sacred syllable, word or phrase, given at initiation by the Guru to the disciple and for that reason of great power. The disciple concentrates upon it in his meditation and keeps it secret at all times.

marg. Way or path.

math. A monastery.

maya. The differentiated phenomenal universe, perceived as illusory when compared with the real, absolute totality which is Brahman.

moksha. State of being released from the birth-death-birth cycle, the condition of the realized man.

mukti. A synonym for moksha; hence mukta, one who is in the state of self-realization.

pan. The little packet of betel leaf and areca nut chewed by many Indians.

pandit. Learned man.

paramahansa. Highest level of sannyasi, released from all social trammels and at one with the Absolute.

parampara. Succession, as in guru-shishya parampara, the continuing line from Guru to succeeding disciple.

prana. Breath, but used to mean the body's vital forces.

pranayama. The control of breathing in hatha yoga, the first and basic exercise leading to control of all the body's vital forces.

prasad. Food or other gift offered to idol or Guru and then distributed among the faithful; the word means 'grace' and to be offered such a morsel is a small mark of the Guru's favour.

Puranas. Eighteen in number, they contain the mythology of Hinduism, and are considered a guide to behaviour almost as important as the *Vedas* and the *Shastras*.

raja yoga. Highest reaches of the path which hatha yoga begins, where mind turns to its own control and on the way to realization gains for the practitioner psychic powers.

Rama. Seventh incarnation of Vishnu and widely worshipped, a hero who defeated Ravana, the ogre king, after the latter had kidnapped his wife Sita.

Ramayana. The second great Hindu epic, of about half the length of the *Mahabharata*, relating the victories, virtues and follies of Rama.

rishi. Sage, usually a hermit; the austerities of the ancient rishis were said to be such that they could coerce even heaven.

sadhana. Spiritual discipline, its details often ordered by one's Guru, leading to realization.

sadhu. Holy man, ascetic, monk; there are estimated to be between five and ten million of them in India.

samadhi. The highest stage of meditation, in which one achieves unity with the Absolute; hence mahasamadhi, the death of a realized person, a saint or ascetic. By extension, his tomb, often a place of pilgrimage, may be referred to as his samadhi.

344

sannyasa. The last stage of Hindu life, in which a man puts away all worldly things and settles until death to contemplation; hence it is the condition of all ascetics who have turned to non-attachment and the effort of self-realization.

sannyasi. A monk who has been given sannyas-diksha and thus initiated into his ascetic order.

shabda. Sound, including both the Word as set out in the *Vedas* and ethereal, self-subsisting sound, pre-existing utterance.

Shaivite. Devotee of Shiva.

shakti. Divine energy, conceived of as female; thus Shakti, the mate and counterpart of Shiva. All female deities are considered to personify this power and so to a lesser degree are all women; it is this divine and female force to which Tantrics pay their devotion.

shaktipat. The transfer, sometimes sudden and unexpected, of divine energy from Guru to disciple.

shastras. Scriptural texts setting out right behaviour.

shishya. Disciple of a Guru.

Shiva. One of the great triad of Hindu deities, he has a dual nature, being regenerator but also destroyer; in the last aspect, he is much feared. God of dance and the arts, but also of asceticism, one of his names being *Mahayogi*; paradoxically the phallus is his most common symbol.

shruti. 'What has been heard': the most ancient and powerful Hindu texts, so-called either because the earliest rishis heard them – that is, were given them through revelation – or because they were handed down by word of mouth.

shudra. The lowest of the four castes, said to have been created out of the feet of Brahma.

shukta. A chapter of the *Vedas*.

siddhis. Occult powers gained by the practice of yoga.

sloka. A short verse, usually of two couplets; but often used for any aphorism or proverb.

smritis. 'What has been remembered': religious works whose authority is only exceeded by that of shruti; thus all post-Vedic religious writing, the word being synonymous with shastras.

sutra. Pithy, aphoristic style of writing, so economical as to be difficult to understand without commentary; most of the smritis are written in this style.

swami. 'Master' or 'lord', the respectful title by which one addresses a sadhu of known spiritual attainment.

tambura. Stringed instrument giving a drone accompaniment.

tapas. Austerities practised by sadhus; hence tapasvin, one who practices such austerities.

tilaka. Caste or sect mark made on forehead, arms or chest in white, yellow or red.

tonga. Horse-drawn cart, for carrying passengers.

tulsi. Sacred plant, the Indian basil.

Vaishnavite. Follower of Vishnu.

vaishya. Third of the four castes, traditionally that of merchants and farmers.

vanaprastha. Third stage of Hindu life, in which the householder relinquishes worldly attachments and prepares to become a sannyasi.

vedanta. Literally 'end of the *Vedas*', this may mean ultimate knowledge or the final section of the *Vedas*, i.e. the *Upanishads*; as usually used, means philosophy basing itself on these scriptures, the *Upanishads*. Sometimes used to refer to the monistic philosophy of Shankara, more accurately called advaita vedanta.

Vishnu. Second God of the Hindu triad, the Preserver, the All-Pervading, whose incarnations are renowned for their victorious struggles against evil.

yoga. Root of English 'yoke'; path to God-realization. Hence yogi, one who has taken such a path.